TABLE OF CONTENTS

THE MOST FAMOUS SOLDIER IN AMERICA		1
CHAPTER I:	FROM CROCKERY CLERK TO MAJOR GENERAL	4
CHAPTER II:	JEFFERSON DAVIS' JAILER	30
CHAPTER III:	RECONSTRUCTION, THE SIOUX WAR, AND THE NEZ PERCE	47
CHAPTER IV:	GERONIMO, CROOK, AND THE APACHE CAMPAIGN	62
CHAPTER V:	THE GHOST DANCE AND THE WOUNDED KNEE MASSACRE	90
CHAPTER VI:	THE PULLMAN STRIKE OF 1894	97
CHAPTER VII:	THE COMMANDING GENERAL AND THE SPANISH WAR	107
CHAPTER VIII:	EMBALMED BEEF	128
CHAPTER IX:	SAMPSON-SCHLEY AND FORMAL CENSURE	144
CHAPTER X:	AT LOGGERHEADS WITH THE PRESIDENT OVER THE PHILIPPINES	155
CHAPTER XI:	RUM, ROMANISM, AND ROOSEVELT	179
CHAPTER XII:	AN APOLOGY FOR AN APOLOGIA	198
CHAPTER XIII:	FORGOTTEN HISTORY	206

ILLUSTRATIONS

	After Page
The Battle of Fredericksburg	15
Winfield Scott Hancock	15
Francis Channing Barlow	15
Lt. Nelson A. Miles	15
The Battle of Spotsylvania	23
The "Muleshoe Salient"	23
George Gordon Meade	23
The Richmond-Petersburg Theater	23
Frederick Remington's "Meeting between the Sioux"	61
Lame Deer Firing at General Miles	61
Remington's "The Crazy Horse Fight"	61
Remington's "Surrender of Chief Joseph"	61
Miles, friends and enemies from the Indian Wars [Miles, Baldwin, Howard, Wood, Maus, Crook, Schofield, Geronimo]	89
Remington's "General Miles & Escort" Harper's Weekly 12/6/90	89
Remington's "Ghost Dance", Harper's 12/6/90	89
Miles promoted to Commanding General, 1895	109
The Mood of the Country, The New York World, 4/4/98	116
The New York World, June 25, 1898	120
Santiago de Cuba	120
Cuba and the personalities of the Cuban campaign [Alger, Shafter, Roosevelt, Wheeler, Lawton, Sampson, Schley]	120
Miles' Return from Puerto Rico, N.Y. World 9/8/98	127
Miles greeted upon return, N.Y. World 9/8/98	127
Mrs. Miles, N.Y. World 9/11/98	127
"No Odious Contrasts Wanted", N.Y. World 9/4/98	127
"It is up to you, Mr. Alger", N.Y. World 9/8/98	127
President McKinley at Camp Wikoff	127
Gen. Shafter and Gen. Wheeler at Camp Wikoff	127
Commissary General Eagan	137
"What General Miles Defends" N.Y. World 2/20/99	137
"Who will haul them down", N.Y. World, 2/4/99	137
Admiral Dewey, Elihu Root, & The Philippines	169
"His First Surrender", N.Y. World, Aug. 1903	178
"After Fourty Years: Get Out and Go Home" N.Y. World 8/9/03	178

PHOTOGRAPHS 46

THE MOST FAMOUS SOLDIER IN AMERICA

A biography of

LT. GEN. NELSON A. MILES

1839-1925

***

Arthur J. Amchan

Amchan Publications
P.O. Box 3648
Alexandria, Va. 22302

THE MOST FAMOUS SOLDIER IN AMERICA

A biography of Lt. Gen. Nelson A. Miles, 1839-1925

by Arthur J. Amchan

Published by:

Amchan Publications
P.O. Box 3648
Alexandria, Virginia 22302

Library of Congress Catalog Card Number: 89-85995
ISBN: 0-9617132-1-6

THE MOST FAMOUS SOLDIER IN AMERICA

On May 15, 1925, the opening ceremonies of a Friday matinee performance of the Ringling Brothers, Barnum & Bailey Circus was coming to a conclusion in Washington, D.C. As the performers entered the arena on horseback, and the flag bearers approached the crowd, a broad-shouldered old man in the third row rose, stood at attention, and saluted. When the flag passed, the crowd sat down and the old man toppled from his chair into the aisle, dead.[1]

The next day, newspapers across America reported the death of Lieutenant-General Nelson Appleton Miles at the age of 85. The obituaries which recounted the events of his life were as much a tale of a bygone era as they were a story of his life. Some of the tributes characterized the old soldier as a "relic," and the Washington Evening Star observed:

> With the passing of General Miles one of the most romantic figures on the vanishing horizon of America's earlier history of expansion has been removed and the final chapter of that crucial era has all but been closed.[2]

The Star and other papers told of General Miles' rise from a Boston store clerk to Major-General in the Union Army at the age of 25, and his heroism in virtually every major Civil War battle in the East. They acknowledged his place as one of, if not the most successful of the Army's Indian fighters. They recalled his successful battles with such famous chiefs as Sitting Bull, Crazy Horse, and Chief Joseph of the Nez Perce. They also mentioned the surrender of Geronimo and his role in

---

[1] The Washington Post, May 16, 1925, 1

[2] Washington Evening Star, May 16, 1925, 2

the Spanish-American War and the conquest of Puerto Rico. However, while there was some allusion to some of the other and more controversial incidents in his career, such as his treatment of Jefferson Davis at Fortress Monroe in 1865 and 1866, and his rivalries and quarrels with a host of military and civilian officials, there was little hint of how unconventional Nelson Miles had been for a professional soldier.

Although he achieved his greatest fame in battles with the Plains Indians, he consistently expressed sympathy with their plight. Similarly, although he was identified with America's imperialist age, he opposed imperialism and was an outspoken critic of the treatment of Filipino prisoners of war by members of the army which he commanded. In a profession in which alcoholism was commonplace, General Miles was a vigorous advocate of temperance, and in a profession which tends to view any war and any increase in the size of military forces as desirable, he expressed disagreement with the belligerence of the nation's leaders. Finally, if his obituaries had been completely candid, they would have noted that General Miles made more enemies over a longer period of time than virtually any public figure in American life.

At the time of his death in 1925, few recognized the name of Nelson A. Miles, but at the turn of the century he was familiar to virtually every American. Mark Sullivan, the most famous chronicler of that period, characterized General Miles as, "head of the United States Army in a symbolic as well as an official sense."[3] His position as the prototypical American soldier is also indicated by H. L. Mencken's characterization in 1917 of the German general August von Mackensen:

> The German beau ideal. An amazing flummery and the highest military genius...The Nelson A. Miles of Germany.[4]

---

[3]Sullivan, Mark, Our Times, Vol. III, Pre-War America (1930), p. 307

[4]Letters of H.L. Mencken, Alfred A. Knopf, 1961, p. 106

Miles was even a subject for the popular turn-of-the-century political humorist, Finley Peter Dunne, "Mr. Dooley," who described him as having "faced death an' promotion in ivry form."[5] Miles' career, however, had by 1925 been overshadowed by World War I. John J. Pershing, who had served under him on the frontier, had emerged as the new model of the American soldier. As time passed, Miles' fame receded further and in many historical accounts of his time he is portrayed as he was by Margaret Leech in The Days of McKinley as "a born troublemaker and a tireless promoter of his own interests."[6]

General Miles' story is worth retelling because no man's life so closely parallels American history from the Civil War through World War I. Moreover, despite the numerous enemies he made, a good case can be made that America never had a military leader who better combined physical and moral courage with tactical skill.

---

[5]Sullivan, Our Times, supra., p. 307

[6] Leech, p. 200

CHAPTER I: FROM CROCKERY CLERK TO MAJOR GENERAL

Nelson Appleton Miles was born on August 8, 1839, in Westminster, Massachusetts, a small town due north of Worcester and near Fitchburg. He came from a distinguished New England family; some of his forebearers had attended Harvard College, and both his grandfather and his great grandfather were veterans of Valley Forge and Yorktown. Nelson's father, however, was not a Harvard man and at the time of his son's birth was engaged in farming and a lumber business in north central Massachusetts.

The first thing that sets the rise of Nelson Miles apart from that of the other "boy generals" of the Civil War is the paucity of his formal education. Unlike men like George Custer (West Point) or Francis C. Barlow (Harvard), Miles never went beyond high school. Afterwards, at the age of 16 he moved to Boston to study business. For the next five years he worked during the day and attended commercial classes at night. His last job prior to the outbreak of the War was working as a clerk in a Boston crockery store.

On nights when he did not have classes, Nelson often went to the Boston Public Library and read books about military history and tactics. Familiar with the military tradition of his family, he fantasized about becoming a soldier himself. As the secession crisis intensified he joined several thousand young Boston men in engaging a retired French Army colonel to teach them military drill and tactics. While Miles was attracted to the coming conflict partially out of a sense of adventure, he also shared the abolitionist sentiment of many of his peers. In his memoirs, he wrote:

> (Slavery) was an institution for which the people of this country, the founders of the Republic...were responsible and will ever be held responsible by future historians, for, in fact, it will ever remain a blot upon our history.[7]

When the South Carolina secessionists fired on Fort Sumter, Nelson Miles, like thousands of other young men in the North, was caught up in a firestorm of patriotic fervor. The young clerk wrote his older brother a few days after the Fort surrendered to the Rebels, "War is all the talk and nothing else is to be thought of."[8] After the first Union military initiative ended in disaster at Bull Run in the summer of 1861, the government embarked upon the raising of numerous additional regiments. United States Senator (later Vice-President) Henry Wilson raised two such regiments in Boston. Young men with money were encouraged to raise companies and were generally rewarded by an appointment as the company commander with the rank of Captain.

Investing his life's savings ($1,000), and borrowing another $2500 from a wealthy uncle, the 22 year-old crockery clerk embarked upon his military career. After raising his company, Miles was elected Captain by his men, a procedure normally honored by the State Governor in issuing commissions. Captain Miles took his company into camp in early September 1861. A month later the Adjutant General of Massachusetts demanded the return of the Captain's commission, presented it to another young officer, William Cogswell, and gave Miles a Lieutenant's commission. Miles' bitterness about this turn of events is expressed in a letter written to his aunt:

---

[7]Miles, Serving the Republic, p. 12 While there is a danger in relying on autobiographies for anything since they are written to make the author look good for posterity, Miles' career indicates a persistent and genuine interest in the plight of the black man in America.

[8]Miles letter of April 18, 1861, Nelson A. Miles Papers, U.S. Army Military History Institute Archives, Carlisle, Pa.

> I feel very sorry about my commission, it was the greatest mistake in the world when I gave it up. I was cheated out of it...[9]

Although Miles initially expressed confidence that this injustice would be rectified when the Governor, John Andrew, became aware of it, he came to hold the Governor personally responsible for this affront. Miles was outraged and he let the Governor of Massachusetts know it. He was told that he was too young to be a company commander, but Miles believed that he was being cheated out of what was rightfully his by political influence peddling. Miles' vociferous expressions of displeasure won him in the person of John Andrew the first in a long list of prominent detractors. Indeed, one might say that his military career began with a snub by the Governor of Massachusetts and ended with a snub from the President of the United States, Theodore Roosevelt.

Lieutenant Miles didn't let his misfortune spoil the grand time he had marching with the 22nd Massachusetts Volunteer Infantry Regiment in front of cheering crowds on Broadway in New York, in Philadelphia, and before President Lincoln when he got to Washington. At the Long Bridge, before crossing into Virginia, Nelson bid a poignant farewell to his brother, Daniel, 12 years his senior, who had accompanied him, and went off to war.[10] After serving only a few weeks with his regiment,

---

[9]Miles letter of October 16, 1861, Miles Papers, Carlisle. The Miles papers and the Register of Massachusetts Soldiers, Sailors, and Marines in the Civil War indicate that Cpt. Cogswell resigned his commission in July 1862, which may mean that he had his fill of military glory after the Peninsula campaign. Miles' adversary is not the William Cogswell who enlisted in the 2nd Massachusetts Infantry and went on to become a general officer and subsequently a Massachusetts congressman. Register of Mass. Soldiers, Vol 1, pp. 88, 135; Vol II, p. 676

[10]Daniel Miles was much like a second father to his younger brother and had been his teacher in school. He died in Lafayette Park, across from the White House in 1912. Nelson Miles happened to be driving by the park when his brother collapsed, and he carried his dying brother to his car.

Nelson was permanently detailed as an aide-de-camp to Brigadier General O.O. Howard, then commanding a brigade at Bladensburg, Maryland.[11]

Soon after his assignment to Howard's staff, the young Lieutenant struck up a friendship with another young officer who would prove to be the closest and most important friend he would have for the next 34 years. This officer was Francis Channing Barlow, a Harvard College graduate five years Miles' senior, who had just begun a career as a lawyer in New York City when the war broke out. After serving a short time as a private in a New York militia unit, Barlow was commissioned and was shortly thereafter appointed regimental commander of the 61st New York Volunteer Infantry by New York's Governor Morgan. During the Civil War Barlow would enjoy a meteoric rise to Major General and would take Nelson Miles along with him as he was promoted. After the War Barlow would enter politics, and as Attorney General of the State of New York would gain favorable recognition for his prosecution of the Tweed political ring in New York City. Returning to the private practice of law in 1876, Barlow would use a fair amount of his spare time until his death in 1896, advancing the military career of Nelson A. Miles.[12]

Howard's Brigade moved into Virginia and established its headquarters at Camp California, four miles from Alexandria, on the road to Fairfax. On December 29, 1861, Lt. Miles and Francis Barlow took time out from their routine of reconnaissance patrols to make a pilgrimage to Mt. Vernon. Miles was sufficiently moved by the visit to write his family a detailed description of Washington's tomb.[13]

---

[11] When the Army of the Potomac was reorganized in the spring of 1862, Howard's brigade became part of its Second Corps.

[12] Barlow military records, National Archives (microfilm roll 241, B583 CB 1866); obituary, New York Times January 12, 1896, 17:7.

[13] Miles papers, U.S. Army Military History Institute Archive, Carlisle, Pa.

Throughout the fall and winter of 1861-2, the Union's Eastern Army outfitted and drilled, but except for a comparatively small and disastrous engagement at Balls Bluff near Leesburg, Virginia, did little fighting. President Lincoln and congressional leaders began to become increasingly impatient and disenchanted with its popular and pretentious commander, thirty-five year old George McClellan. Finally, McClellan was goaded into action and embarked upon a plan to which Lincoln reluctantly assented. Rather than attack the Confederate Army from the north, which would allow him to go on the offensive and defend Washington from attack with the same troops, McClellan decided that the best chance for success was to move the Army by water to the peninsula formed by the York and James Rivers and attack Richmond, the Confederate capital, from the southeast.

In a manner that was to become his hallmark, McClellan's forces arrived in front of Yorktown, Virginia and laid siege to the lightly defended Confederate fortifications in April, 1862. Convinced that the Rebels had many more men than they actually had, McClellan delayed his assault for a month, allowing the Confederates to prepare for the defense of Richmond. After a sharp clash with retreating Rebel forces at the old colonial capital of Williamsburg, the Army of the Potomac advanced to the eastern approaches of Richmond at the end of May, 1862. On May 31, 1862, the Confederate commander, Joseph E. Johnston, launched a counterattack against the Union lines. In this fight Lieutenant Nelson A. Miles saw his first significant action. During the engagement, the battle of Fair Oaks, one of the regiments under General Howard, the 81st Pennsylvania Infantry, was routed when their commanding officer was killed. Lt. Miles was ordered by Howard to take command of the regiment and stop the enemy advance; he did so successfully and received the first of his four war wounds-in the foot.[14] Miles' performance in this battle was the critical juncture in his career because he won the everlasting gratitude and respect of Colonel Barlow,

---

[14]Miles, Serving the Republic, pp 30-33; Official Record of the War of Rebellion (hereafter "O.R."), Series I, vol. 11, pt. 1, pp. 764-771.

commanding the 61st New York Infantry. The Sixty-First New York's position was made vulnerable by the retreat of the 81st Pennsylvania and Miles' ability to move it back into position had rendered Barlow's position secure from attacks from his flanks and his rear.[15]

The battle of Fair Oaks (sometimes also called the battle of Seven Pines) was significant in one other respect. During the battle the Confederate commander, General Johnston, was wounded, and command of the Rebel Army of Northern Virginia was placed in the more than capable hands of Robert E. Lee. As McClellan meticulously prepared and outfitted his Army, Lee decided to launch a counteroffensive at the end of June. On the twenty-seventh of that month, the commander of the Second Corps, Major-General E.V. Sumner, asked for a volunteer to climb a tall pine tree and report to him regarding the state of the Confederate defenses to his front. The first volunteer ascended the tree and was struck by cannon fire; when Sumner asked for another volunteer Miles stepped forward. What he observed from his precarious perch was deeply disturbing. Although the lines in front of his corps were lightly defended, masses of Confederate troops were on the move towards the Union right. Lee's offensive broke the back of the peninsular campaign and McClellan retreated towards refuge on the James River. During the Union retreat to the James (the Seven Days' battles), Miles, now a Captain, served as acting brigade adjutant under General John Caldwell, who replaced Howard.[16] As the Union Army warded off Confederate attacks at Savage Station and Glendale, Virginia on June 29 and 30, 1862, Colonel Barlow reported that Miles brought his regiment reinforcements under heavy

---

[15]O.R. I, vol. ll, pt. 2, p. 67 (Barlow's report of July 5, 1862).

[16] O.O. Howard, Miles' first mentor, lost an arm at Fair Oaks but returned to the Army to distinguish himself as one of Sherman's principal lieutenants in Georgia. After the Civil War he headed the Freedman's Bureau (Howard University in Washington, D.C. thus bears his name). His career during the Indian Wars is less distinguished and led to a break with Nelson Miles over who deserved credit for subduing the Nez Perce and whether Howard unnecessarily got Miles in trouble with his superiors at the time of the surrender of Geronimo in 1886.

fire and obtained an artillery piece for his 61st New York Infantry.[17] General Philip Kearny also praised Miles for leading a counterattack that checked a Confederate advance.[18]

On July 1, 1862, Lee tried to deliver a knock-out blow to the Army of the Potomac at Malvern Hill. Union artillery cut the Confederate infantry to pieces, and McClellan's army was saved from destruction.[19] On the very day of the battle of Malvern Hill, Lincoln asked the state governors for 300,000 additional troops because it had now become quite apparent that the war was not about to come to a quick conclusion. The governors, in seeking officers for their new regiments, sought recommendations from the general officers from their states. First on the list submitted to Governor Andrew of Massachusetts by General Sumner was the name of Nelson A. Miles. Possibly due to his earlier confrontation with the Governor concerning his captain's commission, the young lieutenant was not offered a commission in one of the new Massachusetts regiments. However, Colonel Barlow wrote to Governor Morgan of New York, requesting that Miles be appointed his lieutenant-colonel to replace an officer killed at Fair Oaks. Although it was unusual to give a commission to a resident of another state, Governor Morgan complied with Barlow's request.

While Miles and the rest of the Army of the Potomac sat on the James River, Robert E. Lee turned his attention to the new Union Army of Virginia which Lincoln had established under the command of Major-General John Pope. Pope, fresh from a significant victory against the western Confederates on the Mississippi River, was set up in an independent command due to Lincoln's tremendous dissatisfaction with General McClellan. Pope issued a number of presumptuous communiques and then headed out to capture Richmond from the

---

[17] O.R. I, vol. 11, part 2, pp. 62-68 (Barlow's report of July 5, 1862).

[18] Ibid, 167

[19]Miles believed that had McClellan renewed his offensive after Malvern Hill, he could have taken Richmond. <u>Serving the Republic</u>, p. 37.

northwest. One of the most popular subjects of debate amongst Civil War buffs for the last century and a quarter concerns the reasons for Pope's lack of success. Some believe him to have been unlucky; some believe that he was defeated because McClellan and his friends, particularly General Fitz-John Porter were doing everything within their power to assure that Pope would fail. However, Bruce Catton concluded that the problem was that, in contrast to his prior experiences in the West, Pope "presently found himself up against the first team, and he was woefully outclassed."[20]

The first team was Robert E. Lee, "Stonewall" Jackson, and James Longstreet. Lee, guessing that McClellan had no stomach for renewing his offensive, went after Pope. After a sharp engagement between lead elements of Pope's army and Stonewall Jackson at Cedar Mountain, Pope attempted to destroy Jackson on the Bull Run battlefield. Unfortunately for Pope, Longstreet's troops joined with Jackson's to administer a crushing defeat at the Second Battle of Bull Run (Manassas). McClellan's Army, including the 61st New York Infantry and its new lieutenant colonel, Nelson Miles, withdrew from the James River and slowly reinforced Pope. Miles' regiment was brought north by water and was rushed out to Centreville, Virginia to cover Pope's retreat. Washington was saved, the Army of Virginia was abolished, and the Union forces were reunited under McClellan. Meanwhile, Lee, who had taken the war away from the gates of Richmond and brought it to the gates of Washington in a matter of months, crossed the Potomac and invaded Maryland in early September, 1862.[21]

Flushed with victory, Lee paused in the vicinity of Frederick, Maryland to take care of some unfinished business before pushing on to the East. There was a sizeable Union garrison at Harper's Ferry, that made him uncomfortable. He therefore divided his army to secure

---

[20]Catton, Bruce, This Hallowed Ground, p. 191

[21] The war was going badly elsewhere for the Union, which five months earlier had thought it was on the verge of total victory. In September, Confederates under Braxton Bragg invaded Kentucky and were threatening Ohio and Indiana.

his rear and fell back westward behind the mountain passes. In one of the most inexplicable strokes of luck to occur during the entire war, one copy of Lee's orders to his subordinates was left on the ground wrapped in a couple of cigars near Frederick and was discovered by a Union soldier when McClellan's troops moved into the area. When brought the "lost" order, McClellan's staff determined that it was genuine, and the general realized that he had just been handed an opportunity to destroy the Confederate main force while the other elements of Lee's army were busy at Harper's Ferry. Even so, McClellan moved very slowly. It took him several days to engage the Confederates guarding the passes west of Frederick and move opposite Lee, who had positioned his army west of Antietam Creek, outside of Sharpsburg, Maryland.

When Lt. Colonel Miles and his regiment reached the Sharpsburg area on September 16, 1862, they were treated to a display of bravado that would stick in Miles' memory for the rest of his life. As the armies assembled to prepare for the next day's fight, a couple of Union officers were having a steeplechase race behind their lines. Suddenly, one of the officers rode through the Union picket line and out into the valley separating the two armies. First, thunderous cheers rose from the Union line, and then the Confederates, who could easily have killed both men, joined in. The riders finished their contest and returned to the Federal lines.[22]

In his autobiography, Miles recalls that the evening before the battle he reconnoitered the bridge over Antietam Creek that would become the most famous landmark on the Antietam battlefield. On the evening of September 16, Miles recalled that the bridge was unguarded by Confederate troops, but on the next day several hundred Rebel sharpshooters would hold off the Union Army's Ninth Corps under General Burnside for several hours, thus allowing Confederate reinforcements from Harper's Ferry to prevent a breakthrough in the

---

[22]Miles, Serving The Republic, p. 43

southern sector of the battlefield. Henceforth, the bridge would be known as "Burnside's bridge."

The next morning McClellan launched his attack. The bloodiest single-day battle of the war consisted of three largely uncoordinated attacks on the northern, central and southern sectors of the battlefield, which allowed Lee sufficient opportunity to shift his troops around to meet each Federal thrust. The first attack from the northeast fizzled out in mid-morning. At mid-day a second offensive was launched at the center of the Confederate line. General Sumner's Second Corps, which included the 61st New York Infantry Regiment under the command of Colonel Francis C. Barlow and Lt. Col. Nelson A. Miles, spearheaded this assault. In the area afterwards called "Bloody Lane," the Union attack was successful and the Confederates gave way. After securing his position along a sunken road, Colonel Barlow was seriously wounded by a shell fragment in the groin; Miles took command of the regiment. He ordered his men forward but had to withdraw because no general advance was ordered and his flanks were exposed. McClellan failed to press his advantage and missed his chance to end the war in the east. A lull fell over the battlefield until General Burnside commenced his assault to the south, but his inability to quickly get across the bridge over Antietam Creek allowed A.P. Hill's troops sufficient time to reach the battlefield from Harper's Ferry and save Lee's battered army from destruction[23] The next day Lee bluffed McClellan sufficiently that the Union commander did not renew the battle and the Confederates slipped away back into Virginia. Among the 23,000 casualties at Antietam were Miles' Divisional commander General Israel Richardson, who was killed, and Cpt. Oliver Wendell Holmes, Jr., of the 20th Massachusetts Infantry, who was wounded in the neck but survived to become one of the nation's most famous jurists, dying at the age of 94 in 1935.

---

[23]At Harper's Ferry the Confederates had achieved the surrender of 12,000 Union troops under the command of Colonel Dixon Miles, no relation to Nelson.

General Richardson was replaced by Winfield Scott Hancock, who would become one of the war's greatest heroes and ultimately the unsuccessful Democratic Presidential candidate in 1880. Francis Barlow was promoted to Brigadier-General and Nelson Miles, not quite 23 years old, was promoted to full Colonel, commanding the 61st New York Infantry Regiment. Lincoln finally had his fill of McClellan's insubordination and unwillingness to move aggressively and replaced him with General Ambrose Burnside.

In November, 1862, Burnside moved his army to the vicinity of Fredericksburg, Virginia, halfway between Washington and Richmond. Unfortunately, the pontoon bridges with which Burnside intended to cross the Rappahanock River did not arrive for twenty-three days, which gave General Lee the opportunity to fortify his position, which was centered upon Marye's Heights, a steep hill overlooking the town. Well aware of the criticisms of McClellan and other Union generals who always seemed to have an excuse for not fighting, Burnside decided to assault Lee's positions despite the delay. What followed was one of the most one-sided Confederate victories of the war: Union casualties numbered 9,000; Rebel losses only 1,500. The assault never managed to reach the strongly entrenched Confederates.

The most dramatic phase of the battle was the attack by General Hancock's division of the Second Corps on the well-prepared Confederate positions behind a stone wall below the summit of Marye's Heights. Hancock positioned three brigades 200 paces apart for the assault. After the first two brigades had been repulsed, General John Caldwell's brigade, which included the 61st New York Infantry Regiment commanded by Nelson Miles, made its advance. After being stopped by the Confederate fire, Colonel Miles asked General Caldwell for permission to renew the charge at the Confederate positions in front of him. The request was denied because Caldwell concluded that it would merely result in "a wanton loss of brave men."[24] At about this time, Miles was hit by a minie ball, which entered his neck and exited by his

---

[24]O.R. I, vol. 21, pt. 1, p. 233

left ear; luckily the bullet missed his windpipe, but he left the field. One hundred and eight of his 435 men were either killed or wounded.[25]

In recalling Miles' heroism at Fredericksburg, Charles Fuller, who served in the 61st New York as a sergeant and later as a lieutenant, had a more critical evaluation of his commander's leadership. After characterizing Miles as "equally brave and gallant" as Colonel Barlow, Fuller observed that "a bloody wound in [Miles'] neck spared the regiment a desperate attempt to get a little nearer than other regiments to the invincible lines of the enemy." A little more pointedly, Fuller added:

> It was said at the time that Col. Miles, satisfied that the only thing to do to amount to anything, was to make a rush and take the first picket line, had sent back his conclusion, and requested permission to charge the line with his regiment. About this time an accommodating rebel bullet cut his throat, letting out a liberal quantity of fresh bright blood. This so put him hors de combat that he had to leave the field, somewhat to the longevity account of the Sixty-firsters there present...[26]

After a bivouac on the Rappahanock in the winter of 1862-63, which included an ill-fated maneuver by Burnside known as the "mud-march," Lincoln again was forced to replace the commander of the Army of the Potomac. This time, with substantial reservations, he selected Major-General Joseph Hooker, an officer with a superb combat record but one with an unsavory reputation. Not only had Hooker undercut Burnside's authority when he was the latter's subordinate, but

---

[25] Ibid.; Tucker, Hancock the Superb, pp. 99-106

[26] Charles A. Fuller, Personal Recollections of the War of 1861, (1906), pp. 36, 81.

Major-General Francis Barlow.

General Winfield S. Hancock.

Lieutenant Miles.

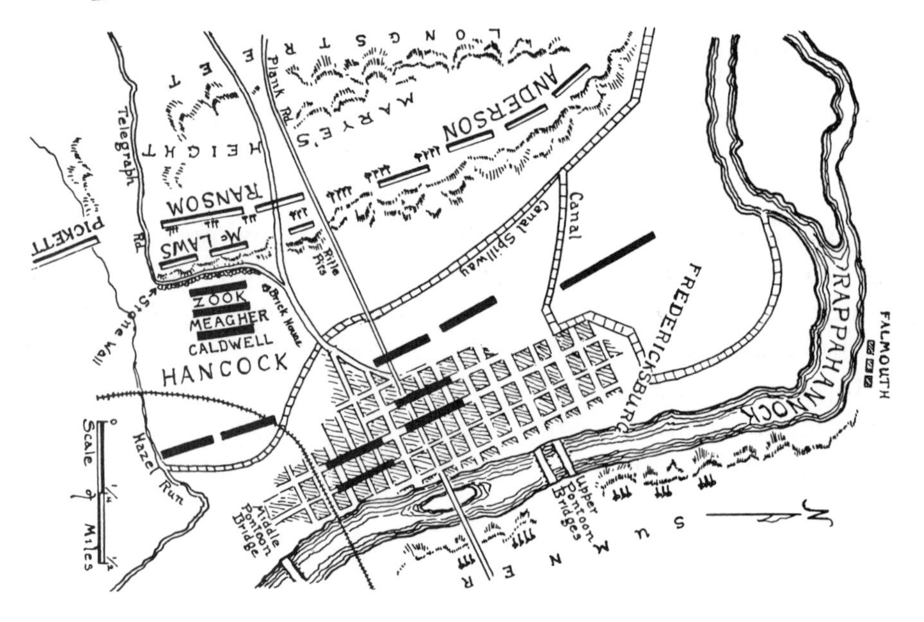

BATTLE OF FREDERICKSBURG, December 13, 1862. Attack by Hancock's Division on Longstreet at the stone wall in front of Marye's Heights, marking the farthest advance of the Right Grand Division of the Federal Army.

he had been heard to repeatedly voice his opinion that what the country needed was a military dictator to replace the inept civilian leadership in Washington. Lincoln wrote the general a letter, now considered a literary masterpiece. The President told Hooker that he was well aware of the controversies surrounding him and had chosen him as commander of Army of the Potomac, in spite of, not because of, these considerations. Lincoln told the general that before one could become the nation's dictator he had first to give the nation military victory and that Lincoln was willing to risk the former if Hooker could provide the latter.

Hooker got off to an impressive start and quickly re-established the morale of his men, which had reached an all-time low after Fredericksburg and the mud-march. By late April, 1863, the new commander was ready to confront Lee and expertly executed the initial stages of his plan. The main force of the Union Army crossed the Rappahanock and the Rapidan to the northwest of the Confederates and then advanced towards Lee, while a smaller segment of the Army of the Potomac under Major-General John Sedgwick prepared to engage the Rebels by attacking once again from the east.

The Second Corps participated in the assault from the northwest. Colonel Miles was ordered to protect the left flank of his corps and, on May 1 and May 2, 1863, fought off several massive Confederate assaults. The Rebels came within yards of his position, and one Confederate colonel fell dead within the regiment's lines. Hancock put Miles in command of three regiments, the 57th, 64th and 66th New York, which established a picket line in a bushy ravine one mile east of Chancellorsville. Given the task of protecting the Second Corps, which constituted the left flank of the Army, as it began to retire from the battlefield, Miles had his men dig rifle pits and fell trees to protect their front.[27] His men successfully kept the attacking Confederates from Hancock's main line until sometime after a bullet struck Miles' metallic

---

[27] Tucker, Hancock the Superb, p. 120

belt plate with great force as he rode up and down his picket line on the morning of May 3. This wound was different from the other two:

> The result was an instantly deathly sickening sensation; my sword dropped from my right hand, my scabbard and belt dropped to the left; I was completely paralyzed below the waist. My horse seemed to realize what had occurred; he stopped, turned, and walked slowly back.[28]

Miles was taken to the Chancellor House, where a dead soldier was removed from a couch and the wounded Colonel put on it. Soon a shell set the house on fire, and he was carried five miles on a stretcher. After spending the night in the woods, he was transported 12 miles over a rough corduroy road to a field hospital and then sent to Washington. His brother, Daniel, then came and took him home. General Caldwell's report, written May 12, 1863, states:

> I greatly regret to report that Colonel Miles was severely, if not mortally, wounded on Sunday morning, while handling the picket line with masterly ability...If ever a soldier earned promotion Colonel Miles has done so. Providence should spare his life, and I earnestly recommend that he be promoted and entrusted with a command commensurate with his abilities.[29]

Providence was indeed kind to Nelson Miles. Two weeks after receiving his abdominal wound he was able to move his right foot slightly, and a surgeon was able to find and remove the bullet which had crushed through the hip bone and lodged in the muscles of his left

---

[28] Miles, Serving The Republic, p. 55

[29] O.R. I, vol. 25, pt. 1, p. 230

leg. His convalescence was also brightened by a letter written to him by General Caldwell on May 19, 1863, in which his commanding officer informed him:

> I have not been neglectful of your interests, but have personally seen in your behalf Generals Hancock, Couch and Hooker. They all speak of you in highest terms. Hancock said Couch was commending you to General Hooker, when the latter asked 'Who is Colonel Miles?' 'Who is Colonel Miles!' said Couch, ' a man that ought to be made Major General today!'[30]

Caldwell also reported that General Hooker (who as yet had not been replaced as commander of the Army of the Potomac), had promised to submit Miles' name to the President for promotion to Brigadier General. As it turned out, Miles would have to wait for this reward and wait much longer for recognition in another form. In 1892, then Major-General Miles was awarded the Congressional Medal of Honor for his gallantry at Chancellorsville.

Ironically, the battle in which Miles achieved his greatest glory was perhaps the most embarrassing Union defeat of all. The Federals had approximately 130,000 troops on the field, the Confederates approximately 60,000. In view of the odds against them, Lee and Jackson executed what was probably the most audacious move of the entire war. Lee divided his forces, keeping half to the east between Hooker's Army and Sedgwick. He sent Jackson to the west across the entire front of Hooker's Army. Jackson then surprised the Union Eleventh Corps and routed it. Hooker lost his nerve, went on the defensive, and then withdrew to the north, suffering 17,000 casualties to Lee's 10,000. However, in the view of many, including Nelson Miles, one of the 10,000 Confederate casualties at Chancellorsville may well have determined the outcome of the entire war:

---

[30]Letter, Caldwell to Miles, May 19, 1863, Miles-Cameron Papers, Library of Congress.

> Up to that time Lee had scarcely lost a decisive battle. After it he had never gained one. When I heard of the death of Stonewall Jackson I considered the event equal to the annihilation of an entire corps of the Confederate Army. It is impossible to know what might have been the result had he lived...[31]

Weeks after Chancellorsville, Colonel Miles, still on crutches, rushed south to offer his services in repulsing Lee's invasion of Pennsylvania. He could not keep up with his regiment and was put in charge of 1,500 men at a State militia camp at Huntington. Miles' troops were sent to guard key mountain passes in the State but the need for their services ended when the Army of the Potomac, now commanded by General George Gordon Meade, defeated the Rebels at Gettysburg, on July 3, 1863. During that battle the Second Corps and its new commander, General Hancock, played a key role. Hancock commanded the Army of the Potomac prior to Meade's arrival and is generally given credit for the decision to fight the battle along Cemetery Ridge [although this credit was contested by General Howard]. Elements of the Second Corps also bore the brunt of Pickett's climactic assault on the third day.

By the end of July Miles was back with the Army of the Potomac, but this time commanding a brigade rather than a regiment. In the fall of 1863 General Meade initiated an offensive in Virginia, but after inconclusive engagements near Bristoe Station on October 13, he returned to winter quarters. Although in global terms nothing much happened in the East between Gettysburg and the spring of 1864, small skirmishes, such as one fought by Miles' brigade at New Hope Church, Virginia, on November 29, 1863, occurred with regularity. During this comparative lull, Miles received a most encouraging letter from his

---

[31]Miles, Serving the Republic, p. 54; Jackson was mortally wounded by Confederate troops in the dark when returning from a scouting mission.

friend, General Barlow, who was recovering from serious wounds received at Gettysburg.[32] Barlow enclosed a copy of a letter that he had written to Senator Henry Wilson on November 28, 1863, which said:

> Cannot something be done to make Colonel Miles a Brigadier General?
>
> He has been repeatedly recommended for this promotion by his commanding officers and among them Generals Hooker, Kearney, Howard, Couch and Hancock. In fact every Brigade, Division, and Corps commander under whom he has served since he became a Colonel has warmly recommended

---

[32] The circumstances of General Barlow's wound at Gettysburg provide the backdrop to one of the more poignant [but according to some, apocryphal] Civil War stories. On the first day of the battle, July 1, 1863, Barlow, commanding the First Division of General Howard's Eleventh Corps of the Army of the Potomac, took up a position north of the town of Gettysburg to confront Confederates pouring in from the northwest. The right of First Division's line occupied a small hill, now known as Barlow's Knoll.

As Rebel troops overwhelmed the First Division, their commander, General John B. Gordon, observed a Union officer get hit while valiantly trying to rally his soldiers. Gordon rode over to the stricken officer, dismounted, offered him water from his canteen, and asked his name; it was General Barlow, who had been hit by a minie ball in the chest. The ball had exited near the spine, and Barlow's legs and arms were completely paralyzed. Both Barlow and Gordon assumed that the Union general's wound was mortal, and Barlow asked Gordon to take a packet of letters from his wife and destroy them. Upon learning that Barlow's wife was a nurse with Union forces at Gettysburg, he sent a soldier under a flag of truce offering her safe passage to attend to her husband.

Gordon assumed that Barlow died at Gettysburg, and Barlow assumed that a Confederate general named Gordon killed later in the war was the officer who assisted him on the Pennsylvania battlefield. Both men were quite surprised to meet each other at a dinner in Washington some fifteen years later. [Storrick, W.C., Gettysburg, pp. 34-37; Tucker, Glenn, High Tide at Gettysburg, p. 160 and n. 18.] Barlow's first wife died as the result of illness contracted as an Army nurse in 1864. He later married Ellen Shaw, the sister of Robert Gould Shaw, commander of the 54th Massachusetts Infantry, the first black regiment raised in the North, who was killed at Ft. Wagner, South Carolina, in 1863.

him and there has never been an official report in which he has not been commended...

These recommendations have not been given as a matter of course...as is so often the case--Everyone who has served with Colonel Miles has seen in him very many of those qualities which go to make up a high degree of military talent--

He is a man of untiring and sleepless energy who does not wait to be told to do a thing, or when and how to do it, but who uses all the means in his power to attain success without waiting to be urged or quickened by anyone--If you need him with a body of troops to accomplish a certain purpose you know that he will do all that under the circumstances skill, determination, and courage can do--To anyone who knows the habit of many military officers of fearing to take any responsibility and of sending at every step for orders and directions and of only doing just enough to escape censure or to obtain a reasonable degree of commendation, what I have said of Colonel Miles will appear high praise.

He has also a remarkable talent for fighting battles. It is not only that he is very brave--for most officers are that, but he has that perfect coolness and self-possession in danger which is much more uncommon. The sound of cannon clears his head and strengthens his nerves and his quickness of perception and skill in taking up positions and availing himself of advantages of ground in action I have not seen equalled. To all this he adds in an unusual degree the faculty of attracting men to him and arousing their pride and enthusiasm without relaxing discipline.

***

> I thought so highly of him from careful observation that I got him made my Lieutenant Colonel over the heads of all my officers though he was then only a Lieutenant and that too in a Massachusetts regiment, while I commanded a New York one.[33]

In his cover letter, Barlow asked Miles if there was any chance of Barlow getting command of one of the Divisions in the Second Corps of the Army of the Potomac. While it is not clear that Miles had any influence in this matter, the two were reunited, with Barlow commanding the First Division of Hancock's Second Corps and Miles one of his brigades.

In May, 1864, Barlow and Miles crossed the Rapidan with 105,000 other Union soldiers to engage Lee once again. Although General Meade was its nominal commander, accompanying the Army of the Potomac this time was the new General-in-Chief of the Union Armies, Lt. General U.S. Grant. Grant, who had a string of successes against the Rebels in the West (Fort Donelson, Vicksburg, and Chattanooga), would make all the strategic decisions in the coming campaign. Miles' brigade camped on the Chancellorsville battlefield on May 4, and the next day his Second Corps led Grant's advance to the southeast. Lee then assaulted the Federal right flank, and a tremendous battle developed in the dense woods known as the Wilderness. Barlow's Division stayed in reserve during the battle. Despite Hancock's order to General John Gibbon, given temporary command over Barlow's Division, as well as his own, to commit Barlow at a crucial juncture in the battle, most of Barlow's troops, including Miles' brigade, saw little or no action. After sustaining 18,000 casualties to Lee's 8,000, Grant, with the Second Corps leading, tried to outflank the Rebels by moving to his left, or southeast.

---

[33]Barlow to Sen. Henry Wilson, November 28, 1863, Miles-Cameron Papers, Library of Congress

On the way southeast to Spotsylvania, Miles' brigade fought off attacks by two Confederate brigades and then, on May 12, led a frontal assault on an angle in the Confederate line.[34] Lee, in tracking Grant's movements, dug in near Spotsylvania Court House, and because of high ground to his front had extended his lines out so that they protruded in a configuration called the "muleshoe salient." This bulge extended approximately three quarters of a mile out from Lee's lines and offered Grant a tempting target. Confederate infantry at the angle in the salient could not effectively concentrate their fire if the Federals attacked their position, and on May 11, Grant ordered Hancock to assault the salient the next morning. Due to his haste, Grant made little attempt to reconnoiter the Confederate positions, which led Miles and Colonel John R. Brooke, whose brigades had been selected to spearhead the assault, to complain openly about the lack of preparation for the attack. At 4:35 on the morning of the 12th, Miles and Brooke started forward and overran the front line Rebel positions. Lee, who fortuitously had moved his artillery in expectation of a Federal attack elsewhere, tried to get some of it back in place, only to lose several cannons to the advancing Union troops. Confederate General John B. Gordon was able to organize a second line of defense a half mile deep in the salient, and the battle line stabilized with desperate hand-to-hand fighting the rest of the day. The initial success of the attack produced no long-term results as Grant did not renew the attack on May 13 but instead moved again to the southeast. By the end of the first week of fighting, Grant had suffered 40,000 casualties with little noticeable effect. In Miles' brigade for the period of May 8-21, 1864, 118 men were killed, 499 were wounded, and 60 were captured or missing.[35]

For their trouble at the Wilderness and Spotsylvania, Barlow was promoted to brevet Major-General and Miles to brevet Brigadier-General (a temporary or honorary rank). As Lee and Grant jousted

---

[34]O.R. I, vol. 36, pt. 2, p. 710; Miles, Serving the Republic, pp. 65-66

[35]O.R. I, vol. 36, pt. 1, p. 120

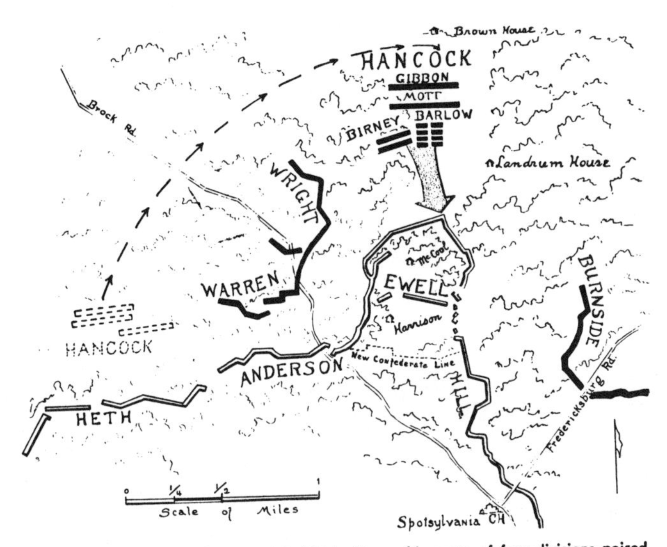

BATTLE OF SPOTSYLVANIA, May 12, 1864. Hancock's corps of four divisions poised for dawn assault on "mule shoe" salient of Lee's fortifications.

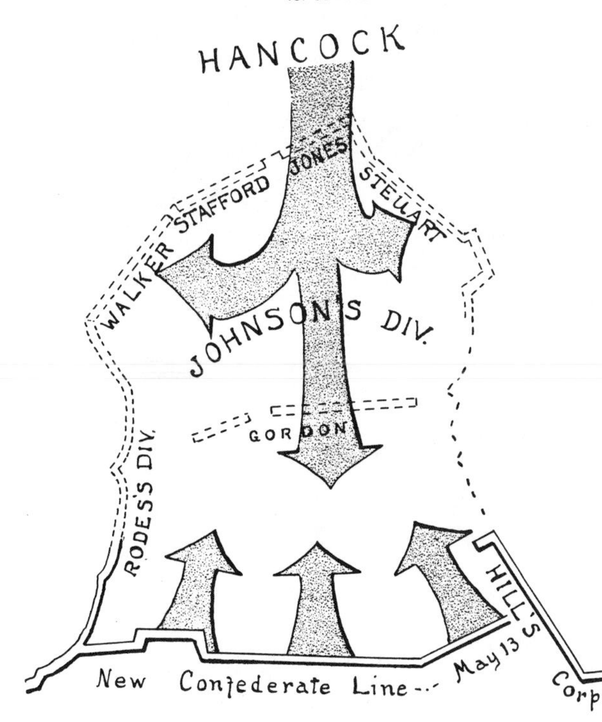

BATTLE OF SPOTSYLVANIA, May 12, 1864, showing Hancock's breakthrough at point of salient held by Jones's brigade and his envelopment and capture of Edward Johnson's division of Ewell's corps.

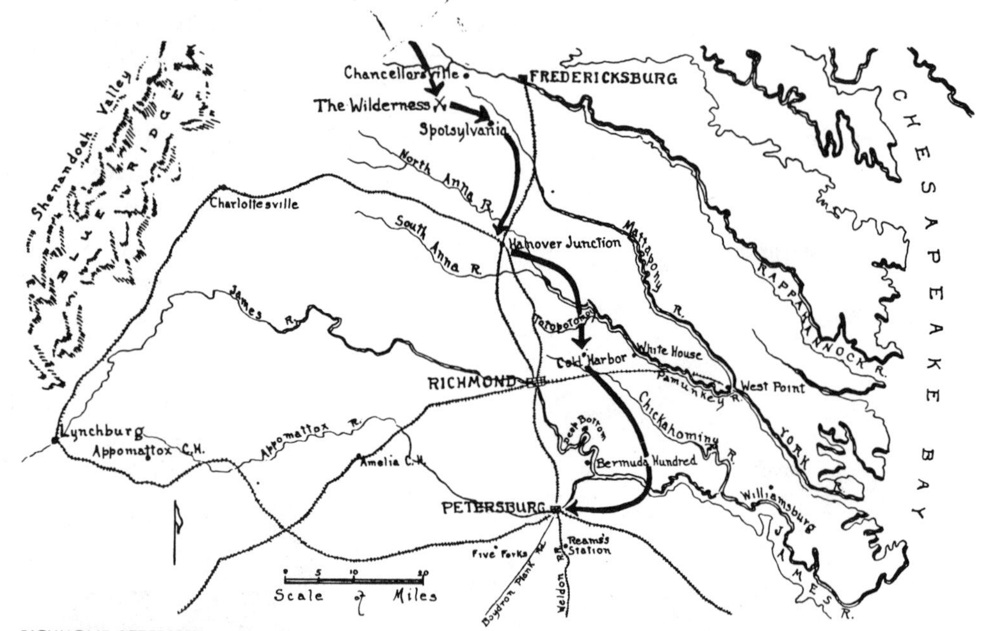

RICHMOND-PETERSBURG THEATER. Route of Grant's army, at times headed by Hancock's corps their way to the southeast, the Second Corps engaged the Confederates at the North Anna on May 24, and had the honor (with two other Army Corps) to be in the front line when Grant tried to break through the Confederate defenses at Cold Harbor on June 3.

As the Union assault began at 4:30 in the morning at Cold Harbor, three Army Corps were positioned along a very broad front. Hancock's Second Corps was on the left of the Union line, with Barlow's and Gibbon's divisions leading the charge. The Sixth Corps occupied the center of the Union line and the Eighteenth Corps the right. The lead brigades for Barlow's advance were those of Miles and Brooke, characterized as "the army's shock troops" by Hancock's biographer, Glenn Tucker.[36] Miles and Brooke captured some forward Rebel positions but were quickly driven back. Elsewhere the attack was even less successful. A little after noon Grant suspended the attack, having sustained as many as 12,000 casualties, including six of his colonels, who were killed.

The relentlessness of the fighting began to take its toll on even as committed a soldier as Nelson Miles. On June 22, 1864, he wrote to his brother Daniel promising to send word every couple of days that he was still alive. He told his brother that "you can not imagine how worn out and tired the army is." The young general indicated an awareness of his incredible luck, noting that he had participated in 25 battles and general engagements in three years and countless additional skirmishes.[37]

On June 27, in a letter to his aunt, General Miles expressed his feelings about the personal tragedy of war:

> I have lost many friends during the last campaign and it seems as if I was about the last of the officers that were in the Division in '62. On the 3rd I lost a very

---

[36] Tucker, supra., p. 223

[37] Miles to Brother Daniel Miles, June 22, 1864, Miles Papers, Military History Archive, Carlisle.

> intimate friend, Col. H. Boyd McKeen. We were Lieutenants together and served through the entire campaign...we have often said it would come our turn next and during the fearful assault at Cold Harbor he fell mortally wounded and died in a half hour. He was a young man of promising ability, a graduate of Princeton College and of a very wealthy family in Philadelphia. We had planned many pleasant trips for the future if we both lived...Since his death I have felt very sad. About the only solace I have is my Brigade band which plays splendid music every evening...

The general also mentioned that he was often entertained by his brigade's glee club. The tunes he chose to mention to his aunt are also an indication that he was experiencing a considerable degree of war weariness; they were "Wounded and Weary," and "Mother I Have Come Home to Die."[38]

Nevertheless, a letter written to his uncle the very next day also indicates that Miles was not totally cured of attraction to war. He took pride in the friendship displayed towards him by General Hancock and told his uncle about an incident that had occurred a few days earlier. Miles stepped up to the firing line to join his men and encourage them, when a solid shot took off the head of the soldier next to him, splattering Miles' coat, cap, and face with brains. Rather than commenting on the horror of the event, Miles observed, "I thought it a pretty close call."[39]

After Cold Harbor, Miles was on the march again as Grant tried once again to outflank Lee by moving to the Southeast and now had brought his army pretty much to where it had been two years earlier when it had been forced to evacuate the environs of Richmond by Lee

---

[38]Letter to "Aunt Mary" [Curtis], June 27, 1864, Miles Papers, Carlisle.

[39]Miles Papers, Carlisle.

and Jackson. The armies circled towards Petersburg, south of the Confederate capital, and after the Federals missed an opportunity to capture the town on June 15, the nine-and-a-half month siege began on June 18. Barlow left his command due to illness, and Nelson Miles became commander of the First Division of the Second Corps of the Army of the Potomac.

On July 30, 1864, the Second Corps was in reserve, massed behind the Ninth Corps, when a regiment of Pennsylvania coal miners dug a mine shaft under the Confederate works and filled it with explosives. A huge explosion blew a gaping hole in the Rebel line ("the Crater") and but for the vacillation of the Ninth Corps commander, Burnside, and one of his division commanders who was drunk, Richmond may have been taken and Lee defeated in mid-summer 1864. For sixteen days in August and September, 1864, Miles sat on a Board of Inquiry investigating the failure to exploit the Crater. The Board's findings resulted in the end of General Burnside's service in the Union Army. Following the Crater and until the next Spring, the war in Virginia consisted primarily of undramatic trench warfare similar to that fought on the western front in World War I.

In August, elements of the Second Corps were sent to Reams Station, south of Richmond, to destroy the railroad which linked the Rebels to their supply line from North Carolina. Miles' and Gibbons' divisions were attacked by large numbers of Confederates under A.P. Hill and were routed. Miles was able to rally part of his division, which launched a counterattack recapturing part of its former position and one of three artillery batteries. The battle, however, was a bitter setback for two of the elite units of the Union army. Miles' report of the battle indicates his tremendous dissatisfaction with the results of the engagement. The general admitted that he could "not say we gained a victory" and that some of the Union troops did not fight. Concluding that the battle was lost by cowardice, he took solace in the fact that "[t]he glorious 61st [New York Infantry] was the only cool regiment on the field..."[40] Despite the blood letting at Reams Station and elsewhere on the Petersburg front, no dramatic change occurred in the battle lines for eight months.

In July, 1864, Miles became permanent commander of the First Division of the Second Corps, which suffered greater losses than any other division in the Union Army: 2,287 killed, 11,700 wounded, and 4,800 missing. In the fall he was promoted to brevet Major-General and for a brief period of time in February, 1865, was in command of the 26,000 man Second Corps of the Army of the Potomac.[41] During the Petersburg campaign he also received a minor wound, his fourth of the war. In September 1864, Atlanta fell to Sherman, and shortly thereafter the Union Army of the Shenandoah won several major victories in the valley that had been so important to early Confederate success. Two days after the final Union victory in the Shenandoah, the battle of Cedar Creek, Miles wrote his uncle and observed that the triumph assured Lincoln's re-election. He also expressed his opinion of the General-in-Chief, saying "Grant is...the most persistent person you ever saw."[42]

Buoyed further by Lincoln's re-election, Miles wrote to his uncle again on November 9, commenting that the Army had great confidence in Grant and criticizing Lincoln's opponent, McClellan, for "mingling" with the enemies of his country.[43] In the closing days of the War, Miles played a significant role in preventing a Confederate breakout from Richmond. On March 31, 1865, Rebels moving southwest in an effort to link up with General Joseph E. Johnston, who commanded the

---

[40]Miles' report, September 3, 1864, Miles Papers, Military History Institute Archive, Carlisle.

[41]O.R. I, vol. 46, pt. 2, p. 577. The Second Corps at this time was about the same size as the entire U.S. Army which Miles commanded at the outbreak of the Spanish-American War.

[42]Miles letter to Uncle October 21, 1864, Miles Papers, Carlisle

[43]Miles Papers, Carlisle.

Confederates in North Carolina, drove the Union Fifth Army Corps from their positions, but were repulsed by Miles' Division[44]

On April 1, Miles was detached from the Second Corps and his Division was ordered to report to General Philip Sheridan, who had been assigned principal responsibility for preventing an exodus of Confederates to the Southwest. On the second of the month Miles attacked the retreating Confederates at Sutherland Station and after a sharp fight drove them back towards Petersburg. Returning to the Second Corps, he led his division in the pursuit of a Confederate wagon train to the vicinity of Amelia Court House and participated in an engagement there on April 6. The First Division fought several small skirmishes the next day, and Grant's first message to Lee regarding surrender passed through its lines. The fighting continued until in front of them Miles' men saw the long-awaited flag of truce, which was followed the same day, April 9, 1865, by the surrender of the Army of Northern Virginia at Appomattox Court House.

As time passed and those who lived through the Civil War died, the fame of all but the most major figures of the struggle has receded. While Grant, Lee, Sherman, Sheridan and Stuart are still familiar figures to many Americans, the next tier of heroes has largely been forgotten. Possibly the best assessment of Nelson Miles' role in the war is contained in a letter written to him by General James H. Wilson,

---

[44] O.R. I, vol. 46, p. 710. I never ceased to be amazed at how the battles of the Civil War continued to be fought for decades after they were over-by soldiers on the same side. Miles testified before a Court of Inquiry at Governor's Island in New York in June 1880 which was instituted by General Warren, the Fifth Corps commander. Warren was removed from his command during the battle of Five Forks on April 1, and fifteen years later was still seeking vindication at the expense of General Sheridan. Miles testified that he suggested to his corps commander, General Humphreys, that he could check the March 31, Rebel advance against Warren by attacking the Confederate flank. Although he mentioned a counterattack by three of Warren's Divisions, he opined that it was his flank attack that made the Rebel positions untenable. [The New York Times, June 29, 1880, 8:1] In his memoirs Miles expressed a great deal of sympathy for Warren, as well as General George Thomas, who was almost relieved by Grant for delaying his offensive at Nashville. Miles, Serving the Republic, pp. 75, 84.

another "minor" hero of the conflict [he led a large and very successful cavalry raid through Alabama and into Georgia at the end of the war]. On the occasion of Miles' retirement from the Army on August 8, 1903, Wilson wrote:

> Looking back over the past you may console yourself with the reflection that you made a place for yourself in the Great War for the Union second to no man of your age, and that is enough.
>
> An old staff officer of General Humphreys [Second Corps commander at the end of the War] told me this morning that in a fight you were the easiest general to find...You were sure to be at the front and in the thickest of it![45]

---

[45]Wilson to Miles, August 8, 1903, Miles-Cameron Papers, Library of Congress, Manuscript Division

CHAPTER II: JEFFERSON DAVIS' JAILER

Jefferson Davis, President of the Confederate States of America, is a figure treated with much ambivalence by American historians. During the Civil War he was an arch-villain in the North, the prototype of the Southern aristocrat who split the country and brought on the War. Once the South seceded, some Northerners speculated that Davis had been planning the break for years and that he had used his position as Secretary of War in the 1850s to prepare his section for the coming conflict. His infamy in the North is best reflected in a verse "we'll hang Jeff Davis from a sour apple tree".

Although popular in the South when the war began, he became the scapegoat for Confederate reverses. His unpopularity increased dramatically with Union success in the West, and he became embroiled in bitter disputes with several Confederate generals, most notably Joseph E. Johnston and P.T. Beauregard over strategy. His conduct of the war became increasingly controversial as a result of his reliance on Braxton Bragg, who to many Southerners seemed incapable of capitalizing on any opportunity to win the war in the West. His increasingly bitter personal dispute with General Johnston was a factor in Grant's victory at Vicksburg and even more so with Sherman's successful drive on Atlanta. Indeed, many historians consider his decision in the summer of 1864 to replace Johnston with John Bell Hood, as commanding general of Confederate forces defending Atlanta, to be the most important decision made by either Lincoln or Davis in the entire war. By making this change, Davis rejected Johnston's strategy of staying on the defensive. Johnston believed that Southern independence was most likely to be achieved simply by holding Atlanta until the Republicans were defeated in the Presidential election in November, 1864.

Johnston's successor, Hood, immediately went on the offensive against Sherman, lost Atlanta, and gave Lincoln one of the victories that led to his re-election. This allowed Lincoln to prosecute the war to its successful conclusion. Despite Davis' responsibility for the Confederate defeat his reputation in the South was rehabilitated in an amazingly brief period of time. Credit for this transformation goes to his wife, Varina Howell Davis, who accomplished this feat partially at the expense of the twenty-six year old Union brevet Major-General, Nelson A. Miles.

On Sunday, April 2, 1865, as Davis sat in a church pew in Richmond, a courier from General Lee arrived to inform him that the Army of Northern Virginia could no longer hold the defenses to the city and was starting its evacuation. Davis and his cabinet immediately escaped to the South. When he learned of General Johnston's surrender to Sherman in North Carolina, Davis continued on his way into Georgia. He intended to reach Confederate forces in Alabama, but if there was no prospect for successful resistance east of the Mississippi, he intended to cross the River and continue to fight with the troops under the command of Kirby Smith and John B. Magruder.

After Lincoln's assassination on April 14, 1865, Davis' fate if he were to fall into the hands of Federal troops became even more problematical. On May 2, 1865, Lincoln's successor, Andrew Johnson, issued a proclamation offering a $100,000 reward for the arrest of Davis. This proclamation stated that it appeared that the assassination of President Lincoln and the attempted assassination of Secretary of State William H. Seward "were incited, concerted and procured between Jefferson Davis...Clement C. Clay...and other rebels and traitors..."

On May 10, near Irwinville, Georgia, Davis and his party were apprehended by Federal troops.[1] Taken to Savannah, they were placed aboard a steamer and were transported to Hampton Roads, Virginia. Here Confederate Vice-President Alexander Stephens, General Joseph Wheeler, (who had volunteered to provide Davis with a cavalry escort through the Gulf states), and others were transferred to a boat taking

---

[1]Several members of the Confederate cabinet who had separated from the Davis party, Secretary of State, Judah P. Benjamin, and Secretary of War, John C. Breckinridge, were able to make good their escape.

them to Federal prisons further north.[2] It was decided that Davis, Clement Clay, and newspaper editor John Mitchell would be incarcerated at nearby Fortress Monroe and that, pursuant to orders issued on May 19, 1865, the commandant of Fortress Monroe would be Major-General Nelson A. Miles.

The selection of Miles for this post made a great deal of sense since, unlike the generals who had attended West Point, Miles had not had close friends from the South before the War and had not acquired any sympathy with their outlook. In the biography she wrote of her husband in 1890, Varina Howell Davis recalled her first meeting with the man she came to regard as one of this nation's arch-villains:

> General Miles and some other officers came on board, and summoned Mrs. Clay and me. He was quite young, about I should think twenty-five, and seemed to have newly acquired his elevated position. He was not respectful, but I thought it was his ignorance of polite usage. He declined to tell me anything of my husband, or about our own destination, and said "Davis" had announced Mr. Lincoln's assassination the day before it happened, and he guessed he knew all about it.[3]

Davis was initially confined in the gunroom of one of the Fortress' casemates. On May 22, Assistant Secretary of War, Charles A. Dana,

---

[2]Wheeler, a twenty-six-year-old Confederate Major-General, managed to survive his imprisonment to become a Democratic congressman and to be appointed a Major-General of United States Volunteers by President McKinley in 1898. In this capacity he commanded the cavalry division during the American invasion of Cuba, which included the "Rough Riders" regiment commanded by Theodore Roosevelt. Wheeler initiated the first skirmish of the campaign and participated in the negotiations for the surrender of the Spanish garrison at Santiago de Cuba, with General William Shafter and Nelson A. Miles, Commanding General of the United States Army.

[3]Davis, Varina Howell, Jefferson Davis, New York, 1890 (2 volumes), p. 650

on a mission to inspect security at the fort, issued the following order to prevent Davis from escaping or committing suicide:

> Brevet-Major General Miles is hereby authorized and directed to place manacles and fetters upon the hands and feet of Jefferson Davis and Clement C. Clay, whenever he may think it advisable in order to render their imprisonment more secure.[4]

A careful reading of this order makes it clear that Miles was not required to put manacles or fetters on Davis but that it was left up to his discretion. The next day, May 23, Miles exercised this discretion and ordered fetters placed on the feet of the Confederate President. To Varina Davis there was no possible justification for this act, which she concluded was motivated solely by a desire to humiliate and torture her husband, and possibly cause his death. Miles, on the other hand, stated that he was notified of several plots to rescue Davis and was ordered to take every precaution to prevent it. He also justified his decision on the grounds that the wooden doors to Davis' cell were in the process of being removed and replaced by metal grating. Workmen were constantly going in and out of the cell to finish this work, and Miles argued:

> It will be remembered that Louis Napoleon escaped through the connivance of a physician and mechanics who were employed in his prison.[5]

Mrs. Davis ridiculed these precautions, claiming her husband's health was precarious, and that no man could have removed the metal grating [which Miles claimed was not yet in place] without mechanical

---

[4]Miles, My Treatment of Jefferson Davis, Independent, 58:413-17 (February 23, 1905)

[5]Ibid.

assistance, swim across the moat that surrounded the fort, elude the sentinels, and make it to freedom. Miles, in 1905, claimed that the poor state of Davis' health had been greatly exaggerated and that Davis himself had indicated that he was looking for an opportunity to surprise a guard, knock him down, and steal his horse.

On balance there is a good case to be made in defense of Miles' decision. In arguing that Davis couldn't possibly have escaped from Fort Monroe, his wife misses the obvious; what Federal authorities were most concerned with was a rescue attempt by others. Indeed, on July 14, 1865, Miles was informed by Secretary of War Stanton that his intelligence sources in Canada expected an imminent attempt to free Davis.[6] In 1878, Miles defended his decision in a letter to the Adjutant General of the Army, noting:

> It will however be remembered that at the time there were hundreds of men outside and some inside that Fortress who had served in the Rebel Army and who were ready to sacrifice an arm to effect his escape.[7]

One must also remember that Miles' shackling of Davis occurred little more than one month after Abraham Lincoln had been murdered. Fear and suspicion of all sorts of conspiracies were rampant and not without justifiable basis. Some Confederate troops west of the Mississippi had not surrendered, and there was a fear that Davis would be spirited away to lead those who refused to accept the verdict of Appomattox. Moreover, there was a conspiracy involved in the Lincoln assassination and, as Miles correctly noted in his 1905 defense, it was not for him to question President Johnson's proclamation that Davis was part of that

---

[6]Stanton to Miles, July 14, 1865, Miles Papers, Carlisle

[7]Miles to Adjutant General October 30, 1878, Miles Papers, Carlisle.

conspiracy.[8] Similarly Miles' concern about a rescue attempt by persons authorized to be at Fort Monroe was not unreasonable in view of the fact that John Wilkes Booth had not worried about security at Ford's Theatre (which turned out to be virtually nonexistent) because he was certain that he would have free access to anyplace in the theatre by virtue of his status as a well-known actor who frequently performed there.

As to Mrs. Davis' assertion that Miles manacled her husband out of a personal vindictiveness, one must note that when she wrote her husband's biography the passions of the Civil War had faded and her husband had become a respectable figure again. There was considerable sympathy for him because he had been imprisoned for two years without ever being brought to trial and because he had erroneously been accused of complicity in the Lincoln murder. In contrast, at the time Miles placed fetters on Davis' feet, the war which had consumed an entire generation had just ended and the beloved Lincoln's corpse was barely cold. Moreover, the one thing that Nelson Miles' career and reputation could not have survived in this assignment was a successful escape. One can hardly blame him for being overzealous about security.

In any event, on May 23, 1865, Cpt. Jerome Titlow, the officer of the day at Fort Monroe, entered Davis' cell with two blacksmiths. According to Mrs. Davis (who was not there) they brought with them "a pair of heavy leg irons coupled together by a ponderous chain".[9] Miles, on the other hand, described this equipment as "light anklets"

---

[8]Indeed, as of this writing, the theory that the Confederate Secret Service was involved in the Lincoln assassination is enjoying a revival. Proponents argue that although Lee had surrendered at the time of the President's murder, much of the Confederacy had not, and that the assassination made some sense as a desperation measure to save Southern independence. One variation also suggests that the assassination was ordered in retaliation for the Union's Dahlgren raid in early 1864. Papers found on Colonel Dahlgren's body after he was killed and the raid failed suggested an intention to kill or kidnap Davis and other Confederate leaders. While the Union disclaimed the authenticity of the documents, the Confederates may obviously have thought otherwise.

[9]Davis, supra, p. 655

which would prevent Davis from running but would allow him to walk about his room.[10]

According to Mrs. Davis, Cpt. Titlow informed Davis that with "great personal reluctance" he had come to execute an order to place him in irons. Davis asked Titlow if Miles had given this order and if so, that Davis wished to talk to Miles. When the Captain informed Davis that Miles had left the fort, Davis asked that the execution of the order be postponed until Miles returned; Titlow replied that his orders did not permit him such discretion.

The Confederate leader made it clear that he had no intention of submitting to the order and told Titlow to have the guards shoot him instead. Titlow ordered the blacksmiths to proceed, and as one stooped down, Davis slung him to the floor. Cpt. Titlow quickly prevented the blacksmith from hitting Davis back and his guards from shooting; then he ordered four men to hold Davis down while the order was carried out. When the deed was accomplished Davis wept, a part of the story mentioned in many accounts of the incident but not that of Mrs. Davis, who was not interested in anything that did not reinforce the image of a stoic Confederate martyr.

Mrs. Davis did, however, allude to the stories that her husband wept. Much of her account of her husband's incarceration and his treatment by General Miles was based on a book sympathetic with Davis that was published in 1866 by Dr. John J. Craven, the post surgeon at Fort Monroe. While she was willing to accept Craven's word as gospel whenever it suited her, she obviously was unwilling to accept any part of Craven's account that didn't serve her purposes. Without mentioning the fact that Craven's book had included an account of Davis breaking down, she euphemistically alluded to it:

> Of the dramatic account published in Dr. Craven's book, he (Davis) said it could not have been written by anyone who ... knew the facts...very little was said by

---

[10]Miles, My Treatment of Jefferson Davis, supra.

> Captain Titlow or by himself, and that whatever was said was uttered in a very quiet practical manner. For himself, he would say he was too resolved and too proudly conscious of his relation to a sacred cause, for such exclamation and manifestation as were imputed to him by Dr. Craven's informant, and given to the public in his book.[11]

At a minimum, this revealing reference is an admission by Mrs. Davis that the Craven book, on which she based so much of her case that Miles mistreated her husband, was not accurate in all respects.

Two chapters of Varina Davis' biography are devoted to the treatment of her husband by Nelson Miles. One is entitled "Cruelties at Fortress Monroe" and the following chapter is entitled "The Tortures Inflicted By General Miles." It is well worth examining closely the specific allegations in Mrs. Davis' book to determine whether Nelson Miles was a sadist, who tortured and harassed a helpless old man to advance his own career, or rather a man with some convictions who simply refused to accord to Mr. and Mrs. Davis the deference to which they were accustomed, and to which they believed they were entitled.

Mrs. Davis wanted her readers to believe that, throughout his imprisonment, her husband was hanging on to life by a thread due to the inhospitable surroundings of his confinement and the mental torture constantly inflicted by Miles. She claimed her husband's health was precarious on his arrival at Fort Monroe and was further compromised by the dampness of his cell, the quality of his food, and his inability to sleep. Her husband complained that he was deprived of his sleep by the guards stationed in his cell who made too much noise when they

[11]Davis, supra, p. 658

changed stations and because they kept a light burning at all times so that they could observe him.[12]

Mrs. Davis notes that Dr. Craven, on whose account she based much of her book, visited Jefferson Davis on May 24, 1865, only a few days after he had arrived at Ft. Monroe. Craven said he found that the prisoner was despondent and emaciated and complained about the noise made by the guards in his chamber. Craven asked Miles that Mr. Davis be allowed tobacco, "the want of which after a lifetime of use, he had referred to as one of the probable causes of his illness".[13] What was General Miles' response to this request? He granted it.

Mrs. Davis complained that her husband ate very little because his food was "shredded" by soldiers searching for weapons--not such an unreasonable precaution given the temper of the times. She also noted that Dr. Craven advised General Miles on May 26 that the removal of the fetters from Davis' legs was essential to the maintenance of his health. Accepting Mrs. Davis' and Craven's belief that Miles removed the leg irons on the basis on Craven's plea, and not, as Miles later claimed, because they were no longer necessary when the metal grating on his cell had been completed, the fact remains that Miles immediately removed these restraints.

Miles initially forbid the Confederate leader any communication with his wife and severely limited his reading material. Whether Miles did so at his own discretion or pursuant to orders from the War Department is not clear.

On June 24, 1865, only one month after Davis' arrival at Ft. Monroe, Dr. Craven requested that the guards be removed from inside Davis' cell so that he could sleep; Miles again complied almost immediately. At the same time Miles announced that the ex-President would be allowed a one-hour walk around the ramparts of the Fortress

---

[12]Miles' orders, received from General Henry Halleck on May 22, 1865, included instructions that a light be kept burning at all times so that Davis could be kept under constant observation. Miles Papers, Carlisle Pa.

[13]Varina Davis, supra, p.660

and would be allowed to have any reading matter that was approved by his headquarters.

Davis was required to take his daily constitutional with Miles and two armed guards. Mrs. Davis wrote that when she was first allowed to visit her husband in May, 1866:

> (He) expressed supreme contempt for the petty insults inflicted hourly by General Miles, who he said, had exhausted his ingenuity to find something more afflicting to visit upon him. Among other things, he told me that General Miles never walked with him on the ramparts...without saying something so offensive and irritating as to render the exercise a painful effort.[14]

In particular she cited Dr. Craven's account of a discussion that Miles struck up with Davis in July, 1865, in which the post surgeon reported:

> ...General Miles...if he was seeking a subject that would not offend the almost dying man, was singularly unfortunate in his choice of a topic...

Dr. Craven then recounted that Miles had asked Davis if he was aware of rumors that John C. Calhoun had become wealthy through unethical business dealings; Davis, according to the surgeon, was outraged that Miles would repeat what he believed to be a malicious lie about one of his idols.[15]

When Miles published his defense in 1905, the New York Times reported that one of the surviving guards at Fort Monroe, a Private

---

[14]Davis, supra., p. 760

[15]Ibid. 673-4

Edwin A. Jones, fully supported Miles. Pvt. Jones recalled that he often saw Miles and Davis walking arm and arm upon the ramparts talking and laughing as if they were the best of friends.[16] While it strains credulity to accept Pvt. Jones' assessment of the relationship between the prisoner and the jailer, the fact that Dr. Craven and Mrs. Davis called special attention to the conversation in which Miles raised the subject of Calhoun, without mentioning any other specific examples of Miles' offensiveness, suggests that Mrs. Davis is not to be believed either.

Surgeon Craven continually referred to the state of Davis' health during 1865 as being critical. Davis suffered from erysipelas on the face and head (a strep infection of the skin) and a carbuncle (similar to a boil) on the left thigh. The doctor asserted that Davis was at death's door despite his ability to walk around the ramparts of Fort Monroe on a daily basis. He was particularly concerned with the dampness of the prisoner's cell and, on October 2, 1865, after a little more than four months in the gunroom, Davis was moved to quarters more to his liking on the second floor of a house built for the officers.

In one telling passage from Craven's book, quoted by Mrs. Davis, perhaps inadvertently, the doctor stated:

> His general treatment, Mr. Davis acknowledged to be good, though there were in it many annoyances of detail--such as the sentry's eye always fastened on his movements, and the supervision of his correspondence with his wife.[17]

Craven ridiculed Miles for prohibiting Davis from sending to his wife a letter describing the prison:

---

[16]New York Times, Feb. 25, 1905, 2:5

[17]Davis, supra, p. 720

> perhaps suspecting that if told where he was Mrs. Davis would storm the fort and rescue him...[18]

Miles, of course, was legitimately concerned with the possibility that Mrs. Davis would pass this information along to people who did have the will and the resources to make an attempt to free the Confederate President. Similarly, the objections to the fact that Mr. Davis was constantly watched while in prison reflects less poorly on Miles and his superiors when you consider that the Allied Powers did precisely the same thing with high-ranking Nazi officials during the Nuremberg trials--to prevent escape or suicide attempts.

Dr. Craven's diary made it quite clear that he had become an unabashed admirer of the state prisoner. In the fall, he purchased Davis an overcoat out of his own pocket, and Commandant Miles became concerned about the rapport between doctor and patient. On November 18, 1865, Miles ordered Craven:

> ...that in the future your conversations with him will be confined strictly to professional matters...[19]

Craven was not only offended by the order but was also inconvenienced. Previously he had sent Davis two meals a day whenever the Confederate President desired them. Miles ordered him to send Davis three meals a day on a fixed schedule, which Craven found to be very inconvenient to himself and to his family, because they generally got their meals at the same time as Davis. Shortly thereafter Craven was relieved of his duties at Fort Monroe, and when his prison diary was published in 1866 it caused a furor in the North as well as in the South.

---

[18] Ibid, 687.

[19] Davis, supra, p.692

In May of 1866, after a year's separation, Varina Davis was allowed to visit her husband and discovered that he was "slowly dying in my sight."[20] Yet she wrote of a visit made to Ft. Monroe at about the same time by President Johnson's Secretary of the Treasury, Hugh McCulloch, whom she quoted as reporting:

> On my arrival at the fortress, Mr. Davis was walking upon the ramparts accompanied by a couple of soldiers. I was glad to notice that his gait was erect, his step elastic, and, when he came nearer, that he had not the appearance of one who was suffering in health by his imprisonment...[21]

In April 1866, Davis' exercise period was increased to two hours pursuant the orders of the new post surgeon, Dr. Cooper, who was every bit as sympathetic toward the prisoner as Dr. Craven. Despite Davis' ability to walk around the ramparts, Dr. Cooper wrote Varina Davis that her husband was growing weaker and sinking. Mrs. Davis was able to enlist Northern and Southern newspapers in her effort to gain her husband's freedom, and an article appearing in the New York World on May 24, 1866 asserted as fact that Davis was at death's door at Ft. Monroe.[22]

Commandant Miles wrote to the Adjutant General's Office on May 28, complaining that he had been faithfully following his orders and that his reputation was being severely damaged by Dr. Cooper's reports

---

[20]Davis, supra, p. 765

[21]Davis, supra, p. 699. This account is corroborated by a June 6, 1866 report by Surgeon General J. K. Barnes that Davis was in good condition. Dr. Barnes reported that Davis told him that his health was much better than had been represented by others. Miles Papers, Military History Institute, Carlisle.

[22] The New York World, May 24, 1866, 4:1; editorial entitled "The torture of Jefferson Davis", citing the report of Dr. Cooper.

regarding Davis' health. He asserted that, "Surgeon Cooper is entirely under the influence of Mr. & Mrs. Davis..." and alleged that Cooper's wife was a secessionist. Miles closed his communique by stating that he had gone out of his way not to make a hero or a martyr out of the Confederate Chief Executive.[23]

Nevertheless, sympathy was growing for Jefferson Davis, and it was becoming clear that the government was not going to put him on trial either for treason or for complicity in the Lincoln assassination. As part of the movement towards his release, Nelson Miles was relieved as commandant on August 29, 1866. Upon Miles' departure from Ft. Monroe, restrictions on Davis were eased even further, and his wife was allowed to live with him in the fortress.

Miles probably would have been very pleased if this unhappy interlude in his career had been totally obscured. By the time Mrs. Davis published her book with its scathing assessment of his treatment of her husband, Miles was one of the senior generals in the United States Army with very realistic ambitions for even further promotion. The publicity of those unhappy days of 1865-1866 could hardly have been welcome. However, buried in Mrs. Davis' book is a passage which perhaps says a great deal as to why she felt such loathing for Nelson Miles:

> We excused much to General Miles, whose opportunities to learn the habits of refined people were said to have been few...[24]

The aristocratic Mrs. Davis could never forgive the upstart Yankee farm boy for failing to acknowledge her husband's social superiority.

Miles was bothered enough by Mrs. Davis' book to, as he put it, "break his forty years of silence" about the circumstances of his shackling

[23]O.R. II, vol. 8, 900, 914, 919

[24]Davis, supra, p. 764

of Jefferson Davis by publishing an article entitled, "My Treatment of Jefferson Davis" in the February 23, 1905 issue of the magazine Independent. Miles noted that it was he who ordered all the improvements in Davis' status and claimed that he also recommended that the prisoner either be released or be brought to trial. Unfortunately for Miles, he committed one egregious tactical error when he referred to a 1865 note from Mrs. Davis thanking him for his consideration. The former First Lady of the Confederacy wrote to the Savannah Press on March 2, 1905, stating that the letter cited by Miles was written during the first few days of Davis' confinement, when she was ignorant of what was being done to her husband. If the letter is genuine, she continued:

> [i]t only serves to put in a clearer light his [Miles] continued infraction of the most obvious rules of veracity...

At the very moment he received her note, Mrs. Davis observed, Miles was "contemplating the immediate subjection of his helpless prisoner to the grossest maltreatment."[25]

Several of Miles' former subordinates at Ft. Monroe came to his aid. In addition to the former Private Jones, mentioned previously, J.W. Sanderson of Beaver Dam, Wisconsin, an officer at Ft. Monroe during Davis' imprisonment, said that while he thought the shackling of Davis to have been unnecessary, he believed from his association with Davis that the Confederate leader "never entertained any bitter feelings" towards General Miles, and Sanderson opined that "no prisoner of state ever received more considerate treatment than did Jefferson Davis."[26]

One C.A. Dorman wrote to a New Haven newspaper saying that he had been a hospital steward at Fortress Monroe throughout Davis'

---

[25]New York Times, Feb. 3, 1905,1:3; Feb. 24, 1905, 1:2;March 5, 1905,9:3.

[26]New York Times, March 12,1905, 7:1.

imprisonment. Noting that he was, in 1905, not of the same "political faith" as General Miles, Dorman observed:

> It will be noticed by those who have read the accounts of cruelty mentioned by Mrs. Davis and her daughter that the only indignity, as they term it, was the placing of anklets upon Mr. Davis for a few days, and why? Because there is nothing else with which to charge General Miles...
>
> As an eye witness of the whole matter, I truthfully and fearlessly declare that the statement that Jefferson Davis was maltreated at Ft. Monroe is a continental falsehood.[27]

As to the fact that her husband never complained in his autobiography about his treatment by Miles, Mrs. Davis attributed the omission to the victim's good nature.[28] Finally, Varina Davis may have the satisfaction of knowing that her husband's year and a quarter under Miles' care may have been a factor in thwarting the general's political ambitions [whether he had any is an open question]. In an editorial following Miles' retirement from the Army in August 1903, the Baltimore Sun commented on his rumored ambitions by observing that nothing could make Miles' arch-foe, President Roosevelt, happier than the prospect of running against Miles. The general was, according to the Sun, the only potential Democratic candidate capable of losing the South.[29] That this assessment had much to do with the controversy over his treatment of Jefferson Davis is evidenced by the fact that the

---

[27]Letter of March 2, 1905 to New Haven Journal & Courier(?) in the Nelson Miles Papers, Military History Institute Archive, Carlisle.

[28]Davis, supra, p. 767

[29]Baltimore Sun, August 10, 1903, p. 4.

Southern Democrats had earlier accepted a Union general as their candidate. In 1880, Miles' former commander, Winfield Scott Hancock, had been the Democrats' standard bearer and carried the South, although he narrowly lost the election to James Garfield.

In reflecting upon Miles' tenure as commandant of Fort Monroe, there is a certain irony in the fact that the first controversial incident of his career involved the treatment of prisoners, and so did one of the last. In 1902, Miles courted trouble by criticizing the treatment accorded Filipino prisoners of war by American soldiers and induced an irate reaction that was reminiscent of his response to the critics of his treatment of Jefferson Davis.

PHOTOGRAPHS

1. Major General Nelson A. Miles, commandant of Fortress Monroe, Virginia, summer 1865--note the armband worn during the mourning period for President Lincoln.

2. Nelson A. Miles, Colonel of the 5th United States Infantry Regiment, circa 1874--wearing the shoulder straps of a brevet major general.

3. The Commanding General of the United States Army, circa 1900--the vertical grouping of four buttons indicates his rank as Lieutenant General; the sash signifies his position as commanding general. Hanging from Miles' neck is the Congressional Medal of Honor.

4. General Miles at Arlington Cemetery circa 1922.

68645

CHAPTER III: RECONSTRUCTION, THE SIOUX WAR, AND THE NEZ PERCE

Virtually all the volunteer officers left the rapidly contracting Army after the Civil War. As one veteran, Colonel Thomas Wentworth Higginson, put it, they left military service to "pursue once again the quiet paths they led."[1] Most of them had had enough adventure and flirtation with violent death to last a lifetime, but Nelson Miles was different.

Actually it is not that difficult to understand Miles' decision to make the Army his profession. Other young men had dramatic success in the war, but unlike many of the others who were not professional soldiers, Nelson Miles had neither impressive educational credentials nor social standing [his friend Barlow, for example, had both]. He was a 26-year-old without a University education, without a promising career to return to, and without "connections" in the civilian world. In the military, by contrast, he was an intimate of Grant, Hancock, Sheridan, and Meade--the men at the very top.

Undoubtedly, Nelson Miles must have given much thought to his future in 1865 and must have considered that what he would be doing in the coming years was going to be very different from the fighting he had done for the great and glorious cause of 1861-1865. The future in the Army promised occupation duty in the South as it was "reconstructed," perhaps some action on the Mexican border, and fighting the Indians, who were trying to preserve their nomadic culture from the expanding white colossus.

In January 1866, in a letter to General Henry Halleck, Miles expressed an expectation that he would soon return to civilian life.[2] However, he did decide to make the Army a career and, upon his departure from Fort Monroe, he received a commission as a Colonel in

---

[1]Higginson, Thomas W., THE HARVARD MEMORIAL BIOGRAPHIES, (1866)

[2]Halleck to Miles, Jan. 16,1866; responding to a letter, Miles to Halleck, Jan. 12, 1866, Miles-Cameron Papers, Library of Congress.

the Regular Army. Given the fact that the Army was in the process of contracting from a million-man organization to one with less than 55,000 overnight, Miles was very lucky to obtain this elevated rank. George Custer, also a brevet Major-General, who was a West Point graduate with an outstanding war record, was reduced to Lieutenant Colonel, and many highly ranked officers found themselves Captains or even Lieutenants in the Regular Army.

Miles was appointed commanding officer of the 40th United States Infantry Regiment and also Assistant Commissioner of the Freedman's Bureau for the State of North Carolina, with headquarters at Raleigh. This assignment was due to his prior association with General O.O. Howard, head of the Freedman's Bureau, the agency through which the federal government intended to guide the former slaves from bondage to citizenship.

In March 1866, while still at Fort Monroe, Miles had expressed an interest in the plight of the former slaves when he wrote to General Howard asking him for assistance in encouraging the blacks camped near the Fortress to resettle in Florida. Miles observed that these uprooted people were hesitant to trust anyone, but that he thought they might listen to Howard, who had acquired the reputation of an ombudsman for the freed slaves.

Howard was very pleased to have Miles assigned to the Freedman's Bureau, and the young Colonel characteristically discharged his duties in North Carolina with much enthusiasm and aggressiveness. He encouraged the Bureau's educational programs with the result that over 8500 black students were studying in 101 new schools in his domain. He also made a concerted effort to encourage the former slaves to vote, an effort that was greeted with a very cool reception by the whites in Raleigh.[3]

Miles was very eager to use his troops to aid the reconstruction government and discourage resistance by North Carolina's white inhabitants. When Miles left North Carolina in 1869, he took with him a testimonial from the Reconstruction Governor, W.W. Holden, that "he has been uniformly true to the loyalists of this State." Miles' enthusiasm for doing the bidding of the Reconstruction government did, however, get him into a bit of trouble that foreshadows much of his future conduct which was deemed insubordinate by his superiors.

In September 1868, Governor Holden asked Miles for assistance in stopping the suspected flow of arms to a white political club in Wilmington, North Carolina. Miles immediately requested his military superior, General Meade in Atlanta, for permission to accommodate the Governor. After being told by Meade that such disposition of his troops was beyond his authority, Miles wrote Meade again on October 4, 1868, renewing his request and observing that "the sequel of the rebellion is now being enacted."[4] Meade's adjutant responded on October 8, informing Miles that the state authorities must deal with this problem without federal military assistance and noted that the commanding general "regrets his difference of opinion with you as to the authority granted by existing laws and instructions."[5]

The next day, General Meade wrote Grant, the Commanding General of the Army, complaining about his overly aggressive subordinate:

---

[3]DeMontravel, Peter R., The Career of Lt. General Nelson A. Miles From the Civil War through the Indian Wars, Phd Thesis, St. Johns Univ. 1977, Library of Congress, pp. 130-146. Miles' support of Negro suffrage is also revealed in a letter to Senator Henry Wilson dated November 18,1865, and his annual report to General Howard dated October 9, 1867. In his report to General Howard, Miles ridiculed the notion that blacks would not exercise the right to vote intelligently. Miles Papers, Military History Institute, Carlisle.

[4]Miles letter of October 4, 1868, Miles Papers, Military History Institute. Carlisle, Pa.

[5]Adjutant Drum to Miles, October 8, 1868, Miles Papers, Carlisle.

> It will be seen from this correspondence that General Miles not only differs in toto, with me as to the authority given by the laws, and instructions of the War Department, but that after the clear and positive enunciation of my views, he continues to make laborious arguments in opposition to the same.
>
> It is hardly necessary for me to say that no one has a higher respect personally for General Miles than myself...

Observing the necessity of having harmonious views between a commanding officer and his subordinates, Meade continued:

> I have to ask a decision on the issue raised, and that the officer whose judgment is not approved whether it be myself or General Miles be relieved from further command in this Department.[6]

Miles backed away from a confrontation with his chief, and on October 13, Meade wrote the Adjutant General in Washington that after speaking with Miles he had concluded that his October 9 letter had misrepresented Miles' intentions. Meade therefore withdrew the request made in that letter for a decision by Grant. In a letter dated October 22, Miles disingenuously contended that his October 4 letter was intended only to explain the rationale of his earlier letter regarding the white political clubs, not to take issue with General Meade. On a larger scale, the dispute between Miles and Meade is indicative of the drift

---

[6]Meade to Grant October 9, 1868, Miles Papers, Military History Institute Archives, Carlisle.

towards relaxed federal control over the Southern states and the reassertion of political control by the former Confederates.

During 1867, Nelson Miles met Mary Hoyt Sherman, a niece of William Tecumseh Sherman who would replace Grant as commanding general; on June 30, 1868, he married her. Another uncle of the bride was United States Senator John Sherman, and many of the groom's detractors would claim that his future advancement was due largely to nepotism. Although Miles was certainly not adverse to seeking every advantage that marriage into the Sherman family could bring, he had made other equally important connections solely on the strength of his performance under fire during the Civil War. His immediate superior in the Second Corps of the Army of the Potomac, Winfield Scott Hancock, was one of only five Major-Generals in the Regular Army, and his closest friend, Francis C. Barlow, Attorney General of the State of New York and later a prominent New York City attorney, was always willing and able to lobby for a promotion for his former comrade in arms.[7] Indeed, his family ties to General Sherman may not have helped Miles very much, because the scourge of Georgia and South Carolina was extremely unreceptive to entreaties from his niece and her husband.

In March 1869, Miles' last ties to the great cause for which he enlisted were severed when he was reassigned to Fort Hays, Kansas. From then on, he would not be fighting to save the Union, to liberate the slaves, or even to protect the freedman; he would be suppressing the Indians. Miles, throughout his career, expressed a great deal of sympathy for the Indians and most probably understood some of the moral implications of his future work. In his memoirs, he wrote:

---

[7]For example, in March 1886, Barlow visited President Cleveland in an effort to convince the Chief Executive to promote Miles to Major-General instead of O.O. Howard. Barlow supported his personal appeal with a letter to the President from Samuel Tilden, former Governor and the Democratic Presidential candidate in 1876.

In an affectionate letter just before his death, Barlow referred to himself as Miles' "old father." He did note that even he had called Miles a "selfish cuss" on occasion. Barlow letters of March 1886 and September 16, 1895, Miles-Cameron Papers, Library of Congress.

> Three hundred years of cruelty, bigotry, and cupidity of the white race, and two hundred years of warfare, had engendered a hostility and hatred that were inherent in both races... It was more intense with the Indians, as they were the unfortunate and subjugated people. Not only was their country overrun, but the vices and diseases brought among them by the white race were more destructive than war and swept whole tribes out of existence. Still they maintained a courage and fortitude that were heroic. In vain might we search history for the record of a people who contended as valiantly against a superior race, overwhelming in numbers, and defended their country until finally driven toward the setting sun, a practically annihilated nation and race.[8]

One may ask, then, if Miles recognized the injustice perpetrated on the Indians, whether that in any way affected his decision to devote his talents to their subjugation. It may be that he was able to rationalize his decision. Possibly the Indian Wars could have been completely avoided only if the Army had prevented white settlement in much of the western part of the country. On the other hand, it is not very difficult to recognize the injustice to the Indians in most of the major conflicts in which Miles participated. In the Red River War, the Indians went on the warpath after being driven to the brink of starvation by white men, who killed off the buffalo herds in violation of the Indian treaty rights. Similarly, the Sioux War was provoked by white disregard of the Indians' treaty rights to the Black Hills. The Nez Perce were peacefully living in Eastern Oregon until driven off their land by whites with the help of the Army. Possibly Miles concluded that the Indians would be better

---

[8]Miles, Serving the Republic, p. 117

off if the Army had officers who understood their dilemma and were sympathetic to it. Most likely, however, he stayed in the Army because he didn't know what else to do and because he loved adventure.

From 1869 to 1874, Miles cooled his heels while others, George Crook, Custer, and Ranald Mackenzie, fought significant engagements with the Indians. Then war with the Cheyennes, Kiowas, and Comanches broke out in Indian Territory (now Oklahoma) and the Texas Panhandle. During that conflict, the Red River War, Miles saw his first significant action against the Indians as commander of a column of troops sent from the Department of Missouri by General John Pope.

After enduring searing heat, Miles engaged 600 warriors on August 30, 1874, and drove them off. He was unable to follow up his success because his supplies were exhausted. While Miles fumed about the lack of logistical support provided to him by his commanding officer, the fleeing Indians ran into another column of troops commanded by Ranald MacKenzie and were badly mauled. In October, Miles renewed his offensive against the remaining hostiles in the Staked Plains of the Texas Panhandle.

In November, elements of Miles' column under the command of Lt. Frank Baldwin[9] attacked a Cheyenne village and, after driving off the occupants, found two white girls, ages 5 and 7. The children had been kidnapped in western Kansas by a band of Indians, who killed their parents and several of their siblings. Miles sent the children to his wife and became their legal guardian. Later, two older sisters were also rescued. As winter came on, much of the Army retired to its quarters. Miles stayed in the field until February 1875 and, due to his persistence and that of MacKenzie, and others, the hostile Indians returned to their reservations, and Indian warfare in the Southern Plains came to a permanent conclusion.

---

[9] Baldwin (1842-1923) was a Civil War veteran who ended his military career as a Brigadier General in the Philippines. After his retirement he was promoted to Major-General.

With a little successful Indian fighting under his belt, Miles went to the Dakotas in June 1876. Blatant violations of their treaty rights to the Black Hills had provoked the Northern Plains Indians into armed resistance. The Army then launched a three-pronged attack against 3,000 warriors led by Chiefs Sitting Bull and Crazy Horse. In mid-June the Indians attacked one of the three columns commanded by General George Crook and defeated it. Then they turned their attention to another column under the nominal command of General Alfred Terry but led in the field by Lt. Col. George Armstrong Custer. The former brevet Major-General divided his command into thirds, and the Indians were able to isolate him with five companies and kill every last man.

In response to this shocking defeat, which cast a very definite pall over the nation's Centennial celebration which began a week later, the Army sent additional units to the area. Colonel Miles was given the task of blocking the Indians' escape route to Canada. At the end of September 1876, most of the Army units tracking the Sioux and their allies began to return to quarters. Miles, on the other hand, decided to continue his campaign and carefully outfitted his men for the expedition. On October 21, 1876, with 394 men in his command, he caught up with Sitting Bull and 1,000 warriors at Cabin Creek, Montana.

After some negotiation, the two men agreed to meet, accompanied by five or six men each, halfway between their assembled forces. Sitting Bull made no bones about his hatred for the white man and his determination to roam the Plains as he saw fit. The Indian leader told Colonel Miles, "God almighty made me an Indian, and he did not make me an agency Indian, and I do not intend to be one."[10] Then, according to Miles:

> While we were thus talking the officers and soldiers, with their rifles ready for action, had been anxiously watching the scene and had noticed a few warriors move

---

[10]Miles, "The Future of the Indian Question", The North American Review, Vol. 152:1-10 at 3 (Jan. 1891).

> down the hills, one at a time, and take a position near Sitting Bull. One was seen to place a short rifle under his buffalo robe...the Indians' object, as I learned afterward, was to encircle and destroy us, as the Modocs had massacred General Canby a few years before in the lava beds of Oregon. I informed Sitting Bull that unless those warriors returned...from whence they came, our conversation would at once terminate.[11]

The chieftain, realizing that Miles was ready to engage him on the spot, ordered his braves back, and the parley ended with a request from Miles that Sitting Bull consider his offer of safe passage to the reservation.

The next day the two men met again; Sitting Bull rejected Miles' offer and a battle began. After several days of fighting and pursuit, 2,000 Sioux (including women and children) and several of their chiefs surrendered and returned to the reservations. Sitting Bull and others escaped northward into Canada. After refitting his men for virtually Arctic warfare, Miles resumed his pursuit of the remaining hostiles in November.[12]

Unlike other Army commanders, Miles believed that because it was harder for the Indians to get food and fodder in the winter, it was the most advantageous time to engage the Sioux. He believed that they could not concentrate their forces as they could in warmer weather. On January 8, 1877, he caught up with Crazy Horse, the military leader of the Sioux at Little Big Horn, and fought a furious pitched battle with him at Wolf Mountain on the Tongue River.

Miles kept the Indians at bay with an efficient use of artillery (the Hotchkiss gun). After the death of a medicine man who defiantly performed a frantic war dance on top of a ridge held by the Indians, resistance broke and the Indians retreated from the field. After several

---

[11]Miles, Serving the Republic, p. 150

[12]Miles wore a coat, lined with bear fur, for which the Northern Plains Indians referred to him as "Bearcoat."

months, large numbers of Crazy Horse's band surrendered, mostly to General Crook, who had not seriously engaged them since his defeat the previous summer, and returned to the reservations. Miles continued his expedition and pursued a band of hostile Indians led by Lame Deer.

On May 7, 1877, Miles found Lame Deer's encampment. At the approach of the troops, Lame Deer and his warriors indicated a desire to discuss surrender. Miles approached the chief:

> He took my hand, and in the intense excitement, as I was trying to assure him of safety, a white scout rode up behind me, and before I could check him, covered the Indian with his rifle. The Indian evidently suspected treachery...he jerked his hand from mine, grasped his rifle, stepped back a few paces, and fired. As he did this I whirled my horse to the right, and his bullet, passing my breast, killed a brave soldier near by. The chief was instantly killed...and the fight continued until fourteen warriors were killed and many wounded.[13]

The remainder of Lame Deer's band was pursued and eventually surrendered at the reservations. This engagement was the last of the Sioux War of 1876-77, and credit for its successful conclusion (from the white man's perspective) was due and given to Nelson Miles. General Sherman, Commanding General of the Army, reported to the Secretary of War, on July 17, 1877:

---

[13]Miles, Serving the Republic, p. 162.

> I now regard the Sioux Indian problem, as a war question, as solved by the operations of General Miles last winter...[14]

In June 1877, Miles rejoined his family for the first time in over a year but soon became involved in possibly the most tragic episode of the Indian Wars, the flight of the Nez Perce.

Since the days of Lewis and Clark, the Nez Perce had maintained a friendly relationship with the few whites they encountered in their lands in the Pacific Northwest. By the 1870s, however, enough white men had reached the area to encroach on their lands. When the Nez Perce resisted, the government decided to move them from their homes in Oregon to a reservation in Idaho. The Army, under Miles' former mentor, O.O. Howard, was entrusted with the task of effecting this move. In what was probably the most brilliant campaign ever waged by any Indian tribe, the Nez Perces, led by their chief, Joseph, defeated the Army and its Crow mercenaries in several skirmishes and embarked upon an epic journey across the Rocky Mountains with the objective of linking up with Sitting Bull in Canada. As the Indians made their way through Yellowstone Park, Miles set out on a two hundred mile forced march from the East to intercept the Nez Perces in northern Montana.

In late September 1877, Miles came upon the Nez Perce camp at Snake Creek near the Bear Paw Mountains, just south of the Canadian border, and immediately attacked. Twenty-three of his men were killed, and forty-five were wounded, with similar losses for the Indians. The Colonel had clearly underestimated the Nez Perce who, unlike the other Indians he had encountered, understood defensive tactics. He withdrew and laid siege to the camp. Although Miles felt confident that the Indians couldn't hold out for very long, there was one extremely

---

[14] Johnson, The Unregimented General, p. 180. Historian Robert Utley also gives Miles top billing in the subjugation of the Sioux. "Neither weather nor fatigue turned Miles from his course, nor did the tendency to overestimate enemy capabilities that afflicted so many after the Custer battle." Frontier Regulars, p. 209.

worrisome possibility. Chief Joseph had sent messengers to Sitting Bull, asking for assistance. If Chief Joseph had gotten reinforcements from the Sioux, Miles would most certainly have met the same fate as his late friend, Custer.

Indeed, to the extent that Nelson Miles was afraid of anything, his pulse must have quickened when, during his siege of the Nez Perce camp, one of his scouts reported seeing a mass of dark objects moving in their direction from the north. Fortunately for Miles, this turned out to be a herd of buffalo, and on October 5, 1877, Chief Joseph surrendered to Miles and to General Howard, who had arrived the day before with an escort of only twelve men. It was to Miles that Joseph's famous "I will fight no more, forever" speech was addressed.

In negotiating with Joseph, Miles promised that his people (numbering between 250 and 400) would be allowed to return to their homes in Oregon. No sooner had the Nez Perce surrendered than Miles was overruled, and Joseph and his band were transported to Indian Country where many died. Both Miles and Howard protested this decision, and Miles persisted in seeking what he regarded to be justice for the Nez Perce. On January 19, 1881, Miles wrote to President Hayes recommending that the tribe be allowed to return to its former home. He told the Chief Executive that the war had not been the Indians' fault and that they had displayed great humanity in their conduct during their flight towards Canada. Although the Nez Perce were allowed to return to the Pacific Northwest after Miles became Departmental commander in the area, they were sent to a reservation in northwest Washington State. On April 7, 1900, Miles, in a letter to U.S. Senator William J. Sewell, stated:

> I believe that their retention [at the Colville Reservation in northwest Washington State] is injudicious and unjust,

> and I earnestly recommend that provision be made which will permit them to return to their former reservation.[15]

The Nez Perce remained at Colville, however, and there Chief Joseph died in 1904.

It is fair to ask whether Miles' promises to the Nez Perce amounted to trickery of the basest kind and whether he must have known that they would not be kept. I'm inclined to conclude from the tenor and the persistence of his efforts on behalf of the Nez Perce that he was sincerely interested in their welfare once they surrendered.[16] Additionally, one must remember that the Indians were hardly in an advantageous bargaining position. Miles had them trapped, and if they resisted further they were either going to die from exposure to the elements or starvation. By promising them a return to Oregon, Miles gave Chief Joseph a means to save face, and, although he may have hoped that the War Department would keep his promise, he could also have justly concluded that morality allowed him to prevent the destruction of the tribe even if it required lying to them.

Miles has also come in for a great deal of criticism with regard to other aspects of the Nez Perce campaign. Miles' initial message to the outside world regarding the Indian surrender was a letter to General Terry in which he failed to mention the presence of Howard, his superior. He explained to Howard years later that this letter was intended to be personal and he did not expect it to be publicized as it in fact was. The official report of the campaign, Miles noted, did

---

[15]Miles' letters of Jan 19, 1881; April 7, 1900; Nelson A. Miles Papers, Archives of the U.S. Army Military History Institute, Carlisle, Pa.

[16] Miles lobbied on behalf of other Indians, who desired repatriation to their former homes, such as the Northern Cheyennes in 1891. However, he is most often remembered for his opposition to the resettlement of the Chiricahua Apaches anywhere west of the Mississippi River.

mention the arrival of Howard.[17] Given the fact that the Nez Perce had evaded Howard and that he arrived at Bear Paw with only twelve men, it is difficult to understand how Howard was entitled to any credit for their capture. Finally, Miles has been accused of violating a flag of truce by holding Chief Joseph hostage during their negotiations. Miles' excuse was that he did this to assure the survival of a Lieutenant being held hostage by the Indians.[18]

On many occasions Nelson Miles expressed his admiration for the Nez Perce and other Indians he fought, and, he indeed compared them favorably with those who could be bought by the white man. In this respect he was not unlike a number of Americans in Vietnam, who as much as they feared and sometimes hated the Viet Cong, saw in their adversaries an idealism and nobility that they never found in their allies. As to the larger moral question of why Miles exerted so much effort in the subjugation of people he admired and whom he believed had suffered a terrible injustice, the short answer is that this was his job. However, Miles stayed in the Army in part because he wanted excitement and challenges, and he was probably forever grateful to the Indians who provided it.

In the summer of 1878, Colonel Miles organized an expedition to explore wagon routes west of Ft. Keogh and to do some sightseeing at Yellowstone Park. Accompanying the ten officers of the expedition were four male civilians, five women (including Mrs. Miles), and three children, one of whom was Miles' daughter Cecilia. After a week and a half of travel, as the party approached Yellowstone, it received word that the Bannock tribe had gone on the warpath in Idaho and that some were coming through the Park. After sending the civilians to the nearest military post, Ft. Ellis (near the present site of Bozeman, Montana), Miles took 75 soldiers and a number of Crow Indian scouts with him to intercept the Bannocks. Splitting his force in two, Miles

---

[17]Miles to Howard, Jan. 26, 1888, Miles Papers, Military Historical Institute, Carlisle.

[18]Serving The Republic, pp. 177-78.

posted his men on what he guessed would be the Indians' most likely route.

The Bannocks were sighted approaching the position occupied by Miles with 35 soldiers and 75 Crows. After having the Bannock camp scouted by his Indian allies, Miles attacked and surprised the hostiles. Fourteen Bannocks were killed and the rest surrendered; Miles' troops and their Crow allies also sustained a few casualties, including a Captain from his 5th Infantry, who was killed.[19]

---

[19]Miles, "A Brush With The Bannocks," The North American Review, Vol. 161:346 (1895).

MEETING BETWEEN THE SIOUX.
"GOD ALMIGHTY MADE ME AN INDIAN, AND NOT AN AGENCY INDIAN."

LAME DEER FIRING AT GENERAL MILES.

THE CRAZY HORSE FIGHT.

SURRENDER OF CHIEF JOSEPH.
"FROM WHERE THE SUN NOW STANDS, I FIGHT NO MORE AGAINST THE WHITE MAN."

CHAPTER IV: GERONIMO, CROOK, AND THE APACHE CAMPAIGN

Following his series of successful campaigns against the Plains Indians, Colonel Miles became increasingly aggressive in seeking activity for his troops and reward for his achievements. In 1879 he repeatedly wrote to General Sherman requesting creation of a military department for Montana with himself in command as a Brigadier General. He also sought authority to pursue Sitting Bull into Canada. His requests alienated the Commanding General. First of all, General Sherman was concerned about the fact that his niece's husband felt free to write to him directly instead of going through the chain of command, i.e., Generals Terry and Sheridan. Secondly, Miles' persistence in seeking authority for a raid into Canada evidenced to Sherman an insensitivity to the delicacies of international relations. Miles based his requests for authority to enter Canada upon the precedent set by a raid made by Ranald MacKenzie into Mexico in 1872. Sherman's response was:

> Because...Generals Sheridan and MacKenzie once consented to act unlawfully and violently in defiance of my authority in a certain political contingency is no reason why I should imitate so bad an example...[1]

When Sitting Bull and his band crossed the border into Montana to hunt in the summer of 1879, Miles drove them out of their camp and back into Canada. While his aggressiveness won him influential friends, particularly among the residents of Montana, it also made him a marked man among his superiors. His wife's uncle thereafter resisted efforts to promote Colonel Miles and extend his authority. Sherman sent General Ruger, who outranked Miles, to Montana and opposed his elevation to Brigadier General.

---

[1]Johnson, The Unregimented General, p. 217, citing letter of March 10, 1879, Sherman to Miles, Sherman Papers, Library of Congress.

In 1880, Miles was promoted to the permanent rank of Brigadier General in the Regular Army despite the opposition of the Commanding General.[2] After his promotion General Miles served as commander of the Department of the Columbia, where much of his energy was devoted to fostering the exploration of Alaska. He then assumed command of the Department of the Missouri at Ft. Leavenworth, Kansas. While he was at Ft. Leavenworth in 1885 an opportunity for additional glory presented itself.

The territories of Arizona and New Mexico had been subject to periodic Apache uprisings ever since their acquisition by the United States in 1847.[3] Miles had been detailed to New Mexico in 1875 as the result of one of these outbreaks and in 1878 observed:

> The Apaches have, in my opinion, been for years the victims of mismanagement and the unscrupulous avarice of government contractors, and this is expressing the case in mild terms. The recent disturbances and acts of hostility were, in my judgment, solely due to those causes.[4]

In March 1883 Apaches under the leadership of Chatto and Geronimo went on the warpath again, killing twenty-six white civilians in six days. Among their victims were a federal judge, H.C. McComas, and his wife; their 6-year old son was kidnapped. The departmental commander, General George Crook, pursued the Apaches into Mexico

---

[2]Sherman's opposition to Miles' promotion was so vociferous that President Hayes noted in his diary that his decision to promote Miles had, with other perceived slights, "presently" lost him the friendship of the Commanding General. Williams, T. Harry ed., Hayes: The Diary of a President, 1964, p. 307 [entry of January 23, 1881].

[3]The southern portions of these territories were part of the 1854 Gadsden purchase.

[4]Miles letter to brother Daniel Miles, Dec. 25, 1875; Miles letter to Assistant Adjutant General, Dept. of the Missouri, Dec. 28, 1878; Miles Papers, Military History Archives, Carlisle.

and was blessed by the arrival of a defector from Chatto's band, who led Crook to the hostile Indians' sanctuary in the Sierra Madre mountains. Crook negotiated a surrender with the Apaches that allowed them to return to their reservation with no punishment. For two years afterwards, Arizona and New Mexico were relatively quiet.

In the spring of 1885, the Army began to crack down on such Apache customs as wife beating and ceremonial drunkenness.[5] As a result, one quarter of the Chiricahua and Warm Springs Apaches who had been on the warpath two years earlier, 35 men and 101 women and children, made their way to the mountains of Mexico. The largest group was led once more by Geronimo. The other three fourths of these bands stayed on their reservation, including Chatto, who offered to help the Army track down Geronimo.[6]

General Crook's strategy for subduing the hostiles was to pursue them into Mexico with small groups of soldiers accompanied by scouts from the same tribe, some who "had close ties to the runaways."[7] By the summer of 1885, the hostiles had killed approximately seventeen civilians in raids across the American border. In November, as the raids continued in both the United States and Mexico, Crook organized an expedition into Mexico under the command of Cpt. Emmett Crawford, which consisted of a small number of soldiers and scouts from Chatto's band. In January 1886, Geronimo asked for a meeting with Crawford to discuss surrender. Before the parley could take place, however, Crawford was mortally wounded in an exchange between the American

---

[5]The Apaches also on occasion mutilated their wives by cutting off the ends of their noses, usually as a punishment for infidelity. Angie Debo, Geronimo, pp. 225, 234.

[6]In fact, Geronimo explained his flight from the reservation as being caused by a plot by Chatto and others to kill him. Debo, Geronimo, p. 256

[7]Debo, p. 238

expedition and Mexican irregular forces, who were also pursuing the hostile Apaches.[8]

A few days afterwards a female emissary came from Geronimo to Lt. Marion Maus, second-in-command to Crawford (and afterwards, for many years, one of Nelson Miles' principal staff officers) to inform him that Geronimo desired a meeting. On January 15, 1886, Maus went to meet Geronimo and his band unarmed and was surprised to find Geronimo and his band armed to the teeth. Maus' initial fears as to the Apaches' intentions turned out to be unfounded. Geronimo promised to follow Maus back towards the American border to discuss surrender terms with General Crook.

At the end of March 1886, Crook arrived at Maus' camp just south of the border and conferred with the hostile Apaches. Crook agreed to Geronimo's terms--the Indians would have to spend two years as prisoners in the eastern United States with their families, and then would be allowed to return to the reservation in Arizona. The General instructed the Apaches to accompany Maus and his scouts back to Arizona; Crook then telegraphed news of the surrender to the War Department in Washington.

That night some of the Apaches got drunk and had a change of heart. Approximately 20 men, 14 women, and six children under Geronimo and Natchez, son of the legendary chief, Cochise, slipped away into the interior of Mexico. Although Geronimo never fully explained his decision to escape, he at one point claimed that he did not trust General Crook and feared that Crook intended to execute him as soon as he got back to Arizona.[9] If this was in fact the reason for his flight it undercuts the conventional appreciation of Crook as one who had a unique rapport with Indians--particularly when contrasted with Nelson Miles. For example, Geronimo's fawning biographer, Angie Debo, evaluates the two men as follows:

---

[8]Although the Mexicans contended that Crawford was shot by mistake, many American soldiers thought otherwise.

[9]Debo, Geronimo, pp 266-7.

> [Miles] lacked Crook's quiet dedication, his understanding of the Apaches and--most important of all--his integrity.[10]

Geronimo's escape put Crook in a very embarrassing position. First, he received a telegram from Lt. General Philip H. Sheridan, the Commanding General of the Army, informing him that the President, Grover Cleveland, would not accept the surrender terms to which he had agreed. Instead, Sheridan said that surrender must be unconditional, "only sparing their lives."[11] Then Crook had to let General Sheridan know of Geronimo's flight.

The Commanding General was not happy. He sent Crook a telegram on March 31, 1886, observing:

> It seems strange that Geronimo and party could have escaped without the knowledge of the scouts.[12]

Crook wired Sheridan that he had no regular troops with him and that it would have been impossible for him to get any in a position where they could capture the hostiles. Sheridan then suggested that Crook adopt a defensive strategy with his regular troops in Arizona. Crook, quite correctly, told Sheridan that the regulars could not protect anyone from the Apaches unless they were within a half mile of the Army camps. Frustrated and sensing Sheridan's lack of confidence, Crook offered to resign his command of the Department of Arizona. General Sheridan immediately took Crook up on his offer.

On April 2, 1886, Sheridan ordered Miles, then at Ft. Leavenworth, to take command of the Department of Arizona; Crook

---

[10]Debo, p. 268

[11]Miles, Personal Recollections, pp. 471-2.

[12]Ibid., p. 472

was reassigned. The Commanding General also informed Crook that in view of Geronimo's escape, any agreement he had with 72 Apaches who surrendered was no longer operative. Therefore, he instructed Crook to send the Indians to Ft. Marion, Florida, without conditions.[13] Sheridan sent a telegram to General Miles on April 3, telling him that although he hesitated to give him specific instructions,

> it is deemed advisable to suggest the necessity of making active use of the regular troops of your command.[14]

In his 1896 autobiography, Miles stated that he did not seek the Arizona command, but the truth is that he was absolutely ecstatic about the prospect of relieving Crook and had actively campaigned for the assignment.[15] Miles is often taken to task for stealing the credit due Crook for the surrender of Geronimo, but Crook has rarely, if ever, been criticized for taking credit for the subjugation of the Sioux, when all he did was accept the surrender of bands which had been defeated in battle by Miles. It is apparent that Miles and his friends greatly resented the capital that Crook derived from the Sioux War and considered Crook's accomplishments inconsequential.

In September, 1885, Miles was quoted by the Denver Tribune and other newspapers as questioning Crook's almost exclusive reliance on Indian scouts who came from the same tribe as the hostiles. He said

---

[13]Fort Marion is now known by its original name, Castillo de San Marcos. Located in St. Augustine, Florida it is one of the oldest permanent structures in North America, having been constructed by the Spanish in the late 17th and early 18th centuries.

[14]Miles, Personal Recollections,p. 476

[15]Ibid.

that although he had often used Indians as scouts successfully, one could not expect them to help the Army against members of their own tribe.[16]

Miles' interest in the Arizona command was intensified by the fact that a Major-General's slot was scheduled to become available in the spring of 1886 by virtue of the fact that General John Pope (the loser of the Second Battle of Bull Run) would reach the mandatory retirement age of 64. Although O.O. Howard was the senior Brigadier General, speculation in Washington in early 1886 was that the promotion would go to either Crook or Miles.[17] Intensive lobbying was being conducted on behalf of both men. An indication of the depth of bitterness between the supporters of both men is derived from a letter written on Miles' behalf by Francis C. Barlow on February 3, 1886.

Barlow first dismissed any claim to a second star for Brigadier-General Alfred Terry on the grounds that his first star was a result of his capture of Fort Fisher, North Carolina, in the Civil War, which Barlow characterized as "a single and isolated exploit." Then Miles' closest friend turned his attention to Crook:

> General Crook was made a Brigadier General by Grant in 1873, over all the Colonels of the Regular Army, and since then he does not appear to have done anything to warrant this new position.[18]

Miles also had an active political ally in the Southwest in the person of Edmund G. Ross, the Governor of the Territory of New Mexico. Ross was the United States Senator who permanently damaged his political career by casting the decisive vote against the removal of President Andrew Johnson from office in 1868. For this act he is the

---

[16]New York Times, Sept. 27, 1885,9:5

[17]N.Y. Times, Jan. 9, 1886, 5:1; Jan. 10, 1886, 1:7.

[18]Barlow letter Feb. 3, 1886 (addressee unknown), Miles Papers, Military History Archive, Carlisle, Pa.

subject of a chapter in President John F. Kennedy's Profiles in Courage. In late 1885 and 1886, Ross maintained an active correspondence with General Miles at Ft. Leavenworth.

On December 8, 1885, Ross wrote Miles that, "Under Crook's management I deem it quite certain that we will have trouble in the spring, as usual..." A month later the Governor informed Miles that he was trying to get him assigned to the Southwest and complained that he was having trouble with "land thieves." Governor Ross concluded by observing that he and Miles had both friends and enemies in common.[19]

While Miles could enlist the aid of such prominent persons as Francis Barlow and his wife's contacts,[20] Crook was not without influential backers. During the Civil War, Crook had been the commanding officer of two future Presidents of the United States, Rutherford B. Hayes and William McKinley. Hayes and his sons remained life-long friends of Crook, and McKinley, who served on Crook's staff at one point, remained close enough to offer a private relief bill on behalf of Crook's wife when the general died in 1890.

Neither lobbying campaign succeeded. Despite the fact that another Major-General's slot opened up due to the sudden death of General Hancock, both Miles and Crook remained Brigadiers. Going strictly by seniority in date of rank, President Cleveland promoted Howard and Terry to Major-General. Speculation regarding the replacement of Crook by Miles in Arizona ceased for several months until Geronimo's abortive surrender in late March.

When Sheridan replaced Crook with Miles in April 1886, the general was not the only person who was elated with the change. Governor Ross wrote:

---

[19]Ross to Miles, December 8, 1885; January 15, 1886, Miles-Cameron Papers, Library of Congress.

[20]His most prominent relative by marriage, General Sherman, was no help at all, but Mary Miles' other Uncle, John Sherman, and her sister's husband, Senator Cameron of Pennsylvania, were very supportive of Nelson Miles' career.

> ...in this change we see an end to Indian troubles in the Southwest...Under Crook's management we were certain to have a repetition of last summer's butcheries this summer, but now confidently hope for avoidance and quiet and safety to pursue the work of development.[21]

Miles was allowed to take only one clerk with him from Ft. Leavenworth to Arizona and thus had to rely on officers and enlisted men who had never served under him previously and had served under Crook for several years. The new commander believed there was a widespread belief among the troops that regular soldiers were incapable of subjugating the fugitive Apaches; he sought out those who believed otherwise.[22]

The general's choice for command of the expedition of regular troops into Mexico was Cpt. Henry W. Lawton, a former protege of Ranald MacKenzie, who was then stationed at Ft. Huachuca. With his selection by Miles, Lawton's career advanced dramatically. He would become one of the principal American commanders in the Cuban campaign during the Spanish-American War and in the Philippines, where as a Brigadier-General, he would be killed in combat. Another soldier whose career took off at this point was Leonard Wood, a 24-year-old Army surgeon and Harvard College graduate. Lawton's principal assistant in the Geronimo campaign, Wood was brought to Washington by Miles as his personal physician in 1895 and then became the personal physician to President McKinley. This position allowed Wood to develop a close personal friendship with the Assistant Secretary of the Navy, Theodore Roosevelt. When the Spanish War was declared, Roosevelt selected Wood as commanding officer of the Rough Riders,

---

[21]Ross to Miles, April 6, 1886, Miles-Cameron Papers

[22]Miles, Personal Recollections, pp. 480-81,486.

and their relationship ultimately gained Wood the post of Chief of Staff of the United States Army.[23]

No sooner had Miles assumed command in Arizona, then Geronimo crossed the border from his hideout in Mexico, stealing livestock and killing several white civilians. Pursued into Mexico by Lawton, the small band of Apaches proved to be very elusive. The officers had to abandon cavalry tactics in the mountains of Mexico and were forced to rely solely on infantry with pack mules. They were able to surprise the Indians on several occasions, capturing nearly all of their supplies and animals, but the Apaches were able to replace their losses by raiding Mexican farms and villages.

In May, one of the Apache band deserted Geronimo after a close call with the soldiers and made his way back to Fort Apache in Arizona. In July, Miles met with this warrior who, according to Miles, reported that the hostiles' morale was low and that they were ready to surrender. Miles sent this brave and another from Chatto's Chiricahua band with Lt. Charles Gatewood to seek out Geronimo.

At about the same time, on July 13, 1886, Lawton and Wood discovered the hostile camp in Mexico. According to Wood:

> We effected the surprise of the camp of Geronimo and Natchez which eventually led to their surrender, and resulted in the immediate capture of everything in their camps except themselves and the clothes they wore.[24]

---

[23]Wood's relationship with Roosevelt would also make a him a mortal enemy of Nelson A. Miles and would render him persona non grata with President Wilson, who went out of his way to make certain that neither Wood nor ex-President Roosevelt played any significant part in World War I. Wood was a leading but unsuccessful contender for the Republican Presidential nomination in 1920. The General was the frontrunner in the early balloting at the convention but a deadlock with his principal opponents led to the nomination of a compromise candidate, the immortal Warren G. Harding. Wood finished his public career by returning to the Philippines as governor-general in the 1920s.

[24]Miles, Personal Recollections, p. 510

Nevertheless, Lawton's supplies ran out and he had to suspend his pursuit of Geronimo. A month later when his quest resumed, Lawton was informed that the Apaches had sought to open peace negotiations with the Mexicans at Fronteras, just below the Arizona border. His troops were 100 miles south of the Apaches.

As Crook and other of Miles' critics have maintained, at the end of almost five months of campaigning, Miles was nowhere near capturing the Apaches. The harsh assessment of Angie Debo is that:

> [Miles] did not kill or capture a single hostile.
> He finally decided to proceed against some Apaches he could catch--about four hundred of them who had remained at the reservation.[25]

In July, Miles recommended to the War Department that 198 Warm Springs Apaches, who had been forcibly transferred to Fort Apache from New Mexico several years earlier, and 236 Chiricahuas, the band to which Geronimo belonged, be removed from Arizona. The general defended his decision on the grounds that the culture of these tribes required the young men to prove themselves by going on the warpath and that he had received "reliable information that another outbreak was contemplated...and was then being arranged."[26]

Miles sent the tribal leaders, headed by Chatto, the leader of the 1883 outbreak, to Washington to negotiate their consent to removal to a mutually agreeable location. Miles informed the War Department on July 7 that he presumed that it was not the government's purpose to keep the 72 Apaches who had previously surrendered at Fort Marion and expressed the belief that Indians from an arid climate would probably experience a very high mortality rate in Florida. He

---

[25]Debo, Geronimo, p. 271

[26]Personal Recollections,p. 497

recommended that all the Chiricahuas and Warm Springs Apaches be removed to Indian Territory, and if that was not possible, that they be settled on high ground at Ft. Riley, Kansas.[27] Meanwhile, he planned to deport the rest of the Indians before they suspected his intentions.

Angie Debo's analysis of Miles' motives were that:

> ...failing to apprehend the eighteen hostiles with their women and children, Miles needed some captives to show.[28]

Nevertheless, she gives the general credit for "humane intentions" in seeking removal of the Apaches to Indian Territory rather than Florida.[29]

While Miles and Colonel J.F. Wade at Fort Apache were planning the deportation of the band remaining at the reservation, Lt. Gatewood and his two Apache scouts joined Lawton and went looking for Geronimo in the vicinity of Fronteras. One of the great unanswered questions which bears heavily on the controversy surrounding Miles' campaign is the reason for Geronimo's peace overtures in August 1886. Angie Debo, who gives Miles no credit for subduing Geronimo, says that the Apache leader claimed to have no intention of surrendering and made peace overtures merely to obtain supplies. Then she says Geronimo was tricked into surrendering by false promises from Nelson Miles.

Debo's analysis is incredibly unfair. Geronimo had supplied himself for some time by simply stealing. His need to enter into peace negotiations to obtain supplies in August indicates some degree of desperation. He certainly had to consider the possibility that the

---

[27]Miles letter of July 7, 1886, Miles Papers, Military History Institute Archive, Carlisle, Pa.

[28]Debo, Geronimo,p. 271

[29]Ibid. p. 272.

Mexicans and even the Americans would slaughter as many of his band as possible at the first opportunity.

General Miles, characteristically, gave himself much credit for the surrender. He pointed to the establishment of a heliostat system (a method of communication using mirrors) and the constant pursuit of Geronimo by regular troops as the key elements leading to Geronimo's surrender. The general claimed success because, "no human being...could endure being hunted persistently without eventually being subjugated."[30]

In his time, Miles was given most of the credit for the surrender of Geronimo, except by Crook and his supporters. The New York Times, in an editorial of September 17, 1886, proclaimed:

> Gen. Miles succeeded to a most difficult task, which he most admirably performed. The dispositions of troops for accomplishing this task were all his own. The only aid he may be said to have derived from his predecessor...consisted in the fact that Gen. Crook had obtained the surrender of a few of Geronimo's warriors and of the greater part of the women and children of his band and had sent them to Florida...this advantage was more than counter-balanced by the relief of Geronimo's force from the charge of about seventy non-combatants, thus making it even more foot-loose and formidable than ever for flight and fight.[31]

In more recent historical accounts of the Geronimo campaign, Miles hasn't fared nearly as well. He is either given no credit for Geronimo's surrender and is accused of accomplishing the feat solely by

---

[30]Miles, Personal Recollections, p.486.

[31]N.Y. Times, Sept. 17, 1886, 4:4

lies and the deportation of innocent people--as he is by Angie Debo--or given lesser credit than Crook. An example of the latter assessment is that of the historian Robert Utley, who concludes that Miles' strategy was different from Crook's only in a matter of degree.[32]

Nevertheless, some still conclude that Lawton's pursuit put Geronimo in a frame of mind to initiate peace talks. Utley concludes:

> Miles' conduct of the Geronimo campaign deserves a better judgment than history has rendered.[33]

Moreover, Utley believed that the deportation of the Chiricahua and Warm Springs Apaches from their Arizona reservation, "cruel and unjust as it was, proved to be the vital factor in assuring the finality of Apache warfare."[34]

One reason Crook has fared better than Miles in conventional historical accounts is that the two eyewitness accounts of the Apache campaign on which almost all books since have been predicated were written by Crook proteges, Lt. Britton Davis and Cpt. John Gregory Bourke. Miles also had dedicated subordinates, such as Lawton and Maus, but they didn't write. Crook and Miles provide a glaring exception to the proposition that history is written by the winners.

Miles was not the only person in the Southwest who gave Crook no credit for ending Geronimo's reign of terror against white settlers. In August 1886, Governor Ross wrote:

---

[32]Robert Utley, Frontier Regulars, 1973, p. 392.

[33]Ibid, pp 391-2.

[34]Ibid, p. 392.

> I am amazed at what Mr. Atkinson tells me of the part that General Crook appears to be taking to defeat your plans.[35]

Ross went on to accuse Crook of being motivated by "petty spite." Similarly, William R. Shafter, later commander of the American expedition to Cuba in 1898, wrote to Miles in October 1886, congratulating him on his success in Arizona:

> I perhaps feel better about it from the fact that Crook ignored the troops in his campaign, a policy which I was strongly opposed to...[36]

The denouement of the Apache campaign provides a substantial basis for concluding that the contemporary critiques of Miles' conduct are more valid than those made more recently. On August 23, 1886, Lt. Gatewood, out in front of Lawton's troops, sent his two Apache scouts to the hostile camp. One of the Indians came back and reported to Gatewood that Geronimo wanted to meet him. Gatewood then went alone to Geronimo's camp. It is important to note that all the accounts of what was said by Geronimo and Gatewood are essentially the same. Gatewood told Geronimo that General Miles would send him to Florida to await a decision as to his ultimate fate, which would be made by the President. Geronimo responded by saying that he would surrender only if he was allowed to return to the reservation in Arizona.

Gatewood rejected these terms and may have hit Geronimo with the revelation that there was no reservation to return to because Miles

---

[35]Ross to Miles, August 14, 1886, Miles-Cameron Papers, Library of Congress.

[36]Shafter to Miles, October 10, 1886, Miles-Cameron Papers

had shipped all the Chiricahuas to Florida.[37] Debo characterizes this news as a "real blow." In any event, Geronimo, after peppering Gatewood with questions about Miles, agreed to accompany the Lieutenant to Lawton's camp, which had been moved close to the Apache's hideout. What is critical is that Geronimo made the first move towards surrender without even a promise that his life would be ultimately spared. Miles' terms left open the possibility that President Cleveland would have him tried for murder and executed. Despite the fact that she makes no contrary factual claims, Angie Debo concludes that when Gatewood assured Geronimo that he could trust General Miles, Gatewood "had unwittingly betrayed him."[38]

At Lawton's camp the next day, August 24, 1886, Geronimo agreed to accompany the troops back to Arizona and to surrender. Once again, all that had been promised was that Geronimo's band would not be harmed prior to determination of their fate by the President--although Geronimo's concessions could have been vitiated by flight at any time.

For eleven days Geronimo and his band moved parallel to Lawton's troops back towards Arizona. On the second day of their journey, the party encountered 180 Mexican soldiers who wanted to attack the Apaches and kill them on the spot. Lawton refused to allow this and sent word to Geronimo that he would resist any attempt by the Mexicans to harm the Indians.

The Mexicans retreated and the party moved on. At one point the main body of troops and the pack train became separated from the Indians. Gatewood, Cpt. Wood, and another soldier, who were traveling with the Apaches, were forced to spend one very nervous night alone in the Apache camp.[39]

---

[37]Debo, Geronimo, pp. 284-5; Miles, Personal Recollections, pp. 517-22. In Miles' account the bombshell news that the reservation Apaches had been deported to Florida was not given to Geronimo until Miles' meeting with him in Arizona on September 3. The removal in fact was not effected until after Geronimo's surrender.

[38]Debo, Geronimo, p. 285.

[39]Miles, Personal Recollections, p. 512

Miles meanwhile resisted all entreaties from Geronimo and Lawton to meet them until they crossed into Arizona. Ever mindful of his career [and who can blame him], he wanted to make sure that if Geronimo had a change of heart, that he would not, like Crook, be held responsible. Miles was also concerned that Geronimo might take Lawton and some others hostage and use them to bargain for more favorable terms.[40]

On September 3, 1886, Miles met Geronimo at Skeleton Canyon, just inside Arizona. According to Miles, all Geronimo demanded was that the lives of his band be spared. The general responded by saying that the United States Army did not kill prisoners but that ultimately his fate would be determined by President Cleveland. Miles then allowed Geronimo to return to his camp, noting "[i]t was one of those times when one has to place confidence even in a savage"--thus conceding that even at this late date Geronimo could have changed his mind and headed back to his mountain retreat in Mexico.[41]

Angie Debo's account of Geronimo's journey back to Arizona and his meeting with Miles gives a very sinister cast to the general's conduct. On August 3l, she notes that Miles directed Cpt. Lawton to "secure the person of Geronimo and Natchez...by any means, and don't fail to hold them beyond the possibility of escape." Debo's interpretation continues, "[i]n a second communication that day he explained the 'means'. Lawton could 'send for them saying you have a message from the President.' Then having lured them into his camp, he could disarm and hold them, 'or you can do whatever you think best.' Clearly, this last hinted at murder. A third message was more emphatic: 'You will be justified in using any means'."

Aside from the fact that it takes quite a bit of extrapolation to infer that Miles' phrases "do whatever you think best" and "using any means" were intended to suggest to Lawton that he murder the

---

[40]Ibid, p. 520

[41]Miles, Personal Recollections, pp. 521-22. Geronimo had sent his brother to Ft. Apache as an indication of his good faith in meeting with Miles.

Apaches, the general's messages were perfectly justifiable on moral grounds. These Indians were not innocent noncombatants but rather were cold-blooded killers of numerous American civilians and countless more Mexicans. Lawton would indeed have been morally justified in using "any means," including trickery or violence, to prevent another escape and a continued reign of terror by Geronimo's band.[42]

Debo's account of Geronimo's meeting with Miles at Skeleton Canyon on September 3 is that Geronimo stated that he had come to meet Miles in order to surrender and then Miles stated terms of surrender which promised Geronimo that his band would be allowed to stay with their families in Florida and would not be harmed. The next day, September 4, Geronimo and his band formally surrendered, and on the 5th the party traveled to Fort Bowie. At this point Geronimo had surrendered, and all Miles had promised was that his life would be spared (and even that was conditioned on the determination of the President, according to Miles) and that the Indians would be united with their families.

Even if the latter promise was made it was violated for a period of only six months. Geronimo and the males of his hostile band arrived at Fort Pickens near Pensacola on October 25, 1886, and were reunited with their families, who had been kept at Ft. Marion in St. Augustine, in April 1887. Thus, Debo is clearly wrong in concluding that Geronimo was "induced by false promises to surrender."[43]

Geronimo's biographer further confused the issue and unjustly tarnished Miles' historical reputation in her account of the events following the surrender. She asserted that once the Indians were at Ft. Bowie [and thus fully within the control of the Army], "Miles continued his friendly reassurance to the leaders" and promised them that all would be forgiven and that Geronimo's tribe would get a separate

---

[42]Indeed, not only did the Apaches kill every white person who crossed their path, they were also believed to have tortured many of their victims, including women. See Miles, Personal Recollections (Wood's account), p. 507.

[43]Debo, p. 308

reservation with new wagons and horses.[44] Aside from the fact that Debo accepted Geronimo's account at face value, any promises made at this point were purely gratuitous and cannot be deemed to have been part of the inducement to surrender.

Thus, Debo's primary thesis, that Nelson Miles tricked Geronimo into surrendering by making promises he either didn't intend to keep or knew were not likely to be kept by others, is simply not supported by the facts on which she predicates her theory. Unfortunately for Miles' historical reputation, her book was well-received and her contentions now have a life of their own.

What makes all this more ironic is that Nelson Miles' career and reputation were in fact jeopardized by his handling of the Geronimo surrender--but for reasons precisely contrary to the charges made by Debo. The general got himself in trouble because it was thought that he had displayed excessive leniency to the Apaches. Almost immediately after the surrender [September 8], he put the hostiles on a train bound for Florida. At almost the same time, a telegram was sent from the War Department informing him that the President had ordered that the Indians be held in Arizona for trial on murder charges in the civil courts. Miles' decision to send them to Florida raised charges of insubordination.

Miles' explanation of this controversy was that it was due to the fact that he reported Geronimo's surrender to his immediate superior, General Howard, who was in California, rather than directly informing the War Department. Howard notified the War Department that the Apache surrender had been unconditional, which caused the President and General Sheridan to send Miles the order to hold the Apaches in Arizona. Miles claimed that, by the time he received the President's order, he had already sent the Apaches on their way to Florida because that was in keeping with the actual surrender terms.

The long-standing friendship between Miles and Howard became a casualty of the Geronimo affair. In 1887 and 1888 the two generals

---

[44]Debo, pp. 294-5

exchanged bitter letters in which Miles charged Howard with causing him unnecessary anguish by failing to inform General Sheridan immediately that he had incorrectly reported the surrender terms to the War Department. Howard mentioned his irritation at Miles for not mentioning his presence at the Nez Perce surrender to General Terry.[45]

The seriousness of Miles' troubles over this affair is indicated by a front page story in The New York Times on October 1, 1886, which concluded that Miles' acceptance of a conditional surrender, when instructions were to accept nothing other than an unconditional surrender "raises a very grave question for the President and the Secretary of War." Apparently nobody in Washington remembered that General Sheridan's instructions to General Crook six months earlier had been that the Apache surrender be unconditional "only sparing their lives."

Controversy surrounding the surrender raged for a good month. On September 29, Miles wired the Secretary of War that the Apaches were prisoners of war and that it would be "simply a mockery of justice" to turn them over to civil authorities in Arizona. Not until mid-October was it confirmed that both Crook and Miles had received orders which allowed them to promise to spare the Apaches' lives as part of the "unconditional" surrender. Nevertheless, among Miles' friends there remained for years an assumption that President Cleveland

[45]Letters, Howard to Miles, April 22, 1887; Miles to Howard, May 12, 1887;Howard to Miles, May 16, 1887;Miles to Howard, Jan. 26, 1888; Nelson Miles Papers, Military History Institute, Carlisle, Pa.

and Secretary of War Endicott bore a grudge against the General on account of his "insubordination."[46]

There were yet two additional controversies surrounding Miles' conduct of the Apache campaign: the deportation of the entire Chiricahua and Warm Springs bands to Florida, and his subsequent treatment of Lt. Charles Gatewood, the officer who first contacted Geronimo in August, 1886. Within days of Geronimo's surrender, Lt. Colonel James F. Wade[47], the commanding officer at Ft. Apache on the San Carlos Indian Reservation, summoned all the Chiricahua and Warm Springs Indians to assemble on the pretext of an informal head count. He immediately surrounded them and put them on a train to Florida.

Angie Debo's perception of this event is that "[t]hus peaceable people living quietly on their reservation, tending their little farms and striving in all ways to conform to government policy were changed into 'prisoners' to be 'confined'."[48] Although, the deportation of these Indians was an extremely popular move among the white citizens of

---

[46]Senate Executive Document No. 117, 49th Congress, 2d session (Library of Congress microfiche, serial no. 2449). It is worth mentioning here that even Angie Debo gives Miles credit for having "his own way of keeping faith." Debo, pp. 297-298. She doesn't explain why a man who she claims actively sought their murder a month before would risk his career to prevent the Apaches from standing trial.

New York Times, October 15, 1886, 4:4

Miles' friends also believed that he made enemies at the War Department for making an issue about what he alleged was the incredibly poor condition of the shoes provided his troops, which were made at the Ft. Leavenworth prison. New York Times, June 11, 1887, 4:4 (editorial "Justice For Gen. Miles").

[47]Col. Wade was the son of Senator Benjamin Wade, a leader of the Radical Republican faction during the Civil War and Reconstruction. The Colonel was a distinguished Civil War officer and, thirteen years after the Geronimo campaign, would sit in judgment of his former commander, General Miles, as a member of the "beef court." He was promoted to the rank of general himself, serving in the Philippines.

[48]Debo, Geronimo, pp 278-9

Arizona and generally approved,[49] General Crook immediately charged that without the help of Chatto and others of his band, Miles would never have obtained Geronimo's surrender, and that Miles had therefore broken faith with these Indians by treating them no differently from those who had gone on the warpath.

To one reading an account of the deportation of this entire tribe in the twentieth century, it evokes an image with chilling similarity to the deportation of the European Jews to the death camps in World War II. However, there are a number of important distinctions to be kept in mind. First of all, the deportation was not indiscriminate. Miles did not deport all Indians, or even all Apaches, from their Arizona homeland. He deported only tribes related to those who had been indiscriminately murdering American and Mexican civilians for over a year. Secondly, the adult males of Angie Debo's "peaceable people" had participated in the even bloodier raids a mere three years earlier. Miles, in a letter to Indian rights activist Herbert Welsh in 1887, acknowledged that most of those Apaches sent to Florida were not on the warpath in 1885-6 but pointed out that "...it is likewise true that nearly every one of them has been engaged at one time or another in murder and pillage."[50]

The deportation of the women and children from the San Carlos reservation is not a legitimate issue. If Miles was justified in removing the adult males from Arizona, it was more humane to send their families with them to Florida then to leave the women and children in Arizona. There is simply no way to determine whether the General had any basis for his assertion that the reservation Indians posed a constant threat to peace in the Territory. Yet even some of those who criticize his actions conclude, as did Robert Utley, that "[i]t was the removal of the

[49]See, e.g. New York Times, Sept. 17, 1886, 4:4

[50]Miles to Herbert Welsh, April 12, 1887, Miles Papers, Military History Institute, Carlisle, Pa.

Chiricahuas, hostile and neutral alike, that brought peace to the Southwest."[51]

If in fact the removal of these Indians did accomplish the end of the Apache reign of terror in Arizona and New Mexico, Nelson Miles was clearly justified in taking this measure as a matter of military necessity. It can also be justified on the basis that the removal of the reservation Indians is thought by many to have been a major factor in Geronimo's decision to surrender. Ironically, when controversy over this decision arose, Miles had an opportunity to pass the buck and claim that he was merely acting pursuant to orders from General Sheridan. To the contrary, he told friends that Sheridan had initially opposed the removal of the reservation Indians and then later took credit for the idea.[52]

Another major distinction between Miles' removal of the Apaches and what happened in Europe in the 1940s is that neither Miles nor anybody else in the United States Army intended that the Apaches die at their destination. The Army, to the contrary, intended to civilize the tribe, educate its youth, and arrest the high mortality rate of the Apaches in captivity.[53]

The Indians died in large numbers at Fort Marion from tuberculosis contracted at the Carlisle (Pa.) Indian School, at Mt. Vernon barracks near Mobile, Alabama, and even at Fort Sill, when allowed to settle there in 1894. Ironically, the one place where they fared well was Ft. Pickens (Pensacola), where only the hostile leaders were initially sent. The causes of the Indian mortality rate baffled Army

---

[51]Robert Utley, Frontier Regulars, p. 390.

[52]Letter Miles to Francis C. Barlow, 1888, Miles Papers, Military History Institute, Carlisle, Pa. In this letter Miles also notes that until Geronimo surrendered in September 1886, nobody had ever suggested that he be held for trial in the civil courts of Arizona.

[53]By 1889 about one-fourth of the deported Apaches had died.

surgeons, and even some Apaches attributed it to certain of the tribe's cultural practices.[54]

In 1889 General Crook and New England Indian rights activists initiated a lobbying effort to allow the Apaches, then at Mt. Vernon barracks, to settle at Ft. Sill in Indian Territory. A resolution to this effect was introduced in the United States Senate in January 1890, and was supported by the President, Benjamin Harrison. General Miles and white residents of the Southwest vigorously opposed the measure. Miles testified before the House Committee on Indian Affairs on January 23, 1890, opposing the resolution on three grounds: that Ft. Sill was malarious; that it was too close to Arizona and that some of the Indians might escape to their mountain retreats and return to the warpath; and that there was no injustice to be rectified.[55] Miles agreed that the Apaches should not be kept in Alabama and that they should be transferred to a site with a cooler, dry climate. His preferred location was next to a Cherokee reservation in North Carolina.[56]

The Washington Evening Star observed:

> At the time of Geronimo's surrender General Miles was anxious that these Indians should be sent to Indian territory and strongly recommended it but now that Gen. Crook wants them there he opposes it strenuously. The feeling between these two warriors is such that they cannot agree on any subject.[57]

Miles' North Carolina proposal died due to resistance from the Governor and citizens of that state, and Crook's proposal was not

---

[54]Debo, p. 377

[55]Schmitt, Martin F. ed. General George Crook; His Autobiography, p. 295

[56]New York Times, Feb. 16, 1890, 10:4; Washington Evening Star, Feb. 22, 1890, 6:2.

[57]Washington Evening Star, Feb. 22, 1890, 6:2 "'That Geronimo Campaign' It is being fought over again at the Capitol."

effectuated due to the opposition of Miles, the western press, white citizenry, and congressional witnesses such as Lawton, then a Lieutenant Colonel in the Office of the Army's Inspector General.[58]

On March 21, 1890, General Crook died suddenly in Chicago and with him died the momentum behind his Fort Sill initiative. The Apaches remained at Mt. Vernon barracks for another four years and then were settled at Fort Sill. The fight over resettlement in Oklahoma is a major factor in the conventional historical judgment that Crook was a far more humane person than Nelson Miles, but on examination he emerges only marginally so, if at all.

One can justifiably attribute Miles' opposition to the transfer of the Apaches to Ft. Sill in 1890 to spite; he demonstrated this unpleasant trait on many other occasions. Nelson Miles clearly qualifies as one of history's great haters, and he and Crook hated each other with a passion. Nevertheless, Ft. Sill was not the Apaches' home [indeed neither was the reservation in Arizona--the Apaches had been forced to live there by the Army] and settlement in Oklahoma was therefore no more "humane" than settlement at any other location that was healthier than Mobile.[59] Moreover, Miles' objections to Ft. Sill on the grounds that the Apaches might die of malaria and its proximity to Arizona had at least a colorable basis.

General Miles is not the only person in the 1890 contest to whom ulterior motives can be attributed. General Crook had a tremendous interest in having his strategy during the 1885-86 campaign vindicated. An essential element of that vindication was the acceptance of his contention that the reservation Indians, and Chatto, in particular, were innocent victims of Miles. Another fact that would lead one to question Crook's motives is that he opposed Apache resettlement in

---

[58] New York Times, Feb. 11, 1890, 7:1.

[59] The true ancestral home of these Indians was in the mountains of Arizona and New Mexico, to which nobody would have been willing to repatriate them.

North Carolina even though it was advocated by his former aide, Cpt. John Bourke, as well as Miles.

The last controversy surrounding Miles' role in the Geronimo campaign is his treatment of Lt. Charles Gatewood and the conventional conclusion that he unjustly deprived Gatewood of his share in the credit for Geronimo's surrender. The first thing to note is that Miles certainly did not attempt to take all the credit for Geronimo's surrender and liberally bestowed accolades on many of his subordinates, particularly Lawton and Wood. Although one can attribute this to an attempt to vindicate his strategic moves, he also liberally praised officers such as Maus, who commanded Crook's 1886 expedition (after the death of Cpt. Crawford).[60]

What about Gatewood? In his October 1886 order announcing the end of the Arizona campaign, Miles noted:

> Lieutenant Gatewood of the Sixth Cavalry, rode into their [the Apache] presence at the risk of his life and without any assurance of a peaceable reception demanded their surrender through two friendly Apaches.[61]

It does appear that somewhere between 1886 and 1896, when Miles published his Personal Recollections, he and Gatewood had a major falling out. Nevertheless, the book accurately portrays Gatewood's role

---

[60] Maus had served under Miles before, most notably in the battle against the Nez Perce at Bear Paw Mountain. An 1874 West Point graduate, Maus was Miles' principal staff officer during the 1894 Pullman strike in Chicago and in Puerto Rico in 1898. His career survived censure for not reporting his concerns about the beef ration during the Spanish-American War and he was ultimately promoted to Brigadier-General by President Taft in 1909; he retired in 1913. A few years earlier, he had a combat command in the Philippines. In 1924, Maus was awarded the Congressional Medal of Honor for gallantry in action on January 11, 1886. New York Times, February 10, 1930, 23:3 (obituary).

[61] New York Times, Oct. 22, 1886, 2:7.

in the surrender.[62] In a footnote observing that many of the officers involved in the Geronimo campaign deserved rewards they never received, Miles names Gatewood as one of approximately ten such officers.[63] However, in closing his account with an effusive tribute to a number of the officers who participated in the campaign, he omits mention of the Lieutenant.[64] It is difficult to believe that this omission was inadvertent, and I am willing to attribute it to the darker side of Miles' personality. However, it is not true that Miles cheated Gatewood out of the credit due him in the subjugation of Geronimo.[65]

Following his success in Arizona, some of Miles' friends and possibly the general himself believed that he ought to consider running for President in 1888. One of his admirers, T.L. Livermore, who served under Miles during the Civil War, wrote to Miles on September 3, 1887, promising his support in such an endeavor, but cautioned the general about giving up his opportunity to become Commanding General of the Army.[66]

The Presidential boomlet appears not to have progressed too far, and Miles exerted most of his energy in securing a promotion to Major-General. The problem was that by this time a precedent had been established that promotions in the Regular Army were to be made strictly by seniority; the most senior Brigadier General was Miles' rival, George Crook.

---

[62]Personal Recollections, pp. 506, 5ll (Wood's account).

[63]Personal Recollections, p. 471

[64]Ibid, p. 532

[65]On the whole, Miles' attribution of credit to others for their participation in the Geronimo campaign compares favorably to some other American historical figures. One need only contrast his willingness to share credit with Theodore Roosevelt's inflated account of his role in the Cuban campaign of 1898 [characterized by Mr. Dooley as "Alone in Cuba"].

[66]Livermore to Miles, Sept. 3, 1887, Miles-Cameron Papers, Library of Congress.

One of Miles' supporters, the prominent lawyer-historian, John C. Ropes of Boston, wrote to Francis Barlow in December 1887, cautioning against any attempt to ignore the seniority system. Ropes recommended supporting Crook for promotion on the theory that Crook would soon reach mandatory retirement age and then Miles would have to be given a second star. Ropes noted that Miles had considerable political appeal in that he represented the "non-West Point" element in the Army, but advised that if the seniority system was not followed:

> Endicott [Secretary of War] and Cleveland, who thought Miles was insubordinate about the Geronimo matter, might run in someone else.[67]

As it turned out, Ropes' advice was even better than he could have anticipated. Crook received the coveted Major-General's rank but died two years later at the age of 61, three years short of the mandatory retirement age. Twenty-six years after he had been promoted to brevet Major-General, Nelson Miles became a Major-General in the Regular Army.[68]

---

[67]Ropes to Barlow, December 30, 1887, Miles-Cameron Papers.

[68] President Harrison apparently had reservations about promoting Miles in 1890, possibly as a result of his opposition to the transfer of the Apaches to Indian Territory. Miles rushed to Washington, met with the President, and saved his promotion. Johnson, The Unregimented General, p. 261-64

NELSON MILES AT HIS PRIME

CAPTAIN BALDWIN.

HOWARD

WOOD

CROOK

CAPTAIN MAUS.

GEN. JOHN M. SCHOFIELD

GERONIMO

"GENERAL MILES AND HIS ESCORT"
BY FREDERICK REMINGTON
HARPER'S WEEKLY, DEC. 6, 1890

THE GHOST DANCE
FREDERICK REMINGTON

CHAPTER V: THE GHOST DANCE AND THE WOUNDED KNEE MASSACRE

In July 1890, rumors surfaced that Army officers intended to push for Miles as the Republican Presidential candidate in 1892.[1] Although he never made any effort to become President and on several occasions denied having such ambitions, his enemies would henceforth attribute every initiative he took to his political aspirations. Whether General Miles fantasized about the Presidency is difficult to determine, but the publication in 1890 of Varina Davis' biography of her recently deceased husband must have brought home to the general that he had one very large skeleton in his closet that would make it very difficult for him to run for national political office.

Although the more vigorous exchange between the two adversaries did not occur for another fifteen years, Miles felt compelled to publicly deny Mrs. Davis' account of her husband's imprisonment in February 1891. He proclaimed that "there is not a particle of truth in the statements made by [Jefferson Davis'] wife".[2] However, the general must have realized that many in the South would conclude otherwise and, since the Republicans were now interested in trying to carry a few Southern states, his candidacy was an impossibility.

Regardless of what General Miles' thought about his chances for the Presidency, Crook's supporters claimed that Miles' opposition to his adversary's plan to move the Apaches to Ft. Sill was fueled by his desire to obtain western political support, and some of his enemies accused him of manufacturing new Indian trouble on the Great Plains to advance his Presidential aspirations.[3] In contrast to the recent historical accounts which tend to treat his overwhelming ambition to be President as fact,

---

[1]New York Times, July 4, 1890, 4:7

[2]New York Times, Feb. 8, 1891, 5:6

[3]New York Times, February 8, 1891, 1:6 & 5:5; February 10, 1891, 1:1.

Miles' friends considered the speculation to be inspired by the malice of his enemies.[4]

Whether or not Nelson Miles wanted to be President, he did want George Crook's second star very badly and traveled to Washington to lobby President Harrison personally. His trip was successful, and as a Major-General he was transferred to command the Military Division of the Missouri. He arrived at his Chicago headquarters just in time for the last tragic episode of the Indian Wars.

Conditions on the reservations had been deteriorating. The Plains Indians were at the point of starvation due in part to drought and in part because their beef ration had been decreased. The latter was the result of a well-intentioned effort by reformers to make them more self-sufficient. Tales of an Indian messiah began to spread among the Plains Indians. With the new cult spread a religious rite known as the Ghost Dance. The essence of the new religion was that the buffalo, the elk, and the deer would return to the Plains, along with the spirits of all the deceased Indians. The tribes would once again be free to roam their former hunting grounds and some versions of the messianic vision predicted the destruction of the white man. As the cult spread to the Sioux in South Dakota, civil authorities began to become panic-stricken. Sitting Bull, whom Miles considered the most dangerous and capable of all Indian leaders, declared himself head of the movement, and some warriors proclaimed that the Ghost Dance and Ghost shirts made them invulnerable to bullets.

In October 1890, Short Bull, a prophet of the new cult, predicted that a new millennium would arrive on December 11, and encouraged the Indians to congregate near the boundaries of the Pine Ridge and Rosebud reservations. Miles, as military commander for this area, sought to isolate the leaders of the cult and pressure the other Indians to return home. To this end, he ordered an increase in the Indians' beef ration and authorized the former scout and showman, "Buffalo Bill" Cody, to take Sitting Bull, who had formerly worked in Cody's Wild

---

[4]Ibid.

West Show, into custody. This authorization was cancelled by President Harrison at the request of the Indian Bureau, and the Indian police were ordered to arrest the famous chieftain. When Sitting Bull resisted arrest, a gun battle ensued, and he was killed.

Miles blamed white corruption and mismanagement by the Indian Bureau (an agency of the U.S. Department of the Interior) for the crisis. On December 20, 1890, he wrote his wife:

> We have taken away their land and the white people now have it. The Indians have been half fed or half starved. Neither I nor any official can assure the Indians that they will receive anything different in the future. They say, and very justly, that they are tired of broken promises.
>
> I do not think the government should disregard its promises and get the Indians into such a condition, and then order the military to prevent an Indian War.[5]

Shortly after he wrote this letter, Miles ordered his troops to disarm and escort a Sioux band under Chief Big Foot, which was moving back towards its reservation. On December 29, 1890, at Wounded Knee Creek, Colonel James Forsyth sent his men into the camp to look for guns; an Indian began the Ghost Dance and shooting commenced. Forsyth's soldiers opened fire with rifles and artillery; many Indians, including women and children were killed. According to some accounts,

---

[5]Johnson, The Unregimented General, p. 282.

the soldiers wantonly slaughtered many Indians attempting to flee, although this is still a matter of great controversy.[6]

General Miles was extremely angry at Colonel Forsyth and his second-in-command, Major Samuel Whitside. After receiving a report on the engagement from his investigators, Cpt. Frank Baldwin and Major J. Ford Kent, Miles concluded that initially Forsyth erred in allowing the Indians to camp in a ravine which would be easy to defend and provided opportunities for escape. However, he was primarily angry at the manner in which Forsyth deployed his troops and what Miles believed was his complete lack of appreciation of the potentiality for violence. The troops, Miles concluded, were placed so that not only were the Indian non-combatants in the line of fire of both the soldiers and Sioux warriors, but also in a manner that they were certain to be hit by the fire of their own comrades. Forsyth compounded his troubles with Miles by allowing himself to be surrounded by Indians the next day and leaving a wounded man on the field. Miles characterized Forsyth's conduct as "incompetent" and suspended him from duty.[7]

In contrast to Miles' rancor over Forsyth's conduct, General Schofield, the Commanding General of the Army in Washington, countermanded the Colonel's suspension and commended him. Schofield concluded that the officers and enlisted men at Wounded

---

[6]This incident is generally referred to as the "Wounded Knee Massacre." There is in fact a great deal of controversy as to whether the large number of Indian women and children killed was the result of their simply being in the line of fire or, additionally, deliberate and wanton slaughter. [See, e.g., Marshall, Crimsoned Prairie, p. 246; Robert Utley, Frontier Regulars, pp. 406-408.] The number of Indians killed has been placed at anywhere from 150 to 300. Frank Baldwin's report to General Miles was that 85 warriors were killed in the battle and 68 non-combatants were also slain. Forsyth lost 25 men killed and 35 wounded, a fact some historians point to in distinguishing Wounded Knee from other incidents in which there is almost universal agreement that Indian noncombatants were wantonly slaughtered by whites.

[7]Miles to Adjutant General, Jan. 31, 1891 and Nov. 18, 1891; Miles Papers, Military History Institute, Carlisle.

Knee took great care in avoiding unnecessary harm to the Indian women and children.[8] Commendation was the last thing Forsyth deserved according to Miles. The general observed that at the time of the Wounded Knee battle the Ghost Dance crisis was under control and almost all the Indians were on their way back to the reservations; Wounded Knee almost provoked a general uprising. As to the cause of the outbreak generally, he observed:

> It is not necessary for me to mention the cause that led to the trouble, other than to say that it was chiefly hunger--want of sufficient food, and the impossibility of the Indians to obtain it.[9]

Months later the General condemned any move to decorate Forsyth and Whitside by saying such action would be an insult to many brave soldiers, living and dead.[10]

Some historians believe that Miles bears some responsibility for Wounded Knee on the grounds that there was no need to disarm Big Foot's band, as the general had ordered.[11] However, Miles at no time desired the wanton slaughter of any Indians. Thus, the judgment of

---

[8]Schofield's report of February 4, 1891, Miles Papers, Military History Institute, Carlisle.

[9]Miles report to the Adjutant General of the Army, February 9, 1891, Miles Papers, Military History Institute, Carlisle.

[10]Miles to Adjutant General, November 18, 1891, Miles Papers, Military History Institute, Carlisle. The only mention I have found by Miles of the deliberate murder of innocent civilians concerns an Indian woman and three children shot at close range while apparently making their way from Wounded Knee to their reservation. Miles believed the circumstances of their deaths indicated cold-blooded murder by mounted soldiers which he condemned in letters to the Adjutant General dated January 31, 1891, and March 2, 1891. Miles Papers, Carlisle. It does not appear that individual responsibility for the crime was ever determined.

[11]Utley, Frontier Regulars, p. 407

some of his enemies, such as Theodore Roosevelt, who intimated that Miles ordered the massacre of women and children, has no basis in fact. Moreover, the general is universally given credit for avoiding further bloodshed after Wounded Knee. His immediate superior, Commanding General Schofield wrote:

> ...by very careful management of the commanding general in the field, Major-General Miles, a general conflict was averted, and the Sioux made their submission...[12]

The currency of Schofield's opinion is particularly creditable in light of the fact that he could be bitterly critical of Miles--as he was of Miles' conduct during the Pullman strike.

Admiration of Miles' handling of the crisis was also recorded by Lt. John J. Pershing of the 6th Cavalry, which had been brought from the Southwest to assist in the crisis:

> A situation that might easily have resulted in protracted and bitter warfare, in which thousands of lives might have been lost, was brought to a quick and satisfactory conclusion because of experienced and judicious military handling. It was an exemplary lesson in what might well be called preventive action.[13]

---

[12]Schofield, John M., Forty-Six Years In The Army,(1897), p. 488. Schofield, Commanding General of the Army 1888-1895, was in command during the major Union victory at the battle of Franklin, Tennessee in November 1864.

Miles also gets credit for defusing the Ghost Dance crisis from historian Robert Utley. Frontier Regulars, p. 409.

[13]Vandiver, Frank, Black Jack: The Life and Times of John J. Pershing, Vol. 1, p. 95, citing Pershing Memoirs.

Whatever credit Miles derived from his handling of the Ghost Dance crisis was more than offset in some quarters by his finger-pointing at the Interior Department's Indian Bureau. In July, 1891, President Harrison issued an order abolishing the three military divisions of the Atlantic, the Pacific, and the Missouri. Henceforth, all the Department commanders would report to General Schofield in Washington, without going through a Division commander.[14]

Although General Howard, commanding the Division of the Atlantic, and General Ruger, commanding the Division of the Pacific, were affected by the order in theory, no one doubted that it was aimed at Miles. Neither Howard nor Ruger lost control over any significant amount of territory, while the order stripped Miles of authority for the Departments of the Platte and the Dakotas, where all the Plains Indians resided. Cpt. Marion Maus of Miles' staff (who as a Lieutenant had met with Geronimo in 1886) bluntly told the press that Harrison's order left Miles with nothing to do. An unidentified Miles' aide (possibly Maus) was quoted as saying:

> It goes without saying that Gen. Miles has been a doomed man at Washington since he let in the light on the Pine Ridge difficulty. He did not hesitate to point out that a system of robbery and cruelty has been carried on against the Indians, and he has never been forgiven since he advocated transfer of the Indian affairs to the War Department.[15]

---

[14]New York Times, July 4, 1891, 5:4

[15]New York Times, July 12, 1891, 2:7; July 6, 1891, 5:2.

CHAPTER VI: THE PULLMAN STRIKE OF 1894

One of the striking things about the United States Army during the period between the Civil War and the War with Spain is the extent to which its activities were removed from the major developments in American society. During this era the United States was changing dramatically. It was evolving from an agrarian society, populated almost exclusively by Protestants from Northwest Europe, Irish Catholics in the major cities, and blacks in the South, to a highly industrialized nation populated by substantial numbers of non-Protestants from Eastern and Southern Europe.

Given the fact that the Army was occupied in protecting the development of the most remote areas of the country, it is not surprising that its officers were largely ignorant of the major trends in American life and generally unaware of the social conditions they created. In March 1893, Grover Cleveland returned to the Executive Mansion after a four-year hiatus and was almost immediately confronted with a major economic depression. As unemployment soared and wages fell, the impetus for industrial workers to organize to protect their interests intensified. In the railroad industry, these conditions led to the formation of the American Railway Union in June 1893, headed by one of the most controversial figures in American history, Eugene V. Debs.

The spark that ignited one of the most bitter confrontations in American labor history occurred ironically among workers regarded as the most satisfied and complacent in the United States. The Pullman Car Company in Pullman, Illinois, was considered a model enlightened company, and its President and founder, George Pullman, was deemed to be a paternalistic employer in the best sense of the word. Pullman had maintained a stable workforce since 1880 and had built a town for his workers, where they lived in houses rented from the Pullman Company.

The living conditions of Pullman workers were regarded to be far superior to those of the typical factory worker. However, when the depression of 1893 began, the railroad industry and consequently, the

Pullman Company, suffered substantially. Pullman laid off some employees and cut wages by as much as 50 percent, partially as Pullman saw it, to obviate the necessity of additional lay-offs. When Pullman lowered his employees' wages, however, he did not lower the rents they paid for company-owned housing.

Faced with this economic squeeze, the Pullman workers joined Eugene V. Debs' American Railway Union in the spring of 1894. In May, a committee of these employees called on Pullman management to seek either a restoration of some or all of their wages or a decrease in the rents they were paying to the company. Not only didn't this committee gain any concessions from Pullman, but immediately after their meetings with management, three committee members were laid off.

Perceiving these lay-offs as retaliatory and indicative of a callousness towards their plight, Pullman's workforce immediately went on strike and closed the Pullman plant. The strike continued to be a localized dispute for over a month until a delegation of Pullman strikers attended the convention of the American Railway Union (ARU) in June. The ARU, which primarily represented workers engaged in operating the railroads as opposed to manufacturing employees such as those at Pullman, asked the Pullman Company to submit to arbitration of its employees' grievances. Pullman refused to receive any communication from the ARU.

On June 21, 1894, the delegates to the ARU convention voted to stop handling Pullman cars unless the company agreed to arbitrate its dispute with its employees. Pullman in turn sought the assistance of the General Manager's Association, a group established ten years earlier to represent the common interests of 24 railroads in Chicago. The General Managers agreed to help Pullman and, when the ARU boycott of Pullman cars began on June 26, the railroads immediately fired any workers who refused to move passenger trains with Pullman equipment. This produced a general conflict between the ARU and the railroads.

Up to this point, the Pullman workers and the American Railway Union had demanded only arbitration, not concession to specific monetary demands; the Pullman company response was in essence that the wages paid and the rents charged to Pullman employees were nobody's business but that of the company's management. The analysis of the United States Strike Commission, which investigated the dispute immediately after its denouement, was:

> The policy of both the Pullman company and the Railway Manager's Association in reference to applications to arbitrate closed the door to all attempts at conciliation and settlement of differences. The commission is impressed with the belief...that a different policy would have prevented the loss of life and great loss of property and wages occasioned by the strike.[1]

In the last week of June 1894 and the first days of July, the sympathetic strike of railroad workers in Chicago continued. Strikebreakers were hired, and crowds of angry strikers congregated in the railyards throughout the city. Members of the ARU, defiantly wearing white ribbons in their lapels, confronted the strikebreakers and began to take action to stop rail traffic in the city. Cars were derailed and overturned and the city's hooligan element began to become prominent in the assemblies of workingmen.

Much of the historical dispute regarding the violence during the strike has never been satisfactorily resolved. The railroads blamed the ARU; the Union claimed that the railroads hired thugs to damage railroad property in order to discredit the ARU. The U.S. Strike Commission concluded that much of the vandalism was caused by mean-spirited young men who were simply out looking for trouble.

Regardless of who was responsible, the federal government began to become very concerned about the growing paralysis of rail traffic in

---

[1]Warne, Colston ed., <u>The Pullman Boycott of 1894: The Problem of Federal Intervention</u> (1955) at pp. 24-25.

the Midwest. President Cleveland's Attorney General, Richard Olney, a former railroad lawyer, appointed another railroad lawyer, Edwin Walker, to be special federal attorney to deal with the strike. Walker obtained a federal court injunction against Eugene Debs and his union. The injunction not only prohibited acts of violence but also any peaceful advocacy by ARU members which encouraged workers to refrain from handling trains with Pullman cars.

The injunction was issued on July 2, and the very next day, President Cleveland convened a meeting at the Executive Mansion to discuss events in Chicago. Nelson Miles, the commander of the military Department of the Missouri, which included Chicago, was in New York when the Pullman strike came to a head. Instead of returning to Chicago, he went to Washington, where on July 3, he attended the meeting at which the use of federal troops in Chicago was discussed. The participants in the discussion included the President, the Attorney General, the Secretaries of State and War, Miles, and General Schofield, the Commanding General of the Army.

Ordinarily, federal troops would be committed in such a situation only upon request by local officials; no such request had been received. However, Cleveland and Olney were very distrustful of Chicago's Mayor Hopkins and Governor John Altgeld of Illinois, whom they perceived as much too sympathetic to the ARU. General Schofield recalled that Miles initially was unenthusiastic about the intervention of Regular Army troops in the strike:

> in reply to my suggestion that his presence was needed with his command, General Miles said he was subject to orders, but that in his opinion the United States troops ought not to be employed in Chicago at that time.[2]

---

[2]Schofield, Forty-Six Years in the Army, p. 494

Miles left for Chicago immediately and arrived mid-day July 4, 1894. His troops preceded him into the city from nearby Fort Sheridan. Commanding General Schofield had ordered that the Regular Army contingent be concentrated by Chicago's lakefront, but instead it had been split up into small groups and dispersed to different railroad yards.

Upon his arrival on the scene, Miles took his time complying with Schofield's instructions, which obviously rankled the hero of Franklin when he sat down to write his memoirs:

> This error [the dispersion of Regular troops] appears to have resulted in some measure from the too great deference paid by commanding officers to the advice and wishes of civil officers to whom they were referred for information, and much more from lack of knowledge of the lawful relations existing between the national troops and the civil authorities, in this country, although those relations had been plainly defined in an order dated May 25...[3]

Schofield also complained about the ignorance of his local commanders [read Nelson Miles] of the proper tactical methods for dealing with an insurrection and concluded that this led to "halting and ineffective" action. The Commanding General issued another order on July 9, calling for the concentration of all U.S. troops at the lakefront, and noted that it was complied with "some time after the arrival of General Miles."[4]

In the view of the Commanding General, the dispersed deployment of the 2000 Regulars in Chicago resulted in greater property damage than if the troops had been kept together and committed en masse wherever trouble broke out. That Schofield held Miles responsible for

---

[3]Schofield, Forty-Six Years, p. 495

[4]Ibid, pp 495-6.

ignoring his orders is evident from the fact that he cited an order issued to Miles on July 5, which stated:

> the troops should not be scattered or divided in small detachments, nor should they attempt to do service in several places at the same time...[5]

Another complaint that Schofield had about Miles' conduct in Chicago and the issue about which General Miles receives the most criticism, was his eagerness to commit his troops to protect railroad property as opposed to federal government property. Schofield believed that his order of May 25, 1894 made it clear that the Army should respond only to orders from the War Department or directly from President Cleveland, and not to orders from U.S. Marshals or other civil officers. Further, as far as Schofield was concerned, the U.S. troops were in the city solely to protect government property, not to preserve peace and order. The latter, he believed, was the sole responsibility of state and local authorities.

Thus, in another thinly veiled criticism of Miles, General Schofield wrote:

> The distinction between the authority of the United States and that of the several states is so clearly defined that there can be no possible excuse on that subject on the part of any officer of the army.[6]

Conceding that these distinctions may not have been clearly defined prior to his May 25 order, Schofield observed:

---

[5]Ibid, p. 500

[6]Ibid, p. 508

> that can hardly excuse continued ignorance of the law a month or more after that order was issued...[7]

While the Commanding General did not specify the manner in which Miles overstepped his authority, the propriety of Miles' conduct has been more directly challenged in a pro-labor account of the strike by Almont Lindsey. Immediately upon his arrival in Chicago, Miles conferred with the railroad's general managers' association, which according to Lindsey, "more than anything else caused labor to view him as an ally of the railroads."[8]

Miles clearly was antagonistic to Eugene Debs and the American Railway Union. He saw his job as encompassing the protection of the movement of trains in interstate commerce as well as the protection of federal property. Indeed, this was one of the primary objectives of committing federal troops to Chicago and Miles saw his authority as extending to dispersion of the mobs which had paralyzed the railyards by derailing and setting fire to the freight cars. Furthermore, Miles believed that the effectiveness of the strike was due solely to threats of violence by the ARU. A month after the strike, Miles wrote that tens of thousands of men in Chicago would have been glad to replace the strikers but did not "on account of the reign of terror that was instigated by the so-called strikers and their sympathizers."[9] Miles also believed that many workers were being forced to wear the white lapel ribbon of the ARU.

Violence and the destruction of property reached their peak in Chicago from July 5 through July 7, 1894. A huge fire of suspicious origin destroyed part of the Columbian Exposition in Jackson Park, and a mob attacked a state militia unit clearing the tracks in a railyard. The

---

[7]Ibid, p. 509.

[8]Lindsey, Almont, The Pullman Strike, p. 174.

[9]Miles, The Lesson of the Recent Strikes, North American Review CLIX (1894), pp. 180-88, Library of Congress microfilm reel # 1626.

state troops fired into the crowd, killing four and wounding twenty. On July 7, Miles sent federal troops along with U.S. marshals to escort the mail trains. After a week, the rioting ceased due to the court injunction, the presence of state and federal troops, and simply because the energy of the mobs had begun to dissipate of its own accord.

General Miles characteristically took much of the credit for restoring order. Local officials disputed him and bestowed the credit on the state militia and city police. However, note should be taken of the evaluation of the conduct of Miles' soldiers by one of his harshest critics:

> The conduct of the federal troops was exemplary. Unwelcomed by the state and municipal authorities and frowned upon by labor, these soldiers were in an unenviable position, which may explain why their conduct was characterized by such caution. Suppression of the riots was accomplished almost entirely by the police and the state militia...In the protection of mail and interstate commerce the regulars were expected to play an active part, but in carrying out this assignment they inflicted no casualties. Among the thirteen people killed, and the fifty-three seriously wounded in Chicago during the strike, none were the victims of federal soldiers. The record of the police was as good, but the same cannot be said for the state troops, who killed five and seriously injured sixteen...[10]

In an overall assessment of Miles' role in the Pullman strike, it is apparent that the General overcame his initial lack of enthusiasm for Army involvement and took the initiative in seeking an active role for his men. The same traits that won him the admiration of men like Francis Barlow in the Civil War ("a man...who does not wait to be told

---

[10]Lindsey, The Pullman Strike, pp. 213-14.

to do a thing, or when and how to do it..."), alienated others later in his career. Once he was sent to the scene of what he deemed a full-scale rebellion, Nelson Miles was not the type of person to sit around at the Chicago lakefront while the entire transportation system of the country disintegrated. He may have had some justification in viewing Schofield's instructions as unnecessary and ill-advised limitations on his authority because the protection of interstate commerce clearly would allow him to use federal troops to keep the mobs from inhibiting the movement of private rail traffic.

Although General Miles may have taken more than his share of the deserved credit for restoring order to Chicago, even Almont Lindsey attributes to the general some responsibility in bringing the rioting to an end:

> ...it seems evident that Illinois could have done very well without federal aid; but it is equally true that this assistance proved a potent factor in the termination of the strike and the collapse of the American Railway Union.[11]

Lindsey also absolves Miles of the most dramatic accusations made by Eugene Debs and his supporters that federal troops forced workers to run the trains at bayonet point:

> such tactics did not represent the policy of the army and were pursued, if at all, in only a few isolated cases, of which General Miles seemed not to have the slightest knowledge.[12]

---

[11]Ibid, p. 214.

[12]Ibid, p. 215

Miles was clearly, however, unsympathetic with the plight of the industrial worker and, when he reflected upon the strike a month afterwards, the only solace he could offer the workers was an observation that "[t]here has been too much concentration in the cities" and a suggestion that those afflicted by economic conditions move to the sparsely populated areas of the Pacific Northwest.[13] He also joined the chorus of those advocating restrictions of immigration.

In 1902, Theodore Roosevelt charged in a private letter to his Secretary of War, Elihu Root, that Miles was endorsing rumors that the Army was being gathered near a number of American cities in order to intimidate labor.[14] Although one has to be cautious about believing anything the President said about Miles, if the general was posing as the champion of the working man in 1902, he has to be viewed as an insincere opportunist in view of his attitudes during the Pullman strike.

Miles' conduct during the strike also had the effect of reinforcing the view of an increasing number of people in the Army and in politics that he was a dangerous individual who tended to be insubordinate and could not be controlled. A year after the Chicago riots, General Schofield reached the mandatory retirement age and Miles as the senior active Major General was in line to replace him. As a result of his impressions formed during the Geronimo campaign and the Pullman strike, President Cleveland was very hesitant to appoint Miles to the top post in the Army.

---

[13]Miles, The Lesson of the Recent Strikes, supra.

[14]Morison, ed., The Letters of Theodore Roosevelt, vol. 3, p. 240

CHAPTER VII: THE COMMANDING GENERAL AND THE SPANISH WAR

In November, 1894, General Miles was assigned to the command of the Military Department of the East headquartered on Governor's Island in New York City. With General Schofield reaching the mandatory retirement age of 64 in little less than a year, Miles, as the senior active Major-General (according to date of rank) was slated to ascend to the position of Commanding General of the Army.[1] However, by the spring of 1895 rumors began to circulate that President Cleveland and Secretary of War Lamont were considering ignoring the seniority principle because of Miles' identification with the Republican Party.

The assignment of T.H. Ruger, the second most senior Major-General, to the War Department in Washington fueled the speculation that General Miles would be passed over.[2] In September, on the eve of Schofield's retirement, the St. Louis Republic published an anonymous attack on Miles which charged that he owed his position largely to his marriage into the Sherman family.[3] As the New York Times pointed out, the charge was patently absurd given the fact that Miles became a brevet Major-General several years before his marriage. The Washington Evening Star observed:

> It is the public impression that objection to General Miles being placed in command of the Army comes almost entirely from those who, being themselves graduates of West Point, are opposed to the supreme elevation of a nongraduate.[4]

---

[1]Since the Civil War this position had been occupied by Sherman, Sheridan and Schofield.

[2]New York Times, May 8, 1895, 4:7

[3]Ibid, Sept. 6, 1895: 4:4

[4]Washington Evening Star, Sept 19, 1895, 6:1.

However, as we have seen from the battle with Crook, one could strongly dislike Nelson Miles for reasons having nothing to do with lack of a West Point diploma. Despite this spirited opposition from within the Army and the administration's reluctance to put him in a position in which they would have to deal with him on a regular basis, Nelson Miles had a great deal of powerful support in his quest for the Army's command. Not only was he related through marriage to Senator John Sherman, who was much more helpful to him than his brother (General Sherman died in 1891), his wife's sister, Elizabeth, was married to Senator James Donald Cameron, the Republican political boss of Pennsylvania.

If being related by marriage to two powerful United States Senators wasn't enough to protect Miles' claim, Elizabeth Cameron was on her way to becoming the grande dame of Washington society. She not only had the ear of her uncle and husband (although her marriage was not a good one), she had a close relationship with John Hay and an even closer one (possibly more than platonic) with the influential widower and historian, Henry Adams.[5] Moreover, as the highest ranking officer who had entered the Army as a volunteer during the Civil War, Miles was the darling of the Grand Army of the Republic and the Loyal Legion, the powerful veterans' lobby. Miles also had support from much of the nation's press.

The New York Times, in an editorial entitled "General Miles and the Army", concluded that:

> Gen. Miles has fully earned and richly deserves the honor of commanding the army...[6]

---

[5]A grandson of John Quincy Adams, and the great grandson of the second most important founder of the Republic.

[6]New York Times, Sept 6, 1895,4:4

Similarly, the Washington Evening Star expressed the view that it could not see how the President could select anyone but Miles as Commanding General.[7]

As much as they would have liked to do otherwise, the President and Secretary Lamont finally designated Miles as Schofield's successor. General Ruger was reassigned to the command of the Department of the East, taking with him Lt. Colonel Henry C. Corbin, his principal aide. Colonel Corbin, as Adjutant General of the Army a few years later, would succeed to Crook's role as Miles' principal enemy within the military. Nevertheless, the public reaction to the appointment was laudatory. The New York Times proclaimed:

> throughout [Miles'] military reports for the last twenty years may be found suggestions of an Indian policy based on just and humane views of the nature and needs of the redmen...

The paper also praised his handling of the Pullman strike, saying that it:

> shows a mingling of energy and calm judgment which form a good source of reliance should there be any repetition of such disturbances.[8]

The first two and a half years of Miles' tenure as Commanding General were fairly uneventful. He occupied himself in trying to keep the American Army current with recent technology. One of his major concerns was getting the country's coastal defenses upgraded. Additionally, he wanted the size of the Army to reflect the dramatic growth in the nation's population. The General suggested that the size

---

[7]Star, Sept. 19, 1895. 6:1.

[8] New York Times, October 3, 1895, 4:5

GEN. MILES CHOSEN

He Will Be Designated to Succeed Gen. Schofield.

HIS GALLANT MILITARY CAREER

Service in the War of the Rebellion and on the Plains.

NOT A WEST POINTER

Maj. Gen. N. S. Miles will succeed Lieut. Gen. Schofield in command of the army. Maj. Gen. T. H. [illegible] will succeed Gen. Miles at New York in command of the military Department of the East. Orders to this effect will be issued by the War Department in a day or two. They would

ing in each department before their submission to the Secretary for final action. This would be a radical change in the existing system, and would add largely to the duties and responsibilities of Gen. Schofield's successor. A diligent inquiry among those conversant with the facts shows that there is no provision of the kind in the revised regulations, now in the printer's hands, so far as they have been completed, and that nothing of the sort is contemplated.

of the Army be fixed by Congress at a minimum of one soldier for every 2,000 persons or a maximum of one soldier for every 1,000 persons.[9] Miles advocated a series of experiments to determine the utility of the bicycle in military operations, noting that the Germans were exploring this possibility.[10] While observing the test of a new artillery piece at Glen Cove, Long Island in April of 1896, Miles and other high ranking officers narrowly escaped injury when the gun exploded.[11]

At about this time an organization called the National Society of New England Women was embarking on a campaign to purchase a colonial mansion in Washington for General Miles and his wife. Members of the finance committee for this project included Colonel Henry Higginson (one of the founders of the Boston Symphony) and General Grenville Dodge.[12] At the same time, Miles' friends in Congress were introducing legislation backed by the Grand Army of the Republic to promote Miles to Lieutenant-General. The bill was actively opposed by Secretary of War Lamont on the grounds that Miles' contribution to the country was not commensurate with that of Grant, Sherman, Sheridan, or Schofield, the only other soldiers so honored since the Civil War.[13] The promotion bill failed, but soon Miles could look forward to the departure of Lamont and Cleveland. In November, 1896, the electorate returned the Republicans to the Executive Mansion in the person of 54 year old William McKinley, a former Major in the Union Army.

---

[9]Miles Annual Report for 1896, Miles Papers, Carlisle.

[10]New York Times, Jan. 5, 1896, 25-5

[11]Ibid, April 14, 1896, 1:3

[12]New York Times; March 1, 1896, 20:7; May 3, 1896, 8:2; February 9, 1897, 6:4

[13]New York Times, June 12, 1896, 12:6.

It is not completely clear when relations between Miles and the McKinley administration began to sour.[14] One must assume that his reputation of being "insubordinate" and difficult to deal with had preceded him from the Harrison and Cleveland administrations. However, there is another factor that may also have prejudiced Miles. William McKinley, destined to be the last Civil War veteran to become President, entered the Union Army at the age of 18 and enlisted in the Twenty-Third Ohio Volunteer Infantry. Almost immediately he became the favorite of one of the regimental officers (later the regimental commander), Rutherford B. Hayes.

McKinley served as the regimental commissary sergeant and was promoted for bringing food and hot coffee to his troops during the battle of Antietam on September 17, 1862.[15] After a stint on Colonel Hayes' staff, Cpt. McKinley graduated to the staff of a superior officer, General George Crook. During the decisive battle of Cedar Creek in October, 1864, McKinley, according to some accounts, played a minor role in taking General Sheridan to Crook on his way to the field from Winchester.[16] One can only surmise whether McKinley's close association with Crook during the war and Miles' bitter feud with Crook in later years had put Miles in McKinley's bad graces from the beginning. Whatever chance Miles may have had for smooth relations with the

---

[14]The General's relations with the new administration were actually pretty good at the beginning, because he was out of the country on an inspection tour of Europe from May 5, to October 10, 1897.

[15]One of the most striking monuments on the Antietam battlefield marks the spot, not far from Burnside's bridge, where the future President accomplished this deed.

[16]The battle of Cedar Creek was the last major battle in the Shenandoah Valley of Virginia. Afterwards, the Confederates lost a major source of their foodstuffs and their avenue for raids into the North. The battle opened with Sheridan, the Union commander, twenty miles north of his troops at Winchester. The Confederates surprised the Federals in a pre-dawn attack and drove them back several miles. Sheridan, hearing the cannons, rode south on his horse, Rienzi, and rallied his soldiers, to turn defeat into a decisive victory. The general's ride is memorialized in a famous poem by Thomas Buchanan Read, entitled "Sheridan's Ride."

McKinley administration was destroyed by the President's selection of Russell Alger as his Secretary of War and the pressures created by the outbreak of the war with Spain.

The origins of the Spanish-American War lie in the United States' long-standing interest in the island of Cuba. Prior to the Civil War, annexation of the island as additional slave territory was often seen as a solution by Southerners to the widening gap in the distribution of wealth and political power between the North and the South. By the 1890s, American interest centered on the Cuban independence movement which was waging a bitter guerilla war against the Spanish.

In 1896 American sympathy with the Cuban rebels was greatly increased by the heavy-handed management of the conflict by General Valeriano Weyler, the Spanish Governor-General. General Weyler decided that the best way to deal with the success of the rebels was to herd the rural population into concentration camps and thus deprive the insurrectos of their sources of supplies and recruits. This policy inflicted great suffering on the Cuban populace and greatly strengthened the hand of those in the United States who were tired of the country's inactivity in the international arena and were waiting for an opportunity to demonstrate the nation's maturity and power to the Europeans. Two prominent young men of this persuasion, called "jingos" and later "imperialists" by their opponents, were Congressman Henry Cabot Lodge of Massachusetts and McKinley's Assistant Secretary of the Navy, Theodore Roosevelt.

In June of 1897, the 39 year old second-in-command at the Navy Department told an audience at the Naval War College in Newport, Rhode Island:

> Better a thousand times to err on the side
> of over readiness to fight, than to err

> on the side of tame submission to injury,
> or cold blooded indifference to the misery
> of the oppressed.[17]

In October, 1897, the crisis in Cuba appeared to have eased when a new Spanish government recalled General Weyler and introduced measures to increase Cuban autonomy. However, extremist elements in the Spanish Army opposed these moves and rioted in Havana on January 12, 1898. President McKinley, in response to requests from the American counsel general in Havana, the ex-Confederate general, Fitzhugh Lee, sent the battleship Maine to Havana Harbor on a transparently "friendly" visit which was intended to intimidate the Spanish militants.

On February 15, 1898, three weeks into its visit, the Maine suddenly exploded, killing 262 American sailors. In his second autobiography, Serving the Republic, written in 1911, General Miles observed:

> The sending of the battleship Maine
> to Spanish waters was most unfortunate
> at that time. Her destruction in the harbor
> of Havana precipitated the war with Spain.
> I have never believed that the disaster was
> caused by the Spanish government nor its officials
> or agents. They certainly had no motive for such
> a crime and every reason to avoid it. Terrible
> explosions have occurred since at the Naval
> Proving Grounds at Indian Head, Maryland...the
> Dupont Powder Works, and at the Mare Island
> Powder Arsenal, California, as well as in

[17] Morris, The Rise of Theodore Roosevelt, p. 569

> other places. I believe that the disaster resulted from internal rather than external causes.[18]

A similar sentiment was expressed to Miles by the famous Confederate guerilla leader John Singleton Mosby in a letter dated March 24, 1898:

> while I have no sympathy with a policy that would provoke war, and do not believe that there is now, or will be, any just ground for declaring war, yet I want you to know that if it comes I shall be with the first who will go to the field...[19]

The views of people like Miles and Mosby were distinctly in the minority. On March 28, 1898, a Naval Court of Inquiry concluded that the forward magazines of the Maine had exploded after being ignited by an external device. Although the Court's report specifically avoided blaming the Spanish, neither the American public nor its leaders really cared. McKinley demanded that Spain declare an armistice with the Cuban rebels and submit to mediation by the United States. Although Spain met most of the American demands, McKinley asked Congress for a declaration of war, which passed easily on April 24, 1898.

Once the War began, the administration had to immediately augment the 25,000-man regular army and decided to do so by calling for volunteers much like Lincoln had done in 1861. Also as in 1861

---

[18]Miles, Serving the Republic, p. 269. In a May, 1899, article for the North American Review, the general was a bit more elliptical. He wrote, "[i]t does not matter how this [the sinking of the Maine] was done; whether or not any Spanish official was concerned...from that moment Spanish rule in Cuba was doomed. The whole nation in one voice demanded its termination." Vol. 168:514.

[19]Miles-Cameron Papers, Library of Congress

there was an overwhelming clamor for an immediate attack on the primary concentration of enemy soldiers, in this case the 80,000 to 125,000 Spanish regulars at Havana. Miles told his superiors that the Army wasn't ready for such an attack and that the Cuban climate made a summer offensive very inadvisable. His concern about the climate was based on his review of a 1762 invasion of the island by the British, who had lost thousands to disease. Miles contended that initially the United States Navy had to secure the Caribbean Sea and that the best way for the Army to be helpful was for it to seize lightly defended Puerto Rico first and then wait until the fall to attack Cuba. Pressure on the Spanish forces in Cuba, Miles believed, could be maintained simply by giving assistance to the large army of Cuban rebels until the yellow fever season was over. In fact Miles thought these measures might force the Spanish to surrender without a full-scale invasion of Cuba. General Miles expressed these views in the following letter written to Secretary of War Alger on April 18, 1898, four days before the declaration of war:

> In my opinion, it is extremely hazardous, and I think it would be injudicious to put an army on that island at this season of the year, as it would undoubtedly be decimated by the deadly diseases, to say nothing of having to cope with some 80,000 troops...
>
> By mobilizing our force and putting it in healthful camps, and using such force as might be necessary to harass the enemy and doing the greatest injury with the least possible loss to ourselves, if our Navy is superior to theirs, in my judgment, we can compel the surrender of the Army on the island of Cuba with very little loss of life, and possibly avoid the spread of yellow fever over our own country.
>
> There is still time ... to put a small force of regular troops... approximately 18,000 men in healthful camps

> until such time as they can be used on the island of Cuba with safety.[20]

The Fifth Army Corps was assembled at Tampa for the purpose of providing aid and arms to the Cubans. General William R. Shafter, who like Secretary of War Alger, hailed from Michigan, was given the coveted position of commander of the expedition.

It is not clear that Shafter's selection was intended to slight Miles, because the mission of the Fifth Corps was not initially intended to be the major land operation of the war. Shafter had a very distinguished Civil War record, having been awarded a Congressional Medal of Honor for gallantry at Fair Oaks, and he had a distinguished record in the Indian Wars (although not nearly as impressive as that of Miles). Although Shafter and Miles were approximately the same age, there was one major difference, which would cause the administration some embarrassment: Miles was in superb physical condition and Shafter weighed well over 300 pounds.

The turn of events which transformed the 5th Army Corps into the principal invasion force began when the Spanish dispatched a squadron to the New World under the command of Admiral Pascual Cervera. In late April the Admiral assembled four armored cruisers, three torpedo boat destroyers, and three torpedo boats in the Cape Verde Islands, and then received orders to sail to the West Indies and defend Puerto Rico. The Spanish squadron was in a serious state of disrepair and was thus far more formidable on paper than in fact. Admiral Cervera, well aware of the relative strengths of the American and Spanish fleets, repeatedly advised against his mission. Unfortunately for Cervera, his superiors were caught in a no-win situation themselves. On April 22, 1898, the American North American Squadron under the command of Admiral William Sampson instituted a naval blockade of Havana. The Spanish

---

[20]Miles to Alger, April 18, 1898, Miles Papers, Carlisle; "The War With Spain", The North American Review, 168:513 (May, 1899)

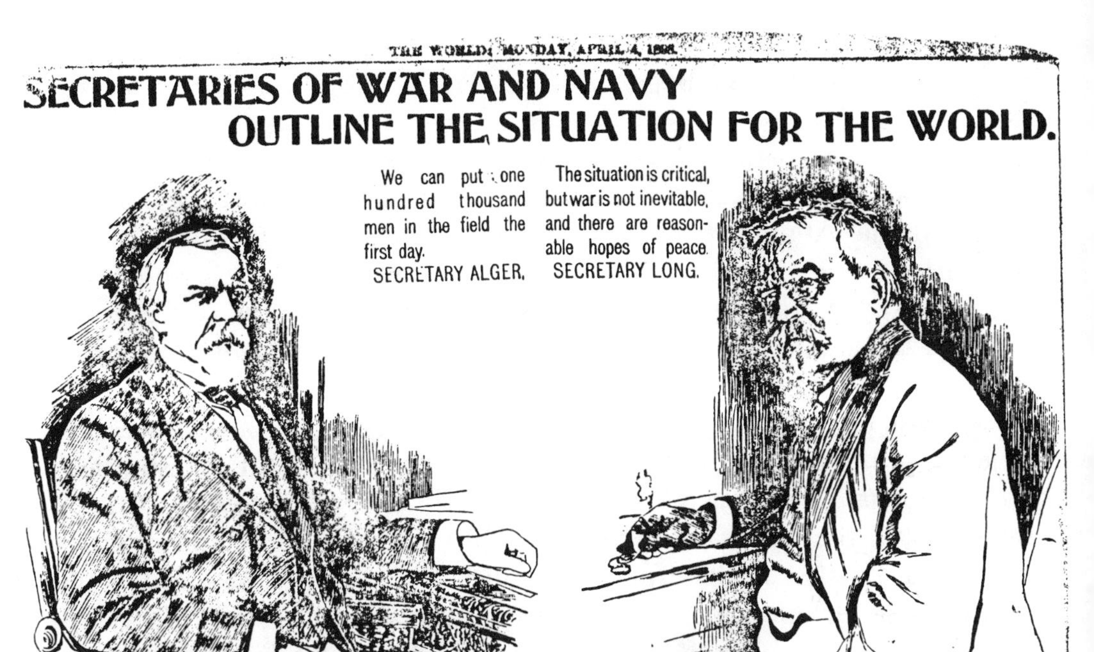

THE WORLD: MONDAY, APRIL 4, 1898.

SECRETARIES OF WAR AND NAVY OUTLINE THE SITUATION FOR THE WORLD.

We can put one hundred thousand men in the field the first day.
SECRETARY ALGER.

The situation is critical, but war is not inevitable, and there are reasonable hopes of peace.
SECRETARY LONG.

SECRETARY OF WAR ALGER AT HIS DESK.

SECRETARY LONG AT HIS DESK.

WASHINGTON, April 3.—Secretary of War Russell A. Alger, whose great influence has been on the side of vigorous action, dictated this statement for The World to-night:

"I have not conferred with the President since yesterday noon, and I do not know that there is any important change in the situation.

"The question is, can Congress be restrained from taking immediate action?

"In case of emergency we can put 100,000 men in the field the first day and a like number the second day

"What we do we should do well."

WASHINGTON, April 3.—John D. Long, Secretary of the Navy, made the following statement this evening to The World:

"I have never thought peace between the United States and Spain was impossible, and I don't think so now. Of course the situation is critical, but, as it is, war is not inevitable, and there are reasonable hopes that there may be a satisfactory and peaceful solution of the trouble.

"I know of no new developments."

FLYING SQUADRON IS SPOILING FOR A FIGHT.

Officers and Men Aboard Commodore Schley's Fleet on Their Mettle.

SHIPS IN WARLIKE TRIM.

Announcement of Spanish Flotilla's Arrival at Cape Verd Was a Great Disappointment.

PUTS OFF NAVAL ENGAGEMENT.

But if There Is a Brush the Brooklyn and Her Mates Will Be Heard From.

THE MOOD OF THE COUNTRY
THREE WEEKS BEFORE THE
DECLARATION OF WAR

Governor-General then began bombarding Madrid with requests for assistance.

For several weeks the U.S. Navy had no information as to the whereabouts of the Spanish warships. Concern about a possible surprise attack on the Atlantic Coast turned into panic in some quarters. A newly formed "Flying Squadron" under the command of Commodore Winfield Scott Schley searched the coastal waters for signs of Cervera's fleet and then sailed to Key West, Florida, when Cervera was reported at Martinique. On May 18, American Naval intelligence reported that the Spanish at Havana were expecting the arrival of their fleet, and Schley was immediately ordered to sail to Cienfuegos, on the southern coast of Cuba. For reasons to be explained later, Commodore Schley's conduct over the next several weeks would provide the background for the formal censure of General Miles by the Secretary of War and would initiate a bitter life-long feud between the General and Theodore Roosevelt.

Cienfuegos was considered to be the most likely destination for the Cervera squadron because it was linked with Havana by rail. Schley arrived off Cienfuegos on May 22, but the next day he received a dispatch informing him that the enemy was most likely at Santiago de Cuba, 315 miles to the East. In fact, Cervera had sailed into the harbor of Santiago undetected on May 18. Schley's orders were to proceed to Santiago and blockade the enemy fleet if he satisfied himself that the Spanish were not at Cienfuegos.

Schley took several days to satisfy himself that Cervera was not at Cienfuegos. Whether he acted reasonably in doing so and whether he proceeded to Santiago as quickly as he should have became issues in one of the bitterest disputes in American military history. According to his detractors, Schley unnecessarily provided the Spanish squadron an opportunity to escape from Santiago harbor and at least prolong the war. Despite being told that the Spanish fleet was not at Cienfuegos on May 24, Schley refused to believe these reports. He was faulted for ignoring signals from Cuban rebels, for making no effort to communicate with them regarding the location of the Spanish squadron, and for taking his time in proceeding to Santiago and insisting that his squadron could not refuel off Santiago. Finally, he was faulted for not engaging the Spanish fleet immediately upon sighting them at the mouth of Santiago harbor on May 29, and for his conduct more than a month later during the climatic naval battle.

The most extreme of Schley's critics charged that his conduct suggested cowardice, but he also had his defenders. Foremost of the latter was Admiral George Dewey who, on May 1, 1898, established himself as the principal American hero of the Spanish-American War by sailing into the harbor of Manila in the Philippine Islands and destroying the Spanish Pacific fleet without losing a man. Another prominent defender of Schley was Nelson A. Miles.[21]

The news that the Spanish fleet was bottled up in Santiago harbor changed the focus of the Army's mission. Immediately it was decided to send the Fifth Army Corps to Santiago to assist in the submission of the Spanish fleet. Unfortunately, it turned out that the facilities at Tampa, particularly the rail links between the military camps and the port, were totally inadequate for the number of troops concentrated there. Confusion and disorder reigned supreme, and fingers began to be pointed. Miles arrived in Tampa on June 1 and issued critical dispatches to the heads of the three staff departments not under his control: the quartermaster general, the chief of ordnance, and the commissary general. The New York Times' reaction to Miles' actions was to support him and to observe that in view of Miles' condemnations, the continuation of Alger as Secretary of War was a "public scandal as well as a national disgrace".[22]

Although most held Secretary Alger rather than Miles responsible for the disarray at Tampa, there was some doubt about the commanding general expressed in one quarter. On June 12, 1898, Lt. Colonel Theodore Roosevelt wrote his friend Henry Cabot Lodge:

---

[21]Dewey and Schley both held the rank of commodore when the war broke out and were both promoted to admiral as a result of their role in the conflict.

[22]New York Times, June 11, 1898, 6:2

Wood [Col. Leonard Wood, Roosevelt's commanding officer] thinks if Miles could be given absolute control he would straighten things out and I earnestly wish the experiment could be tried, though personally I cannot help feeling that Miles might have remedied a great deal that has gone wrong if only he had chosen or had known how..."[23]

Regiments fought each other for space on the trains carrying them to the port and then fought each other for space on the transports. By and large, most of the units assigned to the expedition were regular army units, but a few volunteer units, particularly those with politically influential officers, such as the United States First Volunteer Cavalry or "Rough Riders", were included in the invasion force. On June 8, the troops boarded the transports and almost immediately received instructions to await further orders before they sailed. Secretary Alger had just received a report from Admiral Sampson indicating the sighting of two Spanish ships off Cuba. Miles advised that the troops disembark and that the transports be armed and be sent to help the Navy clear the Caribbean. Alger instead ordered the troops to stay on the transports in the harbor, where they suffered for almost a week. Similarly Miles' requests to assume command in Tampa were greeted by an order to return to Washington to prepare a plan for the invasion of Puerto Rico.

The invasion fleet finally got under way, and on June 22, 1898, approximately 16,000 American troops began to land just east of Santiago. Moving towards the city and its 10,000 defenders, the cavalry

---

[23]Morison, Elting, ed. The Letters of Theodore Roosevelt, vol. 2, p. 840; When War was declared, Roosevelt, ignoring the pleas of friends that he would better serve the war effort as Assistant Secretary of the Navy, resigned, obtained a commission, and organized the First United States Volunteer Cavalry, better known as the Rough Riders. With uncharacteristic modesty, Roosevelt concluded that he was not qualified to command his regiment and thus asked Wood to head the regiment with himself as the regiment's lieutenant-colonel, second-in-command. In Cuba, Wood was promoted to brigade commander and Roosevelt became regimental commander of the Rough Riders.

division's commander, the ex-Confederate Wheeler, initiated an engagement with some Spanish regulars at Las Guasimas. Both sides sustained a few casualties, and then the Spanish executed what was probably a planned retreat. General Wheeler was reported to have yelled, "We've got the Yankees on the run!" Among the American dead was Sgt. Hamilton Fish of the Rough Riders, former captain of the Columbia College crew, and a grandson of Grant's Secretary of State.

By July 1, the Americans had reached the base of San Juan Heights, a low-lying ridge which included San Juan Hill and constituted the last line of defense for the Spaniards protecting Santiago, one mile away, and their fleet. The battle began inauspiciously for the Americans, as the Spanish quickly silenced the invaders' artillery and Shafter had not thought to ask for a naval bombardment of the Spanish positions by the blockading squadron. Nevertheless the assault on San Juan Hill by a regular infantry brigade and the adjacent Kettle Hill by the dismounted cavalry division drove the Spanish from the heights. Theodore Roosevelt, in command of the Rough Riders, found the Spanish gone from Kettle Hill and received permission to join in the charge to the summit of San Juan Hill. Although he did exhibit great courage in the battle and could easily have been killed, he certainly fostered the impression upon his return to the United States that he was principally responsible for the victory, which was not the case. An indication of the contribution of various units in the battle can be gleaned from the casualty figures.

Two hundred and five American soldiers were killed and 1,180 wounded in the day's fighting on the San Juan Heights and at El Caney, a few miles to the north. The brigade of regular infantry commanded by General Jacob Kent, which attacked San Juan Hill lost 89 men killed and 489 wounded; the regular army brigade at El Caney, commanded by Miles' protege, General Henry Lawton, lost 81 killed and 360

C. D. Sigsbee's Daughter
SUNDAY'S WORLD

The World.

"Circulation Books Open to All."

"Circulation Books Open to All."

NEW YORK, SATURDAY, JUNE 25, 1898.

PRICE

HAMILTON FISH, JR., AND TWELVE ROUGH RIDERS AND CAVALRYMEN KILLED IN BATTLE BY SPANIARDS

Fifty Americans, Including Six of the Officers, Were Wounded--Ten Will Probably Die.

SPANIARDS LEFT TWELVE DEAD ON FIELD OF BATTLE.

Gen. Young and Col. Wood Were Reinforced and Now Hold the Position, Which Overlooks the City of Santiago De Cuba.

FIGHT LASTED OVER AN HOUR AND WAS SHARPLY CONTESTED.

The Men Were Making a Reconoissance in Advance of the Army, Which Was Closing In on the City.

COL. LEONARD WOOD. OF THE ROUGH RIDERS.

LIEUT. COL. THEODORE ROOSEVELT.

THE AFTERMATH OF LAS GUASIMAS

WHERE THE BATTLE WAS FOUGHT.

THE HARBOR OF SANTIAGO

MAP OF CUBA.
That portion of Cuba surrendered with Santiago is colored black.

ALGER

SHAFTER, William Rufus,

ROOSEVELT, Theodore,

BRIG. GEN
H.W.LAWTON

SAMPSON

WHEELER

PERSONALITIES OF THE
CUBAN CAMPAIGN

SCHLEY, Winfield Scott,

wounded; the cavalry division, to which the Rough Riders' regiment belonged, lost 35 killed and 328 wounded.[24]

Upon reaching San Juan Heights, General Shafter, who was suffering from the heat, malaria, and gout and could not make it to the front, did not press the attack. Instead he had his troops dig in to guard against a Spanish counterattack. Shafter and Admiral Sampson, now commanding the blockading squadron[25], could not agree on which one should bear primary responsibility in forcing the Spanish fleet from Santiago harbor. Sampson wanted the Army to attack the city and Shafter wanted the Navy to force the issue; indeed, Shafter was considering withdrawing from the San Juan Heights. Back in Washington, President McKinley and Secretary Alger were beginning to get nervous and decided to rush General Miles to the scene with 1500 reinforcements. His orders were to "give such orders as might be required for the welfare and success of the army".[26]

Back in Cuba, some of his subordinates were beginning to have qualms about General Shafter. At a conference on July 2, several of them opposed the expedition commander's proposal that the Americans withdraw from San Juan Heights. Some of them at least welcomed Miles' arrival; General Wheeler, for example, wrote the commanding general, "I am very glad you are here."[27] General Shafter, as we shall see, was less excited by Miles' presence. On July 3, with Miles on his way to Cuba, General Shafter and Admiral Sampson decided to confer to see if they could agree as to what would happen next. Sampson sailed his flagship east towards Shafter's headquarters. No sooner had

---

[24] David F. Trask, The War With Spain In 1898, p. 245; Another soldier present at the battle of San Juan Heights was Lt. John J. Pershing of the Tenth U.S. Cavalry, a unit whose enlisted men were black.

[25] The blockading squadron at this point included Sampson's North Atlantic Squadron and Schley's Flying Squadron.

[26] Miles, Serving the Republic, p. 282

[27] Wheeler to Miles, July 18, 1898, Miles-Cameron Papers, Library of Congress.

Sampson sailed off then the Spanish fleet decided to make a run for the open sea. Steaming out the narrow channel of Santiago Harbor in single file, they tried to elude the blockading squadron, now under the command of Commodore Schley, and were blown out the water. All six ships attempting to leave the harbor were destroyed; 323 Spanish sailors were killed, 151 wounded, and 1,720 taken prisoner. In contrast, one American sailor died in the battle. The fight had eliminated the Spanish Naval presence in the Caribbean Sea. Even in the face of such an overwhelming victory the winners squabbled; Admiral Sampson wired the Navy Department news of the victory and didn't bother mentioning Commodore Schley, who was actually in command during the fight. Some of Schley's detractors wondered about his seamanship. During the battle, Schley's flagship, the Brooklyn, had reversed direction, ostensibly to avoid being rammed by a Spanish vessel. This maneuver forced another American ship to stop and back its engines to avoid being struck by the Brooklyn; to Schley's critics his action was both unnecessary and dangerous.

The situation of the Spanish garrison at Santiago was now desperate. They had no hope of reinforcements or resupply by sea and little hope of reinforcement by land. A small relief expedition from Havana was being held at bay by Cuban insurgents. Nevertheless, Old World notions of military honor would not allow the Spanish commanders to surrender unconditionally. Shafter and General Miles, who arrived in Cuba on July 11, were most sensitive to the Spanish concerns, as well they might be, because they had a little problem of their own. On July 6, the American troops began to come down with the dreaded yellow fever.

General Miles, characteristically and pursuant to his understanding of his orders, sought to take charge of the situation. Since the Army's Surgeon General had concluded that the yellow fever menace existed only at lower elevations, Miles ordered that the troops move to high ground. He also had the field hospitals manned by black soldiers, who mistakenly were thought to be immune to the disease. He also took active measures to improve sanitary conditions. However, he did not, as Shafter expected, place his troops under Shafter's command and set forth his own plans as to how to force the Spanish surrender. Shafter, well aware of Miles' relationship with Crook and the flap over General Howard's role in the surrender of the Nez Perce, indicated his receptiveness to Miles' activities in a cable to Miles on July 17:

> ...Nothing would give me greater pleasure than serving under you, General, and I shall comply with all requests and directions, but I was told by the Secretary that you were not to supersede me in command here...[28]

On July 13, Miles, Shafter, and General Wheeler, who thirty-three years earlier had accompanied Jefferson Davis on the prison ship to Ft. Monroe, began negotiations with the Spanish. Miles backed Shafter in communications with Secretary Alger in Washington. He indicated that the disease situation and the need to commence the Puerto Rican invasion before the advent of the fever season on that island mandated acceptance of the Spanish demands for repatriation to Spain and continued possession of their small arms. On July 17, an agreement along these lines was reached, and Miles made no effort to upstage General Shafter in the surrender ceremony. Four days later, with over 3400 men, Miles was off to Puerto Rico.

While Puerto Rico had none of the historic animosity towards Spanish rule that had turned Cuba into a battleground, Miles believed that in the event of war with Spain, Puerto Rico was more important strategically. He thought that control over the island would allow the United States to control the Caribbean. Now that he was finally on his way to Puerto Rico, he had good reason to expect only token resistance from the 8,000 Spanish regulars and 9,000 militia troops. Like their

---

[28]Miles, Serving the Republic, p. 294. The Commanding General responded by citing an order to him from Secretary Alger authorizing him to accept the surrender of the Spanish or order an assault.

compatriots in Cuba and the Philippines, these soldiers had no hope of being reinforced or resupplied and were equipped with little or no artillery.

Although Miles had informed Secretary Alger that he would land on the northeast coast of Puerto Rico, he surprised, embarrassed, and infuriated his boss by landing on the southeast coast. There is some reason to believe that he changed these plans because he, with good reason, had little faith in security at the War Department.[29] The newspapers were filled with details about the progress of the invasion, which were being given out freely in Washington. Landing unresisted, Miles and General James H. Wilson[30] swept across the island in flanking maneuvers executed by four columns. The Spanish fought little and fell back upon San Juan. Miles rejected suggestions that the island capital be threatened with naval bombardment because he saw no reason to embitter the civilian population towards the United States at the outset of American rule.[31]

---

[29]O'Toole, The Spanish War, pp. 354-55.

[30]Wilson was another of the Civil War's boy generals. As noted at the end of Chapter I, at the age of 27 he led over 12,000 Union cavalry in a raid through Alabama and into Georgia at the end of the War, managing to defeat the legendary Confederate General Nathan Bedford Forrest along the way.

[31]Several dispatches from Miles to Secretary of War Alger indicate substantial friction between the General and Admiral Sampson during the Puerto Rican campaign. On July 18, 1898, Miles complained to the Secretary that he had asked Sampson for a naval escort to Puerto Rico and had gotten no reply; he requested that the Navy be subject to his orders. On August 10, he wrote that he understood that Sampson intended to sail into San Juan Harbor to demand the surrender of the city with the threat of naval bombardment. Miles asked that any such action be prohibited because it interfered with the Army's campaign and would needlessly result in civilian casualties if the Spanish resisted. Alger's response on August 11 assured Miles that there was no cause for his apprehension but that the Secretary would issue orders prohibiting any bombardment of San Juan. [Miles Papers, Military History Institute, Carlisle.] It is possible that Miles' relations with Sampson during the Puerto Rican expedition were a factor in his inclination to support Admiral Schley in his dispute with Sampson as to who deserved credit for the naval victory off Cuba.

As his troops were advancing across Puerto Rico, Miles turned his attention to the troops of Shafter's command, who were falling ill in alarming numbers before Santiago de Cuba. He urged that all available naval resources be committed to immediate evacuation of the Fifth Corps, noting, "I would not delay a single ship notwithstanding our need of cavalry and will order ...every...vessel that can be spared to go with all speed to Santiago."[32]

Before Miles could capture San Juan, the Spanish threw in the towel and hostilities ceased on August 12. On the other side of the world the Spanish garrison at Manila had surrendered to General Wesley Merritt after a sham battle to preserve their honor. Miles' invasion had assured American possession of Puerto Rico in the post-war peace negotiations; the human cost to the United States had been 3 killed, 40 wounded. Miles received little glory or acclaim from the Puerto Rican invasion particularly compared to that heaped upon the regimental commander of the Rough Riders. Still, to some who witnessed both the Cuban campaign and Miles' operation in Puerto Rico, the contrast between the two expeditions was stark. Joseph Pulitzer's New York World, a Democratic newspaper, attempted to promote Miles as the preeminent hero of the War and Alger as the preeminent villain. Upon the commanding general's return from Puerto Rico, the World reported that Secretary Alger had denied Miles' request to parade his Army through New York City because he didn't want city residents to see how healthy Miles' troops were in contrast to those who had served in Cuba.[33]

The most prominent of the Spanish-American War correspondents, Richard Harding Davis, wrote Miles on April 13, 1901:

[32]Miles dispatch, August 6, 1898, Miles Papers, Carlisle.

[33] New York World, Sept. 4, 1898, p. 4

> Thanks to you that expedition was one of the most instructive of any I ever accompanied and without question the best conducted and planned.[34]

The greatest war since his youth was over in less than four months, and while the nation revelled in its newly revealed strength, there had to be a bit of disappointment for the Commanding General, who had missed the main show. Maybe he could understand the acclaim for Dewey, who at least had paid his dues as a junior officer in the Great War with Farragut at Mobile Bay, but the public clamor over Teddy Roosevelt had to have been galling. On November 11, 1898, Miles was the guest of honor at a dinner in the grand ballroom of the Waldorf-Astoria Hotel in New York. The Commanding General's entrance was greeted by a burst of applause, but the New York Times reported that during the serving of the second course, Roosevelt, now Governor-elect of New York, was seen moving through the gallery to take the seat originally assigned to General Shafter (who was either ill or feigning illness):

> a mighty shout went up, and for the moment attention was diverted from the guest of the evening as the Governor-elect made his first public appearance.[35]

The New York World reported the interaction between the two men far more dramatically. In its account, Roosevelt responded to a comment by the evening's master of ceremonies, Joseph Choate, that the soldiers in Cuba were greatly heartened by the news of Miles' arrival by

---

[34]Richard Harding Davis to Miles, April 13, 1901, Miles-Cameron Papers

[35]New York Times, Nov. 12, 1898, 1:7; although relations between the two men remained cordial,at least on the surface, for another three years, one cannot help but believe that Miles resented be upstaged by one whose penchant for self-promotion made Nelson Miles look like an amateur.

shouting, "Here! Here! That's true." The paper also reported that the Commanding General read a quotation from a poem:

> God gives us men!
> A time like this demands
> Strong minds, great hearts, true faith and ready hands
> Men whom the lust of office does not kill
> Men whom the spoils of office cannot buy
> Men who possess opinions and a will
> Men who have honor; Men who will not lie.

While he read, Miles:

> looked squarely at Colonel Roosevelt. For nearly a minute, the two heroes of the war looked into each other's eyes, while the people assembled watched their every action. Colonel Roosevelt did not flinch under the searching gaze of the Commanding General of the Army...[36]

Despite the efforts of the World, it was apparent that the General had missed the main event during the war, but he would get more than his fair share of the action in the post-war finger-pointing.

---

[36] The New York World, Nov. 12, 1898, pp. 1-2 "PEACE HONORS FOR GEN. MILES"

"Circulation Books Open to All."

EPTEMBER 8, 1898. PRICE ONE CENT in Greater New York and Jersey City. TWO CENTS outside of Greater New York and Jersey City and on trains.

MILES FULL OF FIGHT AND READY TO MEET ALGER.

ger Cannot Speak His Mind.

AS ORDERS.

ident Will Not Allow eneral to Be Court-Martialled.

T MUST BE STOPPED.

and Corbin Wanted prisals, but McKinley Wants Peace.

WILL BE CALLED OFF.

ecretary of War Declined to alk on the New Phase of Affairs Last Night.

AL'S FRIENDS GRATIFIED.

elieve that He Has Been Anaired All Along by the Ciilian Head of the Army.

(Special to The World.)

HINGTON, Sept. 7.—There will investigation into the conduct of ar unless Congress athorises it.

Miles desires an investigation participation in the Santiago and Rico campaigns the War Office obably grant his reques: But will be no court-martial proceedainst Gen. Miles

Miles interview will go unnoticed President and the Secretary of n short the Miles Alger-Corbin eray will be stopped, not to ened unless Gen. Miles indulges

MAJOR-GEN. NELSON A. MILES.

(From a photograph by S. R. Honey, World staff photographer, on the deck of the steamship Obdam, taken at 8 o'clock yesterday morning.

General Admits He Made the Charges.

PLAIN TALK.

Interview with World Man in His Cabin on the Obdam.

"DESPATCHES GARBLED."

Laughed at the Possibility of a Court-Martial Being Ordered.

TOOK CHARGE AT SANTIAGO.

Ridiculed the Idea that He Was Only a Spectator Sent with Reinforcements.

FRIENDLY WITH GEN. SHAFTER.

Gen. Miles Was Greeted on Arrival by Cheers of Men and by Steamer Whistles.

Gen. Nelson A. Miles, his family, a large number of regular army officers and 800 men and officers of the Second Wisconsin Infantry Regiment, arrived from Porto Rico yesterday morning on the transport Obdam. The voyage of six days was a pleasant one. The Wisconsin boys arrived in splendid he forming a striking contrast to the human wrecks from Santiago.

Drawn From Mrs. Miles's Latest Photograph.

"IT IS UP TO YOU, MR. ALGER!"

NEW YORK WORLD SEPT. 8, 1898

THE WORLD: SUNDAY, SEPTEMBER 4, 1898

NO ODIOUS CONTRASTS WANTED.

SICK SOLDIERS BEG THE PRESIDENT TO LET THEM LEAVE WIKOFF FOR HOME.

n Company with Vice-President Hobart and Secretary of War Alger Mr. McKinley Visits the Camp and Inspects It.

'ENT FROM WARD TO WARD; SAW SICK AND SUFFERING MEN.

resident, After Being Introduced by Gen. Wheeler, Makes a Speech, in Which He Thanks the Men in the Name of the People of These United States.

SOLDIERS PLEAD WITH THE PRESIDENT AT WIKOFF TO BE SENT HOME.

THE WORLD: SATURDAY, SEPTEMBER 3, 1898.

GENS. WHEELER AND SHAFTER INSPECTING CAMP WIKOFF.

CHAPTER VIII: "EMBALMED" BEEF

Victory should have been enough to allow the American public to forget the confusion and disorganization attending the expedition to Cuba. However, the dreadful toll taken by yellow fever and malaria rekindled interest in investigating the management of the war. The proportions of the epidemic were revealed to the country in a manner that was most embarrassing to the administration. With General Shafter's approval, Colonel Roosevelt wrote him a letter demanding evacuation of the Fifth Army Corps from Cuba. Another letter signed by several officers, including Roosevelt, made the same urgent request. These letters were leaked to the press on August 4, and three days later the troops began to be transferred to Camp Wikoff at Montauk Point, Long Island. In two months on Long Island another 126 soldiers died of disease, and complaints about sanitary conditions increased the pressure on President McKinley. By the time it was disbanded, the Fifth Army Corps had lost 243 men in combat and 771 to disease in Cuba and New York.

In response to the public clamor, the President appointed a War Investigating Commission, headed by Gen. Grenville Dodge. On December 21, 1898, the "Dodge Commission" heard testimony from General Miles and Major-General Wesley Merritt, who had commanded the expedition to the Philippines. Miles testified that much of the meat sent to his troops in Puerto Rico during the war had spoiled in the holds of the transports. He characterized the refrigerated beef provided as "embalmed" and said that he believed that the chemicals in the meat may have been responsible for some of the illness among the troops. Miles said he had received reports that this beef smelled like an embalmed corpse.

The general charged that refrigerated beef had been supplied as an experiment and suggested that the Secretary of War and the Army's commissary department (which was answerable to Alger but not to Miles) should be held responsible. What he had suggested instead,

Miles testified, was that Army paymasters should have accompanied the expedition to purchase live cattle locally for slaughter.

The commanding general also said that much of the canned beef supplied the soldiers was spoiled, and he addressed other errors he thought were made in the prosecution of the war. He said that invading Cuba prior to the destruction of the Spanish fleet had been very risky. Had the Spanish Navy prevailed in the Caribbean, he said, our soldiers in Cuba would have been trapped. He reiterated his view that Puerto Rico should have been seized first to provide a base for naval operations. Finally, he criticized the landing facilities near Santiago as inadequate and opined that inadequate rations and medical supplies made the troops vulnerable to disease.[1]

A day later the Commercial Tribune of Cincinnati quoted Miles as saying that chemicals in the beef supplied the troops were largely responsible for the sickness in the Army during the war. Miles' charges instantly drew a firestorm of reaction, not only from General Charles Eagan, head of the commissary department, but from Swift Beef Co., the meat packer that had supplied the beef to the Army. At the end of December, the Dodge Commission published statements from a number of officers describing the meat provided as unpalatable and even "nasty." Some of these reports, which had been submitted to the Commission by Miles, stated that the beef had given the troops diarrhea. At the same time, General Eagan and the Army's adjutant general, Henry Corbin, testified that Miles' charges were absolutely false.[2]

After some hesitation, the Dodge Commission decided to make a thorough inquiry into Miles' complaints about the beef. Colonel Henry B. Osgood, the chief commissary officer at Tampa and Santiago, asserted that the beef provided the Cuban expedition was every bit as good, or better than, that issued to the Regular Army before the war. However, Osgood acknowledged that he had received many complaints about its

---

[1]New York Times, Dec. 28, 1898, 3:1

[2] New York Times, Dec. 24, 1898, 4:4; Dec. 25, 1898, 5:4, Dec. 28,, 1898, 5:3, Dec. 30, 1898, 3:3 & 6:4.

appearance and that the meat had a green mold or "beard" on the surface. Admitting that this made the beef "repulsive looking," Osgood asserted that under the surface it was as good as freshly killed meat. Osgood also admitted that there was a small experiment made with beef treated with chemicals but that none was ever fed to the troops.[3] Two other witnesses from the commissary department were less helpful to Miles. Col. Henry Sharp, who had served with the commissary at Camp Thomas, a training camp near the Chickamauga battlefield in Georgia, and in Puerto Rico, said the quality of the meat provided by his department was good and took issue with the commanding general as to the advisability of purchasing live beef (or "beef on the hoof") in Puerto Rico. Sharp said the native cattle on that island were infinitely inferior to the refrigerated beef sent from the United States.[4]

More damaging was the testimony of Major John Black, a volunteer officer whom Miles had selected to be chief commissary for his expedition after rejecting the officer provided by Commissary General Eagan. Black said that the general quality of the meat supplied was good. He discussed a shipment of refrigerated beef that had arrived in Puerto Rico on August 10, 1898, on board the transport Manitoba. The meat was spotted and discolored, but Black said the only chemical that he was aware of was the ammonia used in the ship's cooling plant. Although informed that this discoloration did not affect the quality of the beef, several of the Army surgeons in Puerto Rico refused to accept it. Black did confirm that numerous complaints had been received about spoiled canned beef, but he clearly did not support Miles' more dramatic assertions which suggested that the troops had been guinea pigs for an experiment with chemically-treated beef.[5]

Emboldened by the early testimony, Commissary General Eagan went on the offensive against Miles and, in doing so, he moved the

---

[3] New York Times, Jan 6, 1899, 4:5.

[4] Ibid, Jan. 7, 1899, 4:6.

[5] Ibid, Jan. 8, 1899, 11:3

general's charges to the front pages of the nation's newspapers, where they remained for the next four months. Eagan denounced Miles as "an infamous and malicious liar, unfit for the society of decent men." He charged that much of the problem with the acceptance of the beef ration in Puerto Rico had been due to the fact that Miles had selected Major Black, whom he termed an "inexperienced volunteer officer," as the chief commissary for his expedition, over Osgood, the regular Army officer designated by the department. Eagan also took issue with Miles' assertion that the use of canned beef in the Spanish War was something new and unusual, claiming that it had been part of the Army's rations since 1888.[6]

The initial effect of Eagan's denunciation was to create some sympathy for Miles. The commanding general's friends threw a little dirt into the fray by letting the press know that Eagan had been court-martialed for gambling in Arizona in 1878, and they began to press for another court-martial to punish him for the tone of his attacks on Miles. Eagan resubmitted his testimony to the Dodge Commission with his characterization of Miles deleted but with the substance unchanged. Nevertheless President McKinley yielded to the demands for a court-martial over the vociferous resistance of Secretary of War Alger. The response of the New York Times, a pro-Miles newspaper, was to characterize Eagan as "an insubordinate and foul-mouthed officer" and Secretary Alger and his ally, Adjutant General Corbin, as "inefficient and insubordinate clerks." In February, the court-martial recommended that Eagan be dismissed from the Army on account of his outburst; McKinley imposed a sentence of suspension from active duty for six years (which would run to the date of Eagan's retirement).[7]

Miles' friends also went on the offensive against Secretary Alger, who was pressing McKinley to also court-martial Miles. They resurfaced the story that in 1864, General Sheridan had recommended that Alger

---

[6]New York Times, Jan. 13, 1899, 1:7 "EAGAN DENOUNCES MILES AS A LIAR"

[7]New York Times, Jan 14, 1899, 1:7 "GEN. EAGAN IS DENOUNCED"; Jan. 17, 1:5; Jan . 18, 1:2 & 6-1(editorial);Feb. 8, 1899,1:5.

be dishonorably discharged from the volunteer service for an unapproved absence from his post. The commanding general's allies also pointed out that Major-General Wesley Merritt, second to Miles in seniority and one of Sheridan's divisional commanders during the Civil War, had concurred in the recommendation. Rumors were out that Merritt was currying favor with Secretary Alger in the hope of replacing Miles as commanding general, and it was hoped that this revelation would make it difficult for Merritt to side publicly with the Secretary of War.[8]

Miles also got a tremendous boost from another quarter. He made public a letter written to him by Governor Roosevelt on January 14, 1899. The Governor wrote Miles that there was beef on the transport that took the Rough Riders from Tampa to Cuba that he was told was being tried as an "experiment." He said he got complaints from the men living on the forward deck near this beef that the odor from the meat was intolerable. Roosevelt continued:

> I went up, found this to be the case, and so reported it. At first I was told that I must be mistaken and that the beef should be kept.

The Colonel then inspected the beef with one of his surgeons; they determined that it was putrid and, pursuant to their demands, it was disposed of. Roosevelt also observed:

> I was dumbfounded by the reports of many of the officers' testimony and am wholly unable to understand it. I have, however, found that...even brave and good officers are most reluctant to testify where their testimony may get them in trouble and may ruin their future career...but for this reason, when I saw you

---

[8]New York Times, Feb. 4, 1899, 6:1.

> testifying to what I knew to be the truth about the meat, I felt it my duty to write and aid you. Up to the day of our disbandment I never met one officer in the Army of Santiago--and I have conversed with hundreds on the subject--who did not state exactly what I have stated about this beef.[9]

Miles' former protege, General Leonard Wood, was less helpful. Wood testified that, except for some cans of beef that were tainted and thrown away, the quality of the beef provided the troops was good.[10] On the other hand, a Colonel Gibson, who had been the distributing agent for the American National Relief Commission at Santiago, testified that the canned beef furnished the troops was generally unfit for use and should never had been issued. He also stated that the refrigerated beef was bad and was covered with a green beard.[11] At the end of January 1899, amid reports that the Dodge Commission was reacting very negatively to his charges and that Alger was pressing McKinley to institute court-martial charges against him, Miles reiterated his allegations, this time placing more emphasis on the unpalatability of the canned roast beef and its lack of nutritional value.[12]

On February 8, 1899, the Dodge Commission issued its findings on Miles' charges, concluding that the beef furnished American troops during the Spanish War was as good as could be furnished as an

---

[9]Ibid, Jan. 14, 1899, 2:1; Roosevelt to Miles, Jan. 14, 1899. Curiously, Roosevelt's letter closes with a request that it be kept confidential, but Miles immediately made it public and stated that he did so with the Governor's approval. It could be that Roosevelt had a change of heart. Relations between the two men soured much later. When the break came, Roosevelt would intimate that Miles was scheming for a way to ruin McKinley and replace him as the Republican Presidential candidate in 1900; I wonder whether he was imputing his own motives to Miles.

[10] New York Times, Jan. 14, 1899, 2-1.

[11]Ibid, Jan 18, 1899, 1:3.

[12]Ibid, Feb. 1, 1899, 1:5.

"emergency ration" and that it was never intended to be anything else. While finding that some of the canned beef was unpalatable due to the effects of the tropical heat, the Commission opined that the testimony of Miles and his commissary, Maj. Black, was rebutted by a mass of evidence to the contrary.[13] The Dodge Commission's disposition of the controversy was obviously satisfactory to nobody, because McKinley immediately directed the appointment of a new and separate court of inquiry to examine Miles' charges.

On February 20, 1899, Miles testified before the three-member "Beef Court" whose President was Major-General James F. Wade, who thirteen years earlier as commanding officer at Fort Apache had helped Miles deport all the Chiricahua and Warm Springs Apaches from Arizona. The commanding general submitted the statement he had made to the Dodge Commission to the court and then spelled out the course he believed the commissary department should have followed instead of relying on refrigerated and canned beef. Miles testified that it had always been Army practice to transport live cattle to its troops in the field and feed them with freshly slaughtered beef. This had been done during the Civil War, in Arizona, Texas, and even for the expeditions chasing the Apaches into Mexico; he saw no reason why live cattle weren't shipped to Cuba and Puerto Rico.[14] Indeed, he told the court that when he found that native beef was available in Puerto Rico, he immediately told the War Department to cease shipments of the refrigerated meat.

The general appeared to back off a bit from his earlier allegations regarding "embalmed beef." Miles denied ever telling the New York Herald that he had overwhelming evidence that the refrigerated beef had been treated with chemicals. He said he was misquoted and that the only evidence he had was reports from soldiers who claimed that the beef had the odor of an embalmed body and some reports from

---

[13]New York Times, Feb. 9, 1899, 1:5.

[14]New York Times, Feb. 21, 1899, 2:1.

individuals who said they had seen fluid injected into the meat and other indications of chemical treatment. He also backed away from his characterization of the manner in which the decision to supply canned and refrigerated beef had been made. Miles said that although he knew that canned roast beef had been an authorized Army ration since 1888, he had never understood it to be part of the regular Army ration and that this had caused him to testify before the Dodge Commission that it had been provided as "a pretense of experiment." Now, the commanding general said he recognized that his terminology was unfortunate and that he did not intend to suggest a fraudulent intent on anyone's part. He continued to maintain that provision of canned beef to the troops was an experiment and a very unsuccessful one.

Miles told the court that when he had first heard complaints about the beef during the war, he hadn't paid much attention, assuming it was part of the usual complaining soldiers engage in. However, he said that the incidence of disease among the Fifth Corps soldiers in Long Island made him suspicious because he thought the effects of malaria and yellow fever should have ceased. He said he did not report his suspicions to the Secretary of War because he preferred to make his own independent investigation of the matter.[15]

The witnesses who followed Miles largely supported his claims as to the unpalatability of the canned roast beef. As to the refrigerated beef, the testimony varied, and it seemed that one's experience depended on how quickly the meat was transported from the refrigerated hold to the field. The pro-Miles New York Times reported that "the contention of General Miles that the army in Cuba and Puerto Rico should have been supplied with herds of cattle or beef on the hoof, instead of refrigerated beef, was supported by every witness on February 21, who gave an opinion."[16] However, the Times reported that several of these witnesses also testified that in their opinion the

[15]New York Times, Feb. 21, 1899, 1:2

[16]N.Y. Times, Feb. 22, 1899, 6:1 (editorial)

incidence of disease among the troops had nothing to do with the beef supply and that they wouldn't have reported their dissatisfaction with the canned beef if they hadn't been ordered to do so by Miles.

The next day, February 23, former commissary general Eagan and his successor, General J. F. Weston, appeared before the "beef court" to rebut the testimony favorable to Miles. Eagan stated that using beef on the hoof in the tropics was undesirable because the animal heat could not disappear prior to cooking. General Weston testified that the refrigerated beef he observed in Cuba just after the Spanish surrender of Santiago on July 17 was slightly discolored but not spoiled. While Weston denied that preservatives were used on the refrigerated beef generally, he did admit that the "Powell preservative process experiment" was performed on three or four boxes of frozen beef in Tampa. He confirmed that six or seven quarters of this beef were placed on transport ships. Some of these quarters were covered by canvas and some were not; Weston said that the covered meat kept for at least 72 hours but the uncovered portion spoiled quickly.[17] Thus, Weston's testimony did confirm that Miles' charges weren't completely unfounded. Similarly, the testimony of Weston's Assistant, Col. Osgood, that the refrigerated beef appeared offensive but wasn't, also gave some colorable basis to Miles' allegations. The next day Eagan himself made an admission that was somewhat helpful to Miles' position. He stated that the first shipment of refrigerated beef was experimental because it was not certain that it could be used.[18] The testimony supported Miles' view that the commissary department had changed its traditional reliance on live beef by entering into large contracts with Swift without knowing beforehand that the meat provided would be suitable for use in the field.

Among some of Miles' friends there was a perception that after two and a half months of intense publicity the momentum in the beef

---

[17] N.Y. Times, Feb. 24, 1899, 3:4.

[18] Ibid, Feb. 25, 1899, 3:1.

inquiry was finally beginning to turn in the commanding general's favor. On February 20, Senator Joseph Foraker of Ohio warned the general's sister-in-law, Elizabeth Cameron, that "the General is in grave danger."[19] Two weeks later, another U.S. Senator, Cushman Davis, wrote Mrs. Cameron:

> I shall certainly endeavor to help Gen. Miles. I think an overpowering public sentiment will do so. There is no doubt the people are with him in the matter of "embalmed" and putrid beef, and the feeling is growing.
>
> I have been indignant all along at the treatment he has received. He has lacked tact and evidently has not taken good advice in some particulars, if, indeed, [he] has even taken any. But this, of course, does not detract from the justice of his cause. The evidence in the beef investigation is sustaining him every day.[20]

On March 9, the War Department announced that it had decided not to purchase any additional canned roast beef. It also announced that, while it was sending refrigerated beef on the transports bound for the Philippine Islands, it was also shipping live cattle to be slaughtered for use during the voyage. These decisions also appeared to support Miles, because they carried with them a tacit admission that he was partially correct and that his contention that beef on the hoof should be shipped to American troops overseas was not so outlandish as his detractors claimed.

---

[19]Letter of Foraker to Elizabeth Cameron, Feb. 20, 1899, Miles-Cameron Papers, Library of Congress.

[20]Davis to Elizabeth Cameron, March 7, 1899, Miles-Cameron Papers.

JANUARY 28, 1899

EAGAN DOOMED TO LEAVE THE ARMY IN DISGRACE.

Court-Martial Finds: "Guilty Under Both Charges---Sentence, Dismissal From the Service---No Recommendation for Mercy or Executive Clemency."

VERDICT QUICKLY REACHED.

No Hope for Gen. Miles's Accuser Except the Clemency of the President.

POSSIBLE APPEAL TO CIVIL COURT.

Testimony at Last Day of Trial Designed to Show that Eagan Had Lost His Mental Balance.

The World.

Published by the Press Publishing Company, 53 to 63 PARK ROW, New York.

MONDAY, FEBRUARY 20, 1899.

Entered at the Post-Office at New York as Second-Class Mail Matter.

Week Day Issue, in Greater New York and Jersey City	. . . . .	One Cent
Week Day Issue, Elsewhere	. . . . . .	Two Cents
Sunday	. . . . .	Five Cents

TERMS—POSTAGE FREE.

For the United States (outside of the Greater New York, Jersey City and Hoboken), Canada and Mexico.

DAILY AND SUNDAY.		EVENING.	
One Year	$8.50	One Year	$3.50
Six Months	4.25	One Month	.30
Three Months	2.15	THRICE-A-WEEK.	
One Month	.75	One Year	1.00
SUNDAY. One Year	2.50	MONTHLY WORLD, WITH WORLD ALMANAC.	
DAILY ONLY.		One Year	.35
One Year	$6.00		
Six Months	3.00	WORLD ALMANAC for 1899	
One Month	.50	..Price 25 Cents..	

[illegible] allowed to club agents. Sample copies sent free.

For England and the Continent and all Countries in the Universal Postal Union.

DAILY AND SUNDAY:		DAILY ONLY:	
One Year	$15.50	One Year	$12.00
One Month	1.40	THRICE-A-WEEK.	
SUNDAY. One Year	4.50	One Year	2.50

POSTAGE RATES ON THE WORLD.

16 Pages . . 1c. 32 Pages 2c. 48 Pages . . 3c.

Foreign Rates Double.

Address all communications, whether concerning advertisements or subscriptions, to THE WORLD, PULITZER BUILDING, Park Row, New York City. Remit by Express Money Order, Draft, Post-Office Order or Registered Letter.

BRANCH OFFICES:

WORLD UPTOWN OFFICE, 1351 Broadway, corner 36th St. (Removed from [illegible] St. and Broadway.)

WORLD HARLEM OFFICE, 180 West 125th St.

BROOKLYN, 309 Washington St.

WASHINGTON, 1[illegible] Pennsylvania Ave., N. W.

MILES'S OFFENSE.

Nauseating and poisonous beef was furnished to the army by contractors. This fact was certified to by thirty regimental officers of the regular army, whose report on the quality of the food was asked for in the usual way. It was substantiated by a still larger number of volunteer officers, including Col. Roosevelt.

Gen. Miles stated this fact before the War Investigating Commission on the basis of these reports, and also as having come under his own observation in Porto Rico.

For having told the truth in an effort to save the lives and health of the soldiers, and to protect the Government from outrageous and criminal swindling, Gen. Miles is being prosecuted by the Administration under the form of an inquiry into the beef supply.

This is the "Miles case" in brief. The American people are watching the outcome of this conspiracy.

WHAT GEN. MILES DEFENDS.

"For Sales" begin on Sunday. It pays stay in a week. Use new Seven-Time Rat

2,886 For Sales print 778 in next high newspaper.

NEW YORK, SATURDAY, FEBRUARY 4, 1899.

PRICE { ONE CENT in Greater New York and Jersey Ci TWO CENTS outside of Greater New York and J.

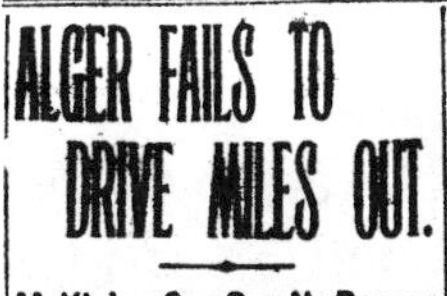

ALGER FAILS TO DRIVE MILES OUT.

McKinley Can See No Reason for His Dismissal or Court-Martial.

MAY BE INQUIRY COURT.

President Loath to Take This Step, as It Would Imply Charges Against the General.

INSPECTION BOARD POSSIBLE.

By This Method the Embalmed Beef Controversy Could Be Thoroughly Investigated.

(Special to The World.)

WASHINGTON, Feb. 2.—It was determined to-day that Major-Gen. Miles should not be deposed from command of the army or be subjected to a court-martial.

Secretary Alger has endeavored to persuade the President to take such action against the Commanding General, but Mr. McKinley could not be made to see that Gen. Miles had offended the Administration in anything he might have said relative to beef furnished the army.

Gen. Miles to-day denied responsibility for some of the interviews attributed to him, and this further disconcerted Secretary Alger, who has been laying much stress upon the published statements.

The subject was discussed in a general way at the Cabinet meeting to-day, but the best information obtainable to-night is that the Cabinet, while favoring a formal inquiry of some kind, left it to the President to take such action as he might deem proper.

President Has Choice of Two Ways.

The President has before him two methods, one of which is through a board of inspection composed of army officers, who would be guided by the rules and regulations prescribed for inspectors-general.

WHO WILL HAUL THEM DOWN?

In late March Miles made what must be termed a political tour of his native Massachusetts. On March 22, he addressed Harvard students in the Sanders Theatre under the auspices of the Harvard Republican Club and was warmly received. University President Charles Eliot praised the general, proclaiming that he had shown the same courage in the face of misrepresentation that he had displayed on the field of battle.[21] The next day the General was the guest of the city of Fitchburg, the largest town of any size near his birthplace, and two days after that received an enthusiastic welcome from the citizens of Springfield.[22]

On March 25, Governor Roosevelt appeared before the beef court. Testifying under oath, he stated that the beef furnished his troops was putrid, unpalatable, unwholesome, emitted a stench, and produced disease. He said that on the transport from Tampa to Cuba the troops were only provided canned roast beef and his men generally complained that it made them sick. Roosevelt said he forced one soldier to eat it and the man vomited. [One must recall that the troops were kept on the transports bobbing up and down in Tampa Harbor for almost a week and one wonders how much of the problem was due to sea sickness.] The New York Governor described the top layer of the canned roast beef as "slime." He said he complained to the War Department about the beef ration on July 21, about the time that his men began to receive the refrigerated beef [about a month and a half after they boarded the transports in Tampa]. The refrigerated meat, Roosevelt testified, was good once the top layer was cut away.

The Governor continued his testimony by recalling that on the way home from Cuba the men had only the canned roast beef which was unfit to eat. He also recalled being told on the first trip that some chemically treated beef was on board his transport and that it was there as part of an experiment. After one day, he remembered, this beef had

---

[21]New York Times, March 23, 1899, 4:5.

[22]Ibid, March 24, 1899, 1:3; March 26, 1899, 1:7.

to be thrown overboard because of the smell. The court was informed that the canned beef was purchased from Swift and Armour; and Colonel Roosevelt, as he liked to be called, was heard to remark as he left the courtroom that the canned beef was a disgrace to the country. The Times' analysis of the proceedings after this session was that General Miles' critics were not nearly so gleeful as they had once been.[23]

The proceedings of the beef court continued until April 21, 1899. Although many of the witnesses and much of the testimony was merely a rehash of what had been considered by the Dodge Commission, there were some startling revelations. Representatives of the Armour meat packing company testified that it had submitted a bid to the commissary department to provide the Army with beef preserved by the "Powell process." Armour also confirmed that a test of meat so preserved was conducted at Tampa with what the company termed "most satisfactory results."[24] The New York Times' reaction to this testimony was that it made commissary general Eagan's outburst at Miles even more outrageous and that Eagan ought to be court-martialed again.[25] On April 8, the developer of the process, Powell, testified before the court.

Powell denied that anything was injected into the meat during his process but that it was "fumigated." He declined to reveal the details of the process on the grounds that to do so would disclose a trade secret. Powell confirmed that there had been a small experiment with his process in Tampa but that no meat so treated was used during the Spanish-American War. Powell denied that his process bore any resemblance to the embalming process, although he did say that it could be used for this purpose. Meat fumigated with his process would not have any characteristic odor, Powell contended, except for the smell of sulfur which would not last for more than one-half hour. Finally, Powell

---

[23]New York Times, March 26, 1899, 2:1.

[24]New York Times, April 7, 1899, 9:3.

[25]Ibid, April 8, 1899, 4:4 (editorial).

stated that his was not the only meat preservative process and that refrigerated beef would not keep for more than 72 hours after it was removed from the refrigerator without preservatives.[26]

Another dramatic witness was General Shafter, commander of the Cuban expedition, who appeared before the court on April 11. Shafter ridiculed Miles' suggestion that it would have been better to have provided the troops in Cuba with beef on the hoof than refrigerated meat. He termed the idea absurd and utterly impracticable largely because there was a danger that the herd would be driven off by the enemy. [Given the situation facing the Spanish troops defending Santiago it is difficult to conceive how they would have accomplished such a feat.] Shafter, obviously very defensive about the conduct of his campaign, took issue with Governor Roosevelt as to the adequacy of the rations and medical supplies available to his commanders. He charged that if there were any shortages it was the fault of the Regimental officers. Shafter denied receiving any complaints about the beef while in Cuba and testified that in his opinion it was entirely satisfactory. With regard to the canned roast beef he said:

> Campaigning in the tropics was new to us, and it was an experimental food. Certainly now we all recognize that the rations were not well adapted to such a campaign, but it was the best we had...[27]

At the closing session of the court on April 21, Major Jesse Lee, appearing as Miles' counsel, summarized the case for the commanding general. Lee said Miles was not saying that bad beef had been supplied to the troops intentionally but that somebody had blundered and that the troops had suffered as a result. The canned beef, argued Lee, had

[26]N.Y. Times, April 9, 1899, 12:1.

[27]N.Y. Times, April 12, 1899, 5:3.

been used without adequate testing and its use had been an "experiment" as Miles alleged. The meat had been accepted on the "reputation" of the packing firms, and Lee rhetorically asked why the beef trust was exempt from scrutiny. Lee took issue with Shafter and said the evidence showed that it was perfectly practicable to have landed herds of cattle in Cuba and Puerto Rico, which would have consistent with the Army's past practices. No sufficient reason for departing from prior practice had been demonstrated, and therefore, Lee concluded, in view of the quality of the meat purchased, a great fraud had been perpetrated upon the government.[28]

What is apparent from reading accounts of Lee's closing argument on behalf of Miles is that the commanding general had retreated considerably from his more dramatic allegations of the past December. The focus of the case had shifted from the "embalmed" or chemically treated refrigerated beef to the adequacy of the canned roast beef. Moreover, his case factually alleged no more than a massive mistake rather than some conspiracy to poison the troops in order to make a few people in the commissary department and in the meat packing industry rich [which is what he was intimating in December]. Before considering the disposition of the court, however, one has to ask whether Miles would look better in this affair if it had occurred at the same time as the agitation that followed the revelations concerning the practices of the meat packing industry in Upton Sinclair's The Jungle in 1906. Additionally, had Miles' attack on the beef trust been made a few years later in conjunction with the trust-busting agitation of the first decade of the twentieth century, the weaknesses in his case might not appear as significant as they did to the beef court in 1899.

Having said all this, Miles' conduct in the "embalmed beef" affair is very difficult to defend. It does appear to me that he ruined commissary general Eagan with very little hard evidence. Although he may have been right about the suitability of some of the canned beef, I believe he quietly could have gotten purchasing practices changed

---

[28]N.Y. Times, April 25, 1899, 4:4

without dragging Eagan's reputation through the mud. Moreover, his assertion that the meat ration was in any way related to the epidemics that were responsible for most of the military deaths was totally unfounded.

Even before the court of inquiry issued its report, there were indications that its findings would not be favorable to Miles. On April 26, 1899, it concluded that the government was responsible for 300,000 pounds of beef delivered to Puerto Rico aboard the "Manitoba" on August 10, 1898, which had been refused by Miles' commissary.[29] Rumors began to circulate that the administration was about to replace Miles as commanding general with Major-General Wesley Merritt, who had been quoted as saying that Russell Alger was the best Secretary of War the country had ever seen.[30]

The "Beef Court" issued its findings on May 7, 1899. It found that Miles' allegations that the refrigerated beef provided to the Army had been treated with chemicals had not been established. On the other hand, it found that his allegations regarding the suitability of the canned roast beef had been sustained. The court censured Miles for not informing the Secretary of War of the unsuitability of the beef when he first concluded that it was unfit for use. In the court's view, when Miles first suspected something was wrong in August 1898, he at least should have had the meat tested. Instead he waited until December 21 [his appearance before the Dodge Commission] to mention the problem to anyone. It also found that he had no sufficient justification for his charges that some of the beef provided was "embalmed" and agreed with Shafter that landing live cattle in Cuba would have been absurd.

Lt. Col. Marion Maus, the inspector general assigned to Miles' staff [Maus was the officer who ended up in command of Crook's expedition after Geronimo in 1885-6], was also censured for not immediately reporting the beef problem to the War Department. The

---

[29]Ibid, April 27, 1899, 3:5.

[30]N.Y. Times, May 4, 1899, 6:1; May 5, 1899, 6:2 & 6:7; May 6, 6:3.

court found that Maus had reports regarding the unsuitability of the canned beef as early as October l, but waited until October 26 to report it to Washington and then did so through regular channels in a manner which would not bring the problem to anyone's attention.

The court also censured commissary general Eagan for what it termed a colossal error in purchasing too much canned beef as an untried ration. Finally, the court exonerated the meat packers, finding that the beef they provided to the Army was as good as that they provided to the public. [Here is where the public perception of Miles' activities would have been markedly different if this affair had occurred in 1906; that the meat packers were providing meat as good as that provided the public would have been perceived as damning in 1906, rather than an exoneration of the industry.] The court concluded its report by recommending that there be no further proceedings conducted with respect to this matter.[31]

The reaction of Miles' friends and supporters to the court's report was predictably hostile. The New York Times termed the report "shameful, indecent, and disgraceful" and charged that the court had seen its primary function as serving of the interests of Secretary Alger.[32] The New York World and other friends also attacked the court, the report, and defended the commanding general.[33] Nevertheless, the fact remained that for the first time in his long career, Nelson Miles had emerged from the fray with egg on his face. On the other hand, if his enemies thought for a minute that the outcome of the embalmed beef scandal would make the commanding general more circumspect, they couldn't have been more mistaken.

---

[31]New York Times, May 8, 1899, 1:6 (includes text of court's findings).

[32]New York Times, May 8, 1899, 6:l (editorial); Also see May ll, 4:4.

[33] New York World, May 8, 1899, 6:2

CHAPTER IX: SAMPSON-SCHLEY AND FORMAL CENSURE

The initial fallout of the Embalmed Beef scandal was the resignation of Secretary of War Alger in July 1899. Miles may well have viewed this as a vindication of his position in the numerous disputes he had had with the Secretary since the outbreak of the Spanish War. However, to the extent that Alger's resignation was a victory for Miles, it was to be pyrrhic because the new Secretary, New York corporation lawyer Elihu Root, would prove to be just as hostile and far more capable.[1]

In September 1899, a Massachusetts Republican politician, Levi F. Cook, mailed a circular to a number of prominent Republicans and Democrats urging them to support General Miles for the presidency in 1900. Cook said that Miles had seen his circular but would not say whether the general had approved of it or not. In any event, no serious attempt to gain either party's nomination was made on his behalf.[2] For the next two years the general stayed out of the limelight except for a minor dispute with General Merritt as to whether U.S. forces in the Philippines should consist of more or less Regular soldiers as opposed to volunteers [Merritt wanted relatively more regulars; Miles gave him relatively more volunteers] and a rumored dispute with General A.R. Buffington, the chief of the ordinance bureau, over some allegedly missing gun carriages.[3]

---

[1]Although probably coincidental, it's intriguing that one of the nastiest confrontations that Elihu Root had in his early professional career was with Miles' benefactor Francis C. Barlow. As Attorney General of the State of New York in 1876, Barlow filed a lawsuit against the Bank of North America, represented by the young Elihu Root. After leaving office Barlow continued to represent the State as "special attorney for the people" and at one point loaned Root a brief and later accused the young lawyer of intentionally failing to return it. According to Root's biographer, the entire matter was a misunderstanding and was quickly resolved. Philip C. Jessup, Elihu Root, Vol. 1, pp 98-99 (1938).

[2]New York Times, Sept. 27, 1899, 6:5.

[3]New York Times, July 18, 1899, 4:2 and 3; May 9, 1900, 2:1; May 10, 1900, 5:4.

Despite all the controversy surrounding the general and the rumors that he had schemed to get the President's job, McKinley, who was then running for his second term against William Jennings Bryan, presented Miles with a Lieutenant General's commission in June, 1900. When the Senate returned to session it confirmed the promotion.[4] Nevertheless, rumors circulated that the administration was looking for a way to retire the general at the first opportunity. In August 1901, upon Miles' reaching the age of 62, it would become possible for the President to retire him for the good of the service, and in September 1901, he could pressure Miles to retire voluntarily upon completing 40 years of active duty.[5] In retrospect, what these reports indicate is that Secretary Root may have been planning Miles' demise long before the events that he seized upon to censure him.

In September, 1901, President McKinley, six months into his second term, was shot in the abdomen at the Pan-American Exposition in Buffalo. After lingering a few days and even showing signs of recovery, the President died, and 42-year-old Theodore Roosevelt became the Chief Executive. There initially appears to have been no friction between Miles and the new President as indicated by a September 30, 1901 note from Roosevelt to the general inviting him to join the President on a ride.[6]

The only overt enemy that Miles appeared to have at this time was Major-General Henry Corbin, the adjutant general, who had allied himself previously with Alger. In Miles' annual report, released at the end of October 1901, he advocated institution of a restricted canteen for the soldiers on post which would sell beer and light wines. The New York Times noted that Miles had previously opposed this concept and favored an off-post canteen, as the best means of promoting temperance among the troops. However, Corbin had apparently come out in favor

---

[4]New York Times, June 9, 1900, 3:2.

[5]New York Times, Feb. 8, 1901, 6:3.

[6]Miles-Cameron Papers.

of an off-post canteen, and the Times suggested that Miles changed his position as a matter of reflex. The paper was critical of both men for putting their spite towards each other ahead of the best interests of the Army.[7]

Two months later, however, Miles would be embroiled in a similar relationship with the President and Secretary of War Root, and the genesis of the feud would be the controversy between Admirals Sampson and Schley over the naval battle of Santiago. The Sampson-Schley controversy was reactivated by the publication of a book entitled History of the Navy by Edgar Staton Maclay, a writer employed by the Brooklyn, New York Navy Yard. After reading the book, which was very critical of his conduct at Santiago, Admiral Schley requested that Navy Secretary John D. Long appoint a court of inquiry to determine whether he was guilty of the misconduct charged in the Maclay book.[8] The presiding officer of the court was Admiral Dewey, the hero of Manila Bay, and the two other members were Admirals Ramsay and Benham. The court met daily in Washington beginning on November 11, 1901 and issued its report on December 13.

The opinion of the majority of the court, Ramsay and Benham, found against Schley at every turn. They found that on May 23, 1898, when off Cienfuegos, Schley should have attempted to communicate with the Cuban rebels to determine the whereabouts of the Spanish fleet. They faulted him for not deploying his ships in a manner which would have allowed him to intercept the Spanish squadron. They criticized him for hesitating during the voyage to Santiago and delaying his entire squadron to wait for one of the smaller ships to keep up. The majority held that Schley should have attempted to capture Cervera's ships at the mouth of Santiago harbor on May 29 and 30, and that when he did attack he failed to do his utmost to sink the largest enemy ship. They

---

[7]New York Times, Oct. 30, 1901, 8:3.

[8]New York Times, Dec. 14, 1901, 2:2.

also faulted Schley for the maneuvering of his flagship during the battle of July 3.

The majority report concluded that "Commodore Schley's conduct in connection with the events of the Santiago campaign prior to June 1, 1898, was characterized by vacillation, dilatoriness and lack of enterprise." It also found that his reports regarding his coal supplies and facilities for refueling were "inaccurate and misleading." However, the majority did not affirm the harshest judgments of Schley's detractors and stated that "[h]is conduct during the battle of July 3 was self-possessed, and he encouraged in his own person, his subordinate officers and men to fight courageously."[9]

The New York Times observed that "[p]ractically the only charge made against Schley that is not upheld by Admirals Benham and Ramsay is that of cowardice." The paper also noted that the filing of a minority report by the president of the court, Admiral Dewey, was "most unusual." The hero of Manila found that Schley's passage to Cienfuegos was made as quickly as possible--giving consideration to the necessity for having sufficient coal for his ships when he arrived. He found that Schley had effectively blockaded Cienfuegos and had made sufficient attempts to discover the location of the Spanish squadron by making inquiries to the British ship that had been in the harbor. The trip from Cienfuegos to Santiago had been made with "as much dispatch as possible while keeping the squadron a unit," according to Dewey, and he said that Schley had effectively blockaded Santiago. The minority report closed with the following observation:

> Commodore Schley was the senior officer of our squadron off Santiago when the Spanish squadron attempted to escape on the morning of July 3, 1898. He was in absolute command, and is entitled to the credit due to such commanding officer for the glorious victory which

[9]New York Times, Dec. 14, 1901, 2:2.

> resulted in the total destruction of the
> Spanish ships.[10]

The publication of the report touched off a firestorm of reaction from friends of Admiral Schley. A Captain Parker of Schley's staff was quoted as saying that Dewey and Schley were the only officers with sufficient experience to judge Schley's conduct, suggesting that Admirals Ramsay and Benham were unqualified because they had never been in command during a serious naval engagement. Rear Admiral George Brown stated his disagreement with the majority opinion, observing that the Spanish squadron had had plenty of opportunity to leave Cuba before Schley's arrival, regardless of what he did.[11]

Schley's friends in Congress also attacked the report. Senator Foraker of Ohio, a Republican, termed the majority opinion "shameful" and "disgraceful" and said Dewey's opinion was the one that should be accepted by the public. Republican Senator George F. Hoar of Massachusetts agreed. The Democrats generally supported Schley, and there was some suggestion that a resolution would be offered in Congress in Admiral Schley's behalf. Nevertheless, even some of Schley's supporters were ready to let the controversy die. As the New York Times noted, there was still a question as to whether Admiral Dewey approved of those findings of the majority on which he remained silent. While the Times decried Admiral Sampson's efforts to discredit Admiral Schley, it concluded that further investigations would only make things worse.[12]

Although there would be no further investigation into the Sampson-Schley affair, there would be plenty of further controversy, most of it centering around Nelson A. Miles. The general was quoted

---

[10]New York Times, Dec. 14, 1901, 2:2 (text of report).

[11]Ibid.

[12]N.Y. Times, Dec. 15, 1901, 3:1 & 8:1; Dec. 17, 1901, 1:3.

during a visit to Cincinnati as saying that he was willing to accept Admiral Dewey's opinion in the matter since he [in contrast to Admirals Ramsay and Benham] has commanded a fleet in battle and understood the responsibilities and anxieties confronted by Schley. Miles concluded by saying, "I think Dewey has summed up the matter in a clear and concise manner, and I believe his conclusions will be endorsed by the patriotic people of the United States. I have no sympathy with the efforts which have been made to destroy the honor of an officer under such circumstances."[13]

On December 19, Secretary of War Root wrote the commanding general asking if he had made the remarks reported in the newspapers on December 17, and asking him for an explanation of those remarks, if he had done so. Miles responded:

> ...Replying to your note of the 19th I have the honor to state my observations, as substantially reported, had no reference to the action, pending or otherwise, of a co-ordinate branch of the service; they were merely my personal views, based on matters set forth in various publications which had been given to the world and concerning which I conceive there was no impropriety in expressing an opinion the same as any other citizen upon a matter of such public interest...

In a second letter to the Secretary dated December 21, Miles observed that Admiral Schley had been assailed by his enemies as a coward for several years and that it was these people to whom he referred when he said he had no sympathy for those trying to destroy an officer. Miles said he did not mean to imply that a coordinate branch of the government [the majority of the naval court of inquiry] had tried to destroy Schley. The same day Root sent Miles a formal letter of censure.

---

[13]New York Times, Dec. 17, 1901, 1:3.

Root started by informing the general that he was communicating the President's conclusions regarding Miles' interview and was doing so at the direction of the President. First of all, the Secretary said, an officer in the Army did not have the same right as a private citizen to express his views on matters of military discipline. Root cited the first article of Army regulations:

> Deliberations or discussions among military men conveying praise or censure, or any mark of approbation towards others in the military service, are prohibited.

The Secretary said that any other rule would be subversive of military discipline and that violations of the regulation would not be tolerated. He observed that there was no reason for the Army or any of its officers to become involved in the Sampson-Schley controversy. The Secretary concluded that the comments made by Miles:

> could not fail to be applied to the naval officers against whose view your opinion was expressed...You had no business in this controversy, and no right, holding the office you did, to express any opinion. Your conduct was in violation of the regulation above cited, and the rules of official propriety, and you are justly liable to censure, which I now express.[14]

On December 21, Navy Secretary Long approved the report of the court of inquiry and in addition approved the majority report where it differed from the minority. The Secretary specifically disapproved of any finding with regard to who was in command of the American fleet on

---

[14]New York Times, Dec. 22, 1901, 1:7 "THE PRESIDENT STERNLY REBUKES GEN. MILES."

July 3, 1898, thus impliedly chastising Dewey for going outside the mandate of his inquiry. Schley's counsel termed Long's action "arbitrary and tyrannical."[15] The New York Times, editorially, agreed.

Nevertheless, the Times opined that Admiral Dewey was indeed guilty of an impropriety in making a finding as to who was in command at Santiago and that Miles clearly violated Army Regulations. Letters to the paper reflected the views of both camps. One writer asked how President Roosevelt could chastise Miles for insubordination in light of the fact that as Colonel of the Rough Riders he had authored a letter to General Shafter demanding removal from Cuba and leaked the letter to the press. Another writer, however, expressed the opinion that Miles' censure was long overdue, citing the "embalmed beef" scandal which the writer said could have been handled by a letter to the commissary general.[16]

The obvious question about the vehemence of the administration's reaction to Miles' comments on the report of the Sampson-Schley court is whether it was precipitated by the interview or whether the interview was merely the opportunity Roosevelt and Root had been waiting for to cut Miles down to size; Roosevelt's letters indicate the latter. In fact, the President's letters also indicate that the President was hardly an unbiased observer of the court of inquiry himself. On July 6, 1901, he observed, "I should have had Admiral Schley court-martialed long ago.."[17] On August 20, 1901, before McKinley's death, the then-Vice President wrote a letter indicating dislike for Schley, Miles, and Admiral Dewey:

> [Dewey] has got the same thirst for notoriety that has helped ruin Miles, and in his soreness at the result of his own folly [a reference to the collapse

---

[15]N.Y. Times. Dec. 22, 1901, 2:1.

[16]Ibid, Dec. 24, 1901, 6:1; Dec. 29, 1901, 5:4.

[17]Morison, Elting ed., The Letters of Theodore Roosevelt, vol. 3, p. 110.

> of Dewey's presidential aspirations], he has become very bitter against the administration. The popular feeling is overwhelmingly for Schley, and I think Dewey now cares very little for the navy people or for the real interests of the navy. In consequence I thoroughly believe that he will yield to the popular clamour and to his feeling against the administration and whitewash Schley...[18]

While the President's letters at the time of the Schley court's report indicate a strong desire to enforce discipline in the armed forces, they also reveal that his actions were largely based on his personal view of the underlying controversy and opinions having nothing to do with the violations of Army regulations in this case. He wrote to James B. Matthews, on December 31, 1901:

> As regards Miles, I feel that any man who fails to back me up is either a fellow wholly incapable of reasoning or else a man who has never taken the trouble to reason, or finally, a wrong-headed person who deliberately desires the growth of a spirit which would render the army and navy not merely useless but a menace to the country...
>
> Three years ago Miles should have been court-martialed for his insubordinate and improper interview attacking the War Department and, on the other hand, Eagan should have been dismissed from the service with

[18]Ibid, p. 128.

> ignominy for his vile outrage against Miles, and at the same time, or before, Schley should have been court-martialed.[19]

One must note how different Roosevelt's assessment of Miles' conduct with regard to the "embalmed beef" was in 1901, when compared to his letter to Miles of January 14, 1899, when he said, "When I saw you testifying to what I knew to be the truth about the meat, I felt it my duty to write and aid you." The reaction of Miles' friends to Roosevelt's censure is typified by a letter to the general from Henry Watterson, editor of the Louisville Courier-Journal, on January 3, 1902:

> ...I know the President to be, and during the twenty years of my acquaintance with him to have been, a most ill-judging, inconsiderate person...my sympathy for you is only exceeded by my respect for the firm and courageous reticence you have observed.[20]

As to Miles' motives in this whole affair, his enemies claimed that he hoped that he could ride public reaction to the Schley controversy to the White House. That assessment is contradicted by a letter the general wrote to George F. Washburn in January 1902:

---

[19]Ibid, p. 213.

[20]Miles-Cameron Papers, Library of Congress. Watterson (1840-1920) was a power in the Democratic Party from the late 1860s to his death. The son of a Tennessee congressman, he met during his lifetime virtually every President from John Quincy Adams to Franklin D. Roosevelt (obviously he met Harding, Coolidge, Hoover and FDR before they were President, and Adams and Jackson after their terms of office). His championing of Miles is all the more interesting in view of the fact that Watterson was a Confederate soldier during the Civil War.

The New York World was also supportive of Miles and critical of Root and Roosevelt. [Dec. 23, 1901, p.6 and December 24, 1901, p. 6]

> I deeply regret these reports. Like many others in the past, they are absolutely unauthorized. They do not emanate from myself nor from my friends...I have not been and will not be a seeker for Presidential honors...[21]

One must allow for the possibility that Miles subtly concluded that by appearing reluctant to seek the Presidency, he would, like Caesar, be more likely to obtain what he wanted. However, unlike Caesar, subtlety was not Nelson Miles' strong suit.

---

[21]New York Times, Jan. 26, 1902, 1:3.

CHAPTER X: AT LOGGERHEADS WITH THE PRESIDENT OVER THE PHILIPPINES

If President Roosevelt thought that his formal censure over the Schley court would make General Miles easier to control, he was sadly mistaken. Throughout the two years between the censure and Miles' mandatory retirement, the two men fought bitterly. The substantive focus of their dispute was the administration's conduct of its war against the Filipino insurgents and the President's army reorganization bill. The administration's reorganization plan proposed abolishing the position of commanding general after Miles' retirement and instituting a general staff system in the War Department.

The more enduring battle was over the Philippines. The Islands became an American possession almost as an afterthought. Naval strategy in our war with Spain (in which Navy Assistant Secretary Roosevelt played a major role), required neutralization of the Spanish Pacific fleet. On May 1, 1898, Commodore George Dewey steamed into Manila Bay and destroyed the enemy fleet without losing a man. Dewey then waited in the harbor for several months while an expeditionary force was put together under Major-General Wesley Merritt to force the Spanish Army garrison to surrender. While Dewey waited, the Spanish were pinned down by the army of the newly proclaimed Philippine Republic, headed by President and General Emilio Aguinaldo.

Upon the arrival of American ground troops in late June and July, it was evident to the Spanish that their position in Manila was untenable; they had no hope of receiving supplies or reinforcements. The Spanish and General Merritt agreed to fight just enough to preserve Spanish military honor. Upon capitulation of the Spanish on August 13, 1898, Merritt left the islands to attend the peace conference between Spain and the United States in Paris and was succeeded by Major-General Elwell Otis. Otis was then confronted by the real challenge to American authority in the Philippines, the Army of the Philippine Republic or, as the Americans described them, the Filipino insurrectionists.

Although President McKinley had decided to recognize the independence of Cuba, he made the opposite decision with regard to the Philippines.[1] The President and his advisors were greatly concerned with the vulnerability of the islands to the imperial designs of other nations, particularly Germany and Japan, the former having a formidable naval presence in Manila Bay. Additionally, the administration came to the conclusion that the Filipinos were not prepared for self-government and would greatly benefit from the tutelage of the United States. On this basis, General Merritt had not allowed the Filipinos to participate in the "battle" for Manila, but afterwards they still ringed the city and had no intention of exchanging one colonial master for another.

Like Lyndon Johnson sixty-five years later, McKinley sought to win the hearts and minds of the Filipinos with good deeds. The Army embarked upon an ambitious program of public works, particularly roadbuilding and school construction. It also instituted a massive public education program. Aguinaldo and his followers, however, were far from placated by McKinley's policy of "benevolent assimilation," and tensions between American troops and the native army intensified.

On February 4, 1899, the shooting war between the Filipinos and the Americans began. Initially the war did not go well for United States, due in part to General Otis' hesitancy to aggressively pursue the rebels. Dissatisfaction with the general developed in the military and at home. On July 18, 1899, the New York Times suggested, in an editorial entitled "Miles For Manila," that the situation in the islands was discouraging and that General Otis should be replaced by the commanding general. The Times observed, "Whatever may be said about General Miles in other respects he is certainly respected throughout the Army as a fighting General."[2]

---

[1]However, the United States reserved the right to intervene in Cuban affairs, a policy which had much to do with the rise of Fidel Castro and the present state of Cuban-American relations.

[2]The New York Times, July 18, 1899, 6:1

Not only was there dissatisfaction with military progress, but an anti-war movement was also developing in the United States. The leadership of this movement was dominated by the Boston-based, aristocratic Anti-Imperialist League. Prominent among the opponents of the war were: Andrew Carnegie, the steel magnate; ex-President Benjamin Harrison; a very conservative Republican Senator from Massachusetts, George F. Hoar; and a number of prominent Civil War veterans and social reformers, including Carl Schurz and Charles Francis Adams, Jr. As the insurrection dragged on, the debate between the administration and its opponents became increasingly nasty. As they did seventy years later, those supporting the war charged that the blood of every American soldier killed in the Philippines was on the hands of the anti-imperialists. Charges of censorship by American reporters in Manila were countered by allegations that the anti-imperialist press was providing aid and comfort to the Filipino rebels.

For McKinley, the approach of the presidential elections added urgency to the need for the appearance of military progress before the fall of 1900. He expected a rematch with the dynamic advocate of easy money, William Jennings Bryan, who had embraced the anti-imperialist cause. In the autumn of 1899, General Otis launched an offensive against the Filipinos. Three columns, led by Generals Arthur MacArthur, Jr., Henry Lawton [who would be killed during the offensive by a Filipino sniper], and Lloyd Wheaton, occupied the entire northern portion of the main Philippine island of Luzon and destroyed the insurrectionists' ability to function as a conventional army. To many it appeared that the insurrection was over; on May 5, 1900, General Otis left the Philippines and was replaced by Arthur MacArthur, Jr., who had commanded a regiment in the Union Army as a teenager but is best remembered for the fact that his third son, Douglas, became one of the most important military and political figures in twentieth century American history.[3]

On June 21, 1900, MacArthur issued a proclamation granting amnesty for prior Filipino violations of the laws of war--in exchange for submission to American authority. Although this was somewhat successful, the summer and fall of 1900 saw a resurgence of activity by Aguinaldo's army, primarily in the form of guerilla attacks rather than large-scale engagements. The Filipinos were hoping that increased American casualties would lead to a Democratic victory in November. At home the Democrats were running against a popular president in a period of economic good times, and they hoped that aversion to the war would carry Bryan into the Executive Mansion.

In addition to their attempt to inflict as many casualties on the American forces as possible before the election, the insurgents also initiated a concerted campaign of terror against Filipinos who aided the American pacification campaign. In turn, some American soldiers and some Filipinos fighting with the Americans began to resort to torture against rebel prisoners. After the election, MacArthur increasingly was forced to rely on Filipinos to suppress the rebellion. Although the general had reservations about this tactic, he had no choice. Over 4,000 American soldiers died in the Philippine insurrection, and troop strength reached a peak level of 70,000. Unlike Lyndon Johnson, President McKinley realized that the public would tolerate such a commitment only for a very short time. The strategy worked largely because the Americans were able to capitalize on the animosity of many of the Philippine ethnic minorities towards the majority Tagalogs, who dominated the insurgent movement.

MacArthur launched an offensive against the guerrillas almost immediately after the election. He severely damaged Aguinaldo's supply and intelligence pipelines from the villages and ordered the arrest of any

[3]During the Civil War, General MacArthur became an officer at 17, fought at Perryville, at Missionary Ridge [for which he received a Congressional Medal of Honor], in the Atlanta campaign [in which he became a regimental commander at 19], and at Franklin, where he was seriously wounded.

Filipino caught assisting the insurrection. The general ceased the practice of releasing unarmed prisoners and deported the captured leaders of the insurrection to Guam.

In March 1901, the most dramatic turn of the war occurred with the capture of the insurgent leader, Aguinaldo, by General Frederick Funston. An insurgent courier, bearing an appeal for reinforcements, betrayed the location of the Filipino leader's headquarters. Funston landed 85 Filipino scouts and five American officers near Aguinaldo's camp in northern Luzon. The party posed as insurrectionist reinforcements bringing in prisoners; the ruse worked and the party overpowered the camp and took the captured Aguinaldo to Manila, where he issued a proclamation urging the surrender of the rest of the revolutionary forces.[4]

Upon the capture of Aguinaldo, MacArthur ordered the release of thousands of prisoners, who agreed to stay loyal to the United States, and transferred authority for civil matters in the islands to the new Civil Governor, William Howard Taft. In July 1901, MacArthur left the Philippines and was replaced by General Adna Chaffee. Just when it looked like the war was practically over, a shocking event transpired which threatened to undo much of the progress previously made in pacifying the Philippines.

On September 28, 1901, in the town of Balangiga, on the island of Samar, insurgent guerrillas, aided by the populace, massacred and mutilated 48 American soldiers of Company C of the 9th Infantry Regiment. Brigadier-General Jacob Smith, sent to pacify Samar, chose to rely on terror as a primary weapon; he issued one order to "kill and burn and make a howling wilderness of Samar."[5] As rumors of this policy began to filter back to the United States, General Miles wrote to Secretary of War Root on February 17, 1902 [less than two months after having been censured], requesting that he be allowed to go to the

---

[4]For the story of General Funston's dramatic capture of Aguinaldo, see Sitting In Darkness: Americans in the Philippines, by David Haward Bain.

[5]Morison, ed., The Letters of Theodore Roosevelt, vol. 3, p. 256,n.l.

Philippines. The commanding general proposed that he take a delegation of Cubans and Puerto Ricans to the Philippines to assist in the negotiation of a peace treaty with the Filipino rebels, noting that such negotiations had often worked in ending hostilities with the Indian tribes. Miles observed that at the time of the letter there were still 40,000 American troops in the Philippines and that the war had been conducted with "marked severity."[6]

On March 5, the Secretary disapproved Miles' request and forwarded it to President Roosevelt. He wrote that Governor Taft and General Chaffee were capable of dealing with the situation in the islands and he took issue with Miles' observations regarding the manner in which the war had been conducted. Rather than "marked severity," said Root, the activities of the United States Army in the Philippines had been marked by humanity and magnanimity. On March 24, Miles wrote Root a second letter denying that he was seeking sensationalist publicity; Root responded by stating that allegations of misconduct by American troops had been referred to General Chaffee, who would investigate them.

The official correspondence between Root and Miles concerning the general's request was made public at the end of March 1902 pursuant to congressional inquiries. What was not revealed was the deep hostility evidenced by the President to Miles and to his proposed journey. Roosevelt wrote to Root the day after Miles' inquiry [February 18, 1902] to tell the Secretary of a meeting he had with the commanding general, during which Roosevelt compared Miles' handling of the Ghost Dance crisis of 1890-91 with American conduct in the Philippines. The President related that he told the general that there had been no attempt to investigate the Wounded Knee incident or punish those responsible [which was untrue; Miles had indeed tried to punish those in command and was overruled by the War Department].

The President said he ridiculed the general's suggestions that he go to the Philippines and bring Aguinaldo and other Filipino leaders

[6]The New York Times, March 30, 1902, 1:7.

back to Washington. Roosevelt observed that Sitting Bull was the Aguinaldo of 1890, and instead of bringing him to Washington, Miles sent the Indian Police to arrest the chief, who was killed [Miles' idea was to have Buffalo Bill Cody convince Sitting Bull to surrender]. The President concluded by telling the commanding general that his trip would "be productive of mischief."[7]

On March 7, the President wrote to Root again asserting that when he had supported Miles in the embalmed beef affair, the general had tried to enlist him in a scheme that would produce a Miles-Roosevelt ticket as the result of the failure of administration policy in the Philippines.[8] His vitriolic letters continued with one on March 19, 1902, which began by accusing Miles of leaking his request to go to the Philippines to congressional opponents of the Philippine War:

> General Miles begins his letter to you with a misstatement of fact. He says that the warfare in the Philippines has been conducted with marked severity. The warfare in the Philippines has been conducted by our troops with very great leniency; far greater leniency than was shown by General Miles and his fellow soldiers in their warfare in the old days against the Indians on the plains. General Miles' course in endeavoring to

---

[7]Letters of Theodore Roosevelt, vol. 3, p. 232.

[8]Ibid, p. 240-l. An undated memorandum in the Miles Papers at the Military History Institute in Carlisle marked "Confidential" gives the general's account of this conversation. Miles recalled meeting Roosevelt in the fall of 1898 and telling him about a letter he received advocating a Miles-Roosevelt ticket in 1900. The tenor of the memorandum is that Miles mentioned this letter to Roosevelt in an off-hand way and had no intention of seriously suggesting that either man do anything to make the suggestion a reality. In this memo the general expressed the opinion that, if he had complimented rather than criticized the efforts of the War Department in supplying the Army, he could have had any position he desired, including the Vice-Presidency. The memo also suggests that Roosevelt knew Miles did not intend to undermine President McKinley. In fairness to Roosevelt, one has to wonder just why the general bothered mentioning the letter to him, if he wasn't thinking that a Miles-Roosevelt ticket wasn't a great idea.

> discredit the army of which he is head by publication or endorsement of untruthful attacks [which by July Roosevelt would have to admit were true] upon it is not creditable to him.
>
> General Miles asks to be sent to the Philippines in the interest of bringing the war to a close. The last time General Miles was employed in Indian warfare was at the time of the Sioux outbreak of 1890. That campaign was a short and very easy one compared to...the scores conducted in the Philippines. Yet the troops in the small army of General Miles, in the fight at Wounded Knee...put to death over sixty women and children...The mere recital of the facts in this case is enough to show the extreme unwisdom of relying on General Miles to mitigate the severity of war.[9]

The President's outbursts and carelessness with the truth were fueled further by General Miles' appearance before the Senate Committee on Military Affairs. Miles allegedly charged that the administration's Army reorganization bill, through which it proposed to abolish the post of commanding general and substitute a general staff system, was motivated by a desire on the part of Secretary of War Root and Adjutant General Corbin to promote their favorite officers. The commanding general charged further that the general staff system was only suited to monarchies having large standing armies, such as Germany and Russia. Miles said the administration plan would "seem to Germanize and Russianize the small army of the United States." It was, he said, incompatible with the principle of democratic government.[10]

---

[9]Ibid, 244-5.

[10]New York Times, March 25, 1902, 1:4; March 21, 1902, 3:3.

Rumors, which were entirely accurate, began to circulate that the President had threatened and wanted to retire Miles immediately but did not do so only because his advisors feared that it might compromise the ultimate success of the Army reorganization bill. Miles' supporters, although far fewer in number than previously, reacted. Henry Watterson, the publisher of the Democratic Louisville Courier-Journal charged that, from the first day that Miles refused to be the President's orderly, he was marked for punishment. Watterson remarked that Miles "was fighting the battles of his country when our puissant Presidential broncobuster was fighting the battle of the nursery."[11]

Herbert Welsh, a Philadelphia-based reformer, who had clashed with Miles over the fate of the Apaches years earlier, also stood behind the Commanding General. In an April 1902, letter to Moorfield Storey, a Boston attorney who was a leader of the anti-imperialist movement, Welsh wrote about a two-hour interview he had had with Miles, during which Miles had shown Welsh a report alleging atrocities by U.S. forces in pacifying the Philippine province of Batangas; Welsh concluded that the report was being suppressed by Secretary Root and continued:

> Whatever his weaknesses may be, the truth places [Miles] in a good light in this matter and Root in only a bad one. Under great difficulties he has done what he could to secure humane and just treatment for the Filipinos, and it is clear to me that the main cause of Root's wrath and indeed the President's towards Miles is due to alarm at the danger of exposures of the awful condition of things they wish to conceal...[12]

However, other of the general's former friends had abandoned him. The enthusiastically imperialistic New York Times concluded:

---

[11]New York Times, March 24, 1902, 1:6, March 23, 1902, 1:3.

[12] Moorfield Storey Papers, Library of Congress

> it is clear that they [Miles' plans] implied the possession on his part of gifts for statesmanship that no one but himself has yet discovered in him...

The Times took the general to task for not letting the matter drop when his proposal was first disapproved. Instead, he had submitted letters "reflecting on the honor of the army and his fellow officers, which he knew to be unproved and under official investigation..." This, the paper concluded, constituted "very serious misconduct."[13]

Several weeks later, the Times called on President Roosevelt to retire General Miles and accept whatever political risks such action entailed. The paper, in an editorial entitled "Gen. Miles," recounted the many controversies of his career, and while it recast several of them less favorably than it had in the past, it was clearly his flirtation with anti-imperialism that irritated the editors. They said he had no right to make public the charges of cruelty on the part of American soldiers in the Philippines and concluded:

> The Lieutenant General of the Army is not in a position to talk about the Commander-in-Chief and the Secretary of War as Mr. Bryan, for instance, may talk about them; and any man in his senses must see that when he insists upon exercising the unrestricted privilege of Mr. Bryan, army discipline suffers to a degree that calls loudly for a remedy...

[13]N.Y. Times, March 31, 1902, 8:1

> ...The theory that General Miles is aching to run for the Presidency explains all his escapades, which nothing else does--not even his vanity, known to be great...[14]

The Times noted that the anti-imperialists were defending Gen. Miles' disclosures on the grounds that if he hadn't leaked them they would never have seen the light of day. The paper ridiculed this position and intimated that such baseless charges were what one would expect from the anti-imperialist camp.

Back at the White House, President Roosevelt's detestation of General Miles was growing daily. He observed to one friend that "Miles is a perfect curse. He has been a detriment to the army for the last eight years. No man of his rank has ever had so purely faked a record as a soldier..." [an interesting allegation from one who had made so much capital from such a brief exposure to the hazards of war, against a man who probably had experienced as much actual combat as any man in history].[15]

Nevertheless, in May the Chief Executive directed Governor Taft to appoint a three-man commission to investigate whether any "brutalities" had been inflicted by the Army upon the natives.[16] Ultimately he conceded that:

> there have been some blots on the record. Certain of the superior officers got to talking with loose and violent brutality...The enemy were very treacherous, and it was well-nigh impossible to find out who among our all our pretended friends really had committed outrages, and in order to find out, not a few officers, especially those

---

[14]N.Y. Times, April 19, 1902, 8:1.

[15]Letters of Theodore Roosevelt, vol. 3, March 24, 1902 to Herman Kohlsaat, letter # 2308.

[16]Ibid, p. 260.

> of the native scouts, and not a few of the enlisted men, began to use the old Filipino method of mild torture, the water cure. Nobody was seriously damaged...
>
> ...it was necessary to recall some of those who were guilty... Brigadier General Smith was an offender of high rank. I had found out from many sources that he was habituated to the use of violent and brutal language...

The President closed by noting that the inspector general had informed him that General Smith had excused his conduct on the grounds that he was "shooting niggers" and Roosevelt conceded that Major Littleton Waller had executed ten native bearers on Samar without trial.[17]

One might well conclude that even without Miles' airing of the improper conduct of some of the American troops, Taft and Chaffee would have rectified the problem, but I do not see how one can fault him for using the weight of his position and reputation to reinforce the principle that torture of prisoners and civilians sympathetic with the enemy was contrary to the official position of the United States Army. Personally, on this basis alone, I would give him far more credit than he is given conventionally.[18]

In any event there was a great deal of pressure on the Army and the administration to thoroughly investigate the charges of brutality and to correct the excesses. In June 1902, a story was leaked from the War Department in a manner similar to the disclosure of the My Lai

---

[17] Letters of Theodore Roosevelt, Vol 3, p. 297, July 19, 1902, to Herman Speck von Sternberg. For a fast paced account of the Balangiga massacre and an engrossing, albeit uncritical account of Major Waller's campaign on Samar and court-martial, see Joseph Schott's The Ordeal of Samar.

[18] On the other hand, his opposition to the Army reorganization bill strikes me as predicated on nothing more than personal resentment. I do not understand how a system which curtails the power of the senior general in the army and makes everyone more accountable to the Secretary of War and the democratically elected President is inconsistent with democratic principles.

massacre in Vietnam 66 years later. An Army private, Andrew K. Weir, charged that American soldiers were using torture methods as bad as any used by the Filipinos. He stated he had observed an American sergeant, pursuant to orders from Lt. Frederick Arnold, 4th United States Cavalry, administer the "water torture" to obtain a confession. The prisoner's mouth was held open with a stick while men sat on his stomach and feet and held his head down. Water was then poured down the prisoner's mouth. Pvt. Weir also charged that the prisoner was whipped, beaten, and hung by his thumbs. According to Weir, Arnold had used other methods of torture, such as strapping prisoners under a horse with their legs touching the ground and then stampeding the horse. When Weir threatened to report Arnold, the Lieutenant threatened to court-martial Weir.[19]

The disclosure of Weir's allegations were accompanied by a report from the inspector general's department that the private's story was corroborated and that a full investigation would probably substantiate them. At almost the same time as this story appeared in the newspapers, President Roosevelt received the report of the court-martial of General Smith. While he may have been appalled and may have acted anyway, the Chief Executive was every bit as angry about the public disclosure of such reports as he was about the conduct of the offending soldiers. Rumors circulated that Roosevelt had ordered Miles back from a trip to Ft. Riley in order to court martial him for furnishing details of the Arnold scandal to Senator Culberson of Texas.[20] Culberson, however, denied that he obtained his information from Miles, and then the War Department denied that the abrupt return of the commanding general from field gun tests had anything to do with the Arnold case.[21]

---

[19]N.Y. Times, June 5, 1902, 1:1.

[20]N.Y. Times, June 6, 1902, 1:3

[21]Ibid, June 7,1902, 1:2.

With the evidence substantiating Miles' February 1902 allegations, the President and Secretary Root had to reconsider the wisdom of denying him his request to go to the Philippines. Thus they approved an around-the-world inspection tour of army facilities. On October 1, 1902, the general, his wife, and the rest of their party sailed on the transport ship "Thomas." After a stop at Honolulu, they arrived on Guam on October 25, where they found Apolinario Mabini, the former Secretary of State of the Aguinaldo government, and a Filipino general at the stockade. Learning that Mabini was still a prisoner due to his refusal to take an oath of allegiance to the United States, several in the party concluded that he should be allowed to return home. Henry C. Rouse, a close friend of Secretary of State John Hay observed, "Mabini is a helpless paralytic, and why our Government persists in keeping those poor devils there...is one of the mysteries of the politics of the times."[22]

The Miles party arrived in Manila on October 30, 1902, where the general met with Governor Taft and American military leaders. Miles also conducted a thorough inspection of U.S. troops and military facilities. Henry Rouse observed, "The general still loves to get up early and make forced marches. He is a great old man." Miles took special interest in reviewing his old unit from the frontier, the 5th United States Infantry Regiment, and found one soldier, the color-bearer, who had served with him in Montana; he called the man out of ranks for special recognition. During his month-long visit Miles visited every major island except Mindoro, saw 25 military posts, and reviewed half the American troops in the islands.

The Commanding General also spent a significant amount of his time talking to Filipinos. After hearing accounts of alleged atrocities by

---

[22]Letters of Henry C. Rouse: Around the World with General Miles, Privately Printed 1904, Copy inscribed to John Hay in Library of Congress Rare Books Division.

In a letter to General Henry T. Allen dated July 22, 1903, Rouse, President of the Missouri, Kansas, and Texas Railroad, told Allen that he could not assist him in securing a promotion because his friendship for General Miles had "queered me with the present administration and its War Department." Allen Papers, Library of Congress.

American troops and Filipino troops commanded by American officers, he issued an order to Major General George Davis, then commanding in the islands. The order, dated November 28, 1902, directed that any orders or personal instructions that suggested or permitted acts of cruelty be cancelled and that such acts be strictly prohibited. Miles concluded, "The excuse that the unusual conditions justify the measures...is without foundation and cannot prevail. The Lieutenant General is gratified to know that a very great many officers of the Army, including yourself" [have renounced the use of torture and upheld the standards of the United States Army].

When news of the Miles' order reached Secretary of War Root, he immediately challenged Miles to name the officers who encouraged cruelty to the Filipinos. The General responded:

> [The] object [of the order] was to correct an evil resulting from instructions that seriously affect discipline and establish dangerous precedents, also to correct still prevailing impressions in the minds of many that acts that have been officially condemned were justifiable.
>
> No specific names or orders were referred to, but I had in mind the statements of Colonel, now Brigadier General, Funston to his officers at Caloocan regarding prisoners, and the letter of General Chaffee to General Hughes, September 30, 1901, which justifies use of any means for certain purposes. Also the written orders of Generals Bell and Smith and verbal instructions of General Hughes, and especially verbal instructions of General Smith regarding the use of water and other torture.[23]

[23]Miles Papers, Military History Institute Archives, Carlisle, Pa.

AMERICA'S FIRST ASIAN WAR

DEWEY

ROOT

In late November the Miles party set sail for China; during the trip General Miles was dreadfully sea sick.[24] After touring China, Miles visited Japan, and then he and his party boarded the Trans-Siberian Railroad for a trip to St. Petersburg. The trip across Russia during the dead of winter was marred further by the death of one of the party from smallpox [if what Miles was after was a pleasure junket at taxpayer's expense, he certainly had peculiar tastes]. From Russia, the party went to Europe and returned home.

Even while he was traveling, Miles was causing the President some discomfort. On December 23, Roosevelt wrote Senator Hoar of Massachusetts:

> Curiously enough in the mail containing your letter of December 20th about Mabini there comes a letter from Governor Taft dated November 9th, in which occurs the following sentence: "General Miles has [hurt] us as much as possible by telling the Filipino ex-insurgent generals that came to call upon him that he had recommended the release of Mabini. Mabini it is true is a paralytic. His station in life is such that he is more comfortable a prisoner than in any other way, so that it costs him but little to be a martyr. He is a plotter and never misses an opportunity to say in his published letters something mean and nasty about the United States. If he declines to take the oath of allegiance, I do not see why he should be brought to the islands to become a burden upon us, and to be the center of all the plotting by the irreconcilables."
>
> Secretary Root had already told me that he believed we might cause serious harm to a great many people if we took back Mabini at this time. I read through the papers of his which you sent me last evening, and I was struck by their ability. But, frankly, I thought the reasons he gave for not

[24]Rouse, supra.

> taking the oath both trifling and disingenuous. He makes a technical plea that he ought to take the oath in the Philippines and not in Guam, and that he does not know what the situation is in the Philippines...[25]

The President's view of Miles and anyone else who disagreed with him about the Philippines is reflected in a letter he wrote to Governor Taft in the islands a few days after speaking to Senator Hoar:

> ...there had been a great outburst here for the restoration to the islands of Mabini. So far as this represents merely petitions by Carl Schurz, Charles Francis Adams, Herbert Welsh and other foolish irreconcilables, I have not deemed it worthy of my attention, but Senator Hoar comes in a somewhat different category...[largely because unlike some other Republican anti-imperialists he did not defect to Bryan in 1900]...[I] explained that Miles' action in telling the ex-insurgent chiefs that he was going to ask for Mabini's return might render it out of the question to return him...[26]

Upon his return to the United States, General Miles filed, on February 19, 1903, a report regarding his tour of the Philippines. The report was not made public until May [and then only due to agitation by the anti-imperialists and other administration opponents] and drew a scathing response regarding his motives from his detractors. In assessing the vehement denunciations of the general's report, it is essential to read what he actually said.

In keeping with his long-standing concern for alcoholism in the Army, he observed that "the discontinuance of the liquor feature of the canteen has been beneficial to the army." He also asked that more

[25]Roosevelt Letters, vol. 3, p. 394.

[26]Roosevelt Letters, Vol. 3, pp. 398-99.

attention be paid to providing wholesome recreation for the troops. Turning to our relations with the Filipinos, he recommended that all heavy artillery be removed from the islands because there was no legitimate use for it and because the guns were needed at home. He also recommended that use of church property by American soldiers cease because he feared that damage to the buildings would result and the United States would end up having to pay for restoration. He recommended fortifying Subic Bay, observing that the Philippines was just as vulnerable to attack as it had been in 1898. The general also advised that parts of the Philippines faced a threat of famine.

Turning to more controversial issues he discussed his trip to Batangas on November 9, 1902. He said that at Lupay, one of the towns in the province, a delegation of leading citizens had come to him and complained of the harsh treatment administered by the Americans and their Philippine scouts. He recounted tales of use of the water torture, an incident in which a man was allegedly burned to death inside his house, and another in which 600 people were herded into one building and several suffocated. The general stated, "I have no reason to disbelieve their statements; in fact the instances of torture and the case of the man Luna having been tortured and burned to death are confirmed by other reports."[27]

The general also mentioned reports of atrocities in a Filipino newspaper dated November 2, 1902 and a torture squad headed by an American major, Edwin F. Glenn. He questioned whether General Hughes, Glenn's superior, was aware of his activities. He then observed:

> These facts came to my notice in a casual way and many others of similar character have been reported in different parts of the archipelago. In fact, I was informed that it was common talk at places where

[27]The Philippine Report by Lt. Gen. Nelson A. Miles, reprinted from the Army and Navy Journal May 2, 1903, published by the Anti-Imperialist League, Boston, 1909, Library of Congress.

> officers congregated that such transactions had been carried on either with the connivance or approval of certain commanding officers. It is, however, most gratifying to state that such atrocities had been condemned by such commanders as Generals Lawton, Wade, Sumner, Lee, Baldwin and others.
>
> I found that with certain officers the impression prevailed that such acts were justifiable and I felt it my duty in order to correct such an erroneous and dangerous impression, and to prevent the possibility of such acts being committed in the future, which must impair the good name of American arms and bring discredit to our service for all time, to address the following letter of instructions.

The general then quoted the order he issued from Manila on November 28, 1902 prohibiting the use of torture, mentioned reports he had received alleging that 400,000 civilians had been forcibly relocated in Southern Luzon, and noted allegations that the Army's Commissary Department [always one of his favorite targets] was selling rice to the natives at exorbitant prices.[28]

Aside from the die-hard anti-imperialists, reaction to the general's report was hardly enthusiastic. The New York World cited the report as proof of the evils of imperialism.[29] Herbert Welsh's City and State called Miles this country's "noblest living soldier" and concluded:

> The report of the Commanding General...only confirms what was already known. Its value consists in being

[28] Ibid. The officers singled out for praise by Miles were men who had been closely associated with him in the past. General Jesse Lee had served as the Commanding General's counsel before the "Beef Court"; Baldwin had been his chief of scouts in the Red River War.

[29] New York World, April 28, 1903, 1:1, 6:2

the testimony of an expert, thoroughly competent to speak of the matters with which he deals."[30]

The New York Times, on the other hand, concluded that the issue raised by the report was not so much whether its allegations were true but rather why Miles had publicized them. The paper thought the circumstances of the general's charges suggested that he had solicited them, and the Times accused him of relying on purely hearsay accounts. In this editorial the Times concluded that Miles' report contributed little to anyone's knowledge of the situation in the Philippines.[31]

The general's report received a little more favorable reception from The Outlook, one of the more popular national magazines. After noting that a "considerable portion of the report is given to an account of cruelties alleged to have been perpetrated by our soldiers in the Philippines," The Outlook observed that "[u]nfortunately, it is an open secret that General Miles has political aspirations for the Presidency." The magazine took the commanding general to task for not mentioning the "splendid philanthropic work which many army officers have been engaged in," but it conceded that, with regard to the atrocities, the U.S. high command had not been "eager to bring the guilty parties to exposure and punishment." The Outlook's evaluation of the report concluded that it contained little new information but that it might serve a purpose in calling public attention to the matter.[32]

Aside from the incentive of the imperialist press to criticize anything that might call into question our benevolence in the Philippines, it is difficult to comprehend the basis for the criticisms heaped upon Miles in this affair. That there was some question as to commitment of all those in authority in the Philippines to humane treatment of the Filipinos is evidenced by the defense raised by Major Edwin Glenn at

---

[30]City and State (weekly-Philadelphia), May 7, 1903, p. 368; May 21, 1903, p. 404

[31]N.Y.Times, April 28, 1903, 8:2.

[32]The Outlook, May 9, 1903, p. 99.

his court-martial in January 1903. Charged with the murder of seven Filipinos and resorting to the water torture, Major Glenn defended himself by asserting that his instructions from Generals Smith and Chaffee authorized such measures to determine the location of the insurrectos. Glenn's request to call the generals as witnesses in his trial was denied.[33] Miles' report was clearly not a wholesale denunciation of the U.S. Army in the Philippines and appears to me to be a laudable effort to reinforce the standards of conduct of the Army which he commanded. [That such standards are apparently not self-evident was proved again at My Lai in 1968.]

The last months of Miles' active military career and tenure as commanding general were relatively uneventful. President Roosevelt instituted a requirement that all Army officers on active duty prove their physical prowess by riding 90 miles in three days. On July 14, 1903, less

---

[33] Washington Post, Dec. 14, 1902, 1:4, Jan. 7, 1903, 1:6. One cannot help but notice the obvious omission of General Chaffee from the list of officers that Miles mentioned in his report as having condemned the use of torture. Chaffee admitted that an order issued in his name after the Balangiga massacre stated, "...that no matter what measures may have to be adopted, information as to the whereabouts of the [insurrecto] force must be obtained." He contended that his order could not be reasonably construed to approve the water torture as Major Glenn alleged. New York Times, Jan. 9, 1903, 9:1.

Major Edwin Glenn was convicted by a court-martial in July 1902 of employing the water torture and was sentenced to one month's suspension from duty and fined $50. New York Times, July 23, 1902, 1:1. Tried again in December 1902 and January 1903 for unlawfully executing seven Filipinos, Glenn alternatively denied ordering the executions and argued that they were consistent with his orders. He was acquitted, although Major-General George Davis approved his acquittal with a disapproval of the orders given by Glenn. Washington Post, Jan. 9, 1903, 1:7, Jan. 16, 1903, 1:3; New York Times, Feb. 19, 1903, 7:2. Glenn as a Major-General commanded the 83rd Division in World War I on the Italian-Austrian front.

Other American officers accused of atrocities were either acquitted by court-martial or received very light sentences. For example, Marine Major Littleton Waller, who admitted to summarily executing at least ten native bearers on Samar, was acquitted and retired many years later as a general and a Marine Corps legend.

than a month before reaching mandatory retirement age (64), Miles went to Ft. Sill, Oklahoma and completed the ride in 9 hours and 10 minutes.[34]

On August 8, 1903, his birthday, the general retired, and almost every newspaper reporting the event noted the absence of a congratulatory message from the President. Indeed, almost all of them printed, for purposes of contrast, the glowing farewell message eight years earlier from President Cleveland to General Schofield. On January 22, 1904, Roosevelt explained his decision to a friend, George B. McClellan Harvey, editor of Harpers Weekly:

> When Root and I decided that we could not conscientiously issue an order of commendation for Miles on his retirement, we did it with our eyes open. We knew that there were plenty of designing people who would mislead ignorant people into the belief that we were doing wrong to a gallant veteran, and we deliberately faced this because we felt that we had no moral right to condone and justify conduct in the Lieutenant General of the Army, which if it became common among his subordinates, would literally lower our whole army to the level of some South American State where each man is playing for his own hand with utter indifference to the welfare of either the army or the country. Of course, I cannot say this publicly...When I was Governor of New York he asked me to enter into an arrangement with him by which I should run as Vice-President on a ticket with him as President, and he then explained to me that he based his hope of our overthrowing McKinley upon the prospect of disasters to the army in the Philippines. In other words, he, the Lieutenant General of the Army, was hoping and praying that the army under him would be beaten and disgraced, so that it might help him to political advancement at the expense

[34] N.Y. Times, July 15, 1903, 1:4.

> of the chief whose military adviser he was supposed to be. By the way the writer of this paragraph in question must have forgotten that Miles owed his great advancement at the end of the Civil War, by which he was put over the heads of so many men whom I regard as his superiors, purely to the social and political influence of the Sherman family in which he had married...[35]

The President's misstatements regarding Miles' meteoric career cast tremendous doubt upon his veracity with regard to the alleged conversation regarding McKinley. Miles' rise to prominence in the military occurred several years prior to his marriage to Mary Hoyt Sherman. Moreover, his record of achievement between the Civil War and the War with Spain was unmatched by any other officer, with the arguable exception of Crook and Ranald MacKenzie, both of whom were dead by the time Miles became commanding general. The proposition that Miles openly wished for the failure of the U.S. Army is inconsistent with his conduct in other episodes in which he energetically participated despite qualms about their justification [e.g. the pursuit of the Nez Perce, the Spanish War]. Moreover, Miles had close friends in the Philippines, such as Lawton, on whom I do not believe he would ever have wished disaster.

The general's retirement was mourned by few. The magazine Nation observed that his gallant career was marred by "several instances of insubordination and total inability to get on with his civilian superiors." The editors did attribute Miles' difficulties to his desire to serve his country well, citing the "embalmed beef" inquiry and "his recent bold criticism of the army for its ghastly cruelties in the Philippines."[36] In Georgia, however, one state official decorated the State Capitol with

---

[35] Letters of Theodore Roosevelt, Vol. 3, p. 704-5.

[36] Nation, Aug. 13, 1903, Vol. 77:126.

Confederate flags and portraits of the Confederate leadership as commentary on Miles' treatment of Jefferson Davis.[37]

A few of his friends stuck up for the general to the last; the New York World characterized him as "the most distinguished American soldier now living."[38] The Louisville Courier-Journal, owned by Miles' friend Henry Watterson, observed:

> For the past two years the doctrine has been industriously propagated that any criticism of the Administration's military policy is abuse of the army, which is regarded with as much horror in Administration circles as is lese majesty in Germany. To this, however, there has been one conspicuous exception. Abuse of the Commanding General has not only been treated as excusable, but praiseworthy. Whoever desired to curry favor with the civilian authorities of the army found an easy way in poking fun at him, in criticizing his utterances and discrediting his honorable desire to render some public service. This is now ended. With the retirement of Gen. Miles the army has become exempt from criticism. The officers who are left behind have no such distinguished service behind them to which they can point when assailed, so that it is obviously inexpedient to subject themselves to criticism to the same extent that Gen. Miles has been...[39]

---

[37]The Louisville Courier-Journal, August 10, 1903.

[38] New York World, August 9, 1903, pp. 1-2.

[39]Louisville Courier-Journal, August 9, 1903, 4:2.

HIS FIRST SURRENDER.

NOTE: THE DATE OF MILES' RETIREMENT IS INCORRECT; HE RETIRED ON AUGUST 8.

The World

"Circulation Books Open to All." | "Circulation Books Open to All."

FIVE CENTS — NEW YORK, SUNDAY, AUGUST 9, 1903. — Copyright, 1903, by the Press Publishing Company, New York World.

AFTER FORTY YEARS: "GET OUT AND GO HOME!"

CHAPTER XI: RUM, ROMANISM, AND ROOSEVELT

Upon Miles' retirement, the general devoted himself to business pursuits. Despite all the speculation about his political ambitions, he not only did not actively seek the Presidential nomination of any party, he affirmatively discouraged efforts to promote his candidacy. In March 1904, the prominent Boston anti-imperialist, Gamaliel Bradford, wrote a letter to the New York Times decrying the lack of a creditable candidate who could effectively advance the Democratic party's position on America's foreign relations. Bradford suggested that the party nominate General Miles as the "peace candidate."[1] However, Miles refused to talk about such a candidacy when asked by the press and spurned an overture from the Prohibition party to be its candidate.[2]

Miles' name was placed in nomination at the Democratic party convention in St. Louis in July, but his political activity was limited to criticizing President Roosevelt and the Republican party on the issue of imperialism and more specifically its policy towards the Philippines. Possibly the general realized that Theodore Roosevelt was immensely popular and he was thus willing to let New York Judge Alton B. Parker play the role of sacrificial lamb in the 1904 Presidential election. It could also be that he realized that any active candidacy as a Democrat was simply not viable given the fact that Varina Howell Davis and her husband's skeleton were lurking in his closet.

The general did what he could to help the Democrats [or hurt Roosevelt] in 1904. In May, for example, before the Boston Reform Club he criticized the administration for its treatment of the Filipinos.[3] Miles was deeply affected by the sudden death of his wife, Mary, who succumbed to a heart attack while visiting their son Sherman at West

---

[1]N.Y. Times, March 14, 1904, 2:4.

[2]Ibid, May 24,1904, 1:5; June 29, 1904, 2:6.

[3]New York Times, May 26, 1904, 3:2.

Point in early August 1904.[4] Nevertheless, he took time immediately afterwards to lavishly praise Judge Parker's acceptance speech.

As part of his effort to aid the Parker campaign, Miles wrote a public letter to Colonel Finley Anderson on October 10, 1904, entitled "Letter to a Civil War comrade." In this letter he asserted that American expansionism and colonialism were contrary to the principles for which America had gone to war with Spain, namely the liberation of the Cuban people from the colonial yoke. He continued that, "[t]he theory that we must hold in absolute subjection for an indefinite term of years the millions of people on the other side of the globe until they are prepared for self-government appears to be utterly unwarranted." Miles closed with an appeal for Parker's candidacy and a thinly veiled critical reference to the service of the new Philippine Governor in the Confederate Army.[5] The pro-Roosevelt press heaped criticism on the General on both counts.

Typical of the hostile reaction of much of the press to Miles' political activities is an editorial in the Washington Evening Star of August 20, 1904, entitled "General Miles in Politics." The Star proclaimed that "General Miles, as everyone knows, is anxious to contribute to the defeat of Theodore Roosevelt on personal grounds. But he should leave the gushing to his oil wells in Texas. As a gusher himself he is not effective."[6] Of course, Roosevelt thrashed Parker in the general election, demonstrating immense popularity by carrying even

---

[4]In assessing Miles' character, attention should be given to his relationship with his wife. Unlike a host of other military and public officials, there is not even a hint of scandal in his private life and every indication that he was a devoted husband and family man. As for Mary Miles, she was described by Elizabeth Custer (George's widow) in a condolence letter to the General dated August 23, 1904, as the perfect mate who enabled Miles to "meet those whose jealousy will never leave you alone." Miles-Cameron Papers, Library of Congress [Elizabeth Custer had been very close with the Miles at Ft. Hays, Kansas before the battle of the Little Big Horn].

[5]Henry Watterson Papers, Library of Congress.

[6]Washington Evening Star, August 20, 1904, 4:1; also see Oct. 24, 1904, 4:2 for reaction to "Letter to a Civil War Comrade."

Missouri, which was considered a Democratic bastion. Although Miles must have been galled by the fact that his arch-enemy appeared to have become the most popular living American politician of all times, he would have the satisfaction of seeing Theodore Roosevelt's ambitions thwarted on several occasions, although he would have to wait eight years. He would also have the satisfaction of outliving the President by six years.

Miles may have found Roosevelt's overwhelming electoral victory sobering because he withdrew somewhat from public life afterwards. He was appointed inspector general of the Massachusetts state militia in December 1904 and aroused a brief controversy as to whether he could draw his federal retirement pay and a salary from the state at the same time. Although he made himself available for numerous ceremonial occasions, many of them relating to nostalgic recollections of the Civil War, he appears to have stayed aloof from national politics until after Theodore Roosevelt left office and began to fight with President Taft over who should run for President in 1912. The general was only more than willing to do whatever he could to make the former Rough Rider's life difficult.

In 1910, the ex-President made critical statements concerning several Supreme Court decisions which adversely affected his anti-trust program. General Miles again returned to the front pages of the nation's newspapers by lambasting his foe:

> In condemning and criticizing the decision of the Supreme Court of the United States and its venerable bench, Theodore Roosevelt is guilty of treason.
>
> Look at his political tracks since he returned from the African wilds. It is a trail of discontent, bombast, disaffection and even treason. And without one word of commendation for the existing administration--which, in my opinion, has been eminently proper and dignified and a great improvement on the administration that preceded it--this politician starts a

> one-man tour, a personal political campaign, haranguing the people, inciting discontent, mixing with malcontents, embarrassing those in authority and power without an excuse or reason for such unprecedented conduct.
>
> It is disgusting, this constant exhibition of a former President running loose over the country surrounded by newspapermen for whose edification he walks, talks, eats and sleeps, hungrily swallowing calcium at its strongest pressure and revelling in the concentrated rays of the light of what should be to a sane man undesirable publicity. But that is what he lives for, and the real people are getting wise.[7]

At about this time the general found a new outlet for his great energies. Unfortunately, it is the aspect of his career that is the least defensible. On June 9, 1911, an organization called The Guardians of Liberty was founded in Washington, D.C. Among its officers were Charles D. Haines, a former congressman; the controversial Civil War general and politician, Daniel E. Sickles[8]; and Nelson A. Miles, whose position in the organization was "Chief Attorney." The society issued a declaration of principles that proclaimed that it was established to assure complete separation of church and state. Another of the stated aims of the organization was "to protect and preserve the free institutions of our country, especially our public educational system, against any foreign or menacing influence." The founders declared further that, "We

---

[7]N.Y. Times, Oct. 4, 1910, 1:7.

[8] Sickles, as a Democratic congressman from New York, committed one of the capital's most sensational crimes when just before the Civil War he shot and killed his wife's lover, Philip Barton Key, son of the author of "The Star Spangled Banner," on the street near the Executive Mansion. During the war he was a brave and energetic political general, who almost singlehandedly lost the battle of Gettysburg by moving his Corps forward and breaking the integrity of the Union's defensive line along Cemetery Ridge.

particularly protest against the diversion of any public funds or lands to any religious purpose whatsoever."[9]

The Literary Digest noted that although the declaration of the organization's principles did not specifically mention the Catholic Church, its speakers left no doubt as to the fact that the activities of the Church were its primary concern. Some Protestant religious journals defended the organization from charges that it represented a revival of the Know-Nothing movement of the mid-nineteenth century, stating that the formation of the Guardians of Liberty was a necessary response to the danger of Church domination of American life and the activities of the Knights of Columbus.

In January 1913, several of the founders of the Guardians, including Haines, the Chief Guardian, quit and formed a competing group. General Miles then became the head of the organization. The organization denied being Anti-Catholic, but in its magazine, "The Guardian of Liberty," it accused the Catholic hierarchy in the United States of "sedition and treason."[10]

The most visible activity of the organization in its fifteen years or so of operation was its leadership in a campaign to prevent the New York City school system from adopting "the Gary Plan." Faced with a shortage of space to accommodate all the students in the city, New York City had many of its children going to school for only a half day and began to explore ways to keep its students more fully occupied. It began to study a program devised by William Wirt, the superintendent of schools in Gary, Indiana, which sought co-operation from various religious organizations to provide instruction during the periods the students were not in school. The "Gary" plan also attempted to arrange for technical and physical training programs off school property.[11]

---

[9]Literary Digest, Vol. 45, #4, July 27, 1912, pp. 152-3.

[10]New York Times, January 7, 1913, 22:2.

[11]New York Times, Jan. 2, 1916, IV, 17:1; Jan. 9, VI, 1:1; Jan. 18, 10:7.

On January 20, 1916, the Guardians of Liberty held a meeting at the Cooper Union in New York to protest the adoption of the Gary Plan. The main speaker that evening was the Chief Guardian, Nelson A. Miles. The New York Times reported that "[i]n the main, speeches dwelt upon the alleged efforts of Catholic teachers to force their pupils to attend the Catholic Church." The Times also reported that some of the Guardians' speakers alleged that a Catholic could not be a "single-minded" servant of the United States and that some Catholic teachers were trying to use the schools to make the United States a Catholic nation.[12]

A review of several issues of the Guardian of Liberty reveals the articles authored by General Miles to be vague, difficult to understand, and mildly inflammatory. For example, in November, 1922, he wrote a piece critical of a California court decision forbidding purchase of the King James version of the Bible by a public school district on the grounds that it was sectarian. Miles proclaimed:

> The Bible is the acknowledged authority for 176 creeds in this country. Protestant is a generic word, and is not confined to any one creed...A Protestant is one who protests against the vagaries of Rome. The Mohammetan, Bhuddist, Persian, Greek or Shinto is Protestant.
>
> ...as most of it is a history of the Jewish people, its text is inert, so far as creed ...is concerned. It [the decision to prohibit purchase of the King James Bible] is, however, on a par with the recent efforts to prevent the teaching of biology in the schools. The true inwardness of it is that the

[12]N.Y. Times, Jan. 21, 1916, 12:2.

> objectives come from people who are so shaky in their own creed they are afraid the truth may put them out of business.[13]

After the congressional elections of 1922, the 83 year-old general wrote:

> Both parties have demonstrated total inability to resist the growing menace of political Romanism, to enact adequate laws to shut out the tide of ruinous immigration, to remove the shame of illiteracy from the nation, to uphold and strengthen the public schools and purge them of sinister alien propaganda.[14]

The major objective of the Guardians of Liberty can be characterized as the weaning of Catholic children from the Catholic schools and the destruction of any sectarian influence in the public schools. Despite the organization's protestations that it was not anti-Catholic, it is clear that Miles and the Guardians found Catholicism consistent with American citizenship only if its adherents abandoned the essence of Catholicism. While making no excuses for Miles, one must point out that his views were consistent with those of many New England Protestants of his time. The religious wars of Europe were not as remote to these people as they were today, and they truly feared the power of the Papacy. Moreover, many like Miles held grudges stemming from the opposition of many Irish immigrants to the Union cause during the Civil War and their prominence in the draft riots of 1863, when troops had to be rushed from the Gettysburg battlefield to restore order in several large American cities. The alliance of the Irish Americans

---

[13] The Guardian of Liberty, Vol VIII, # 11, Nov. 1922, pp.122-23 (Library of Congress, Periodical Division)

[14] Ibid, Vol. VIII, No. 12, Dec. 1922, p. 133 (Library of Congress)

with the Democratic party was another black mark against the American Catholic among the nativists.

On the other hand, not all New Englanders of Anglo-Saxon descent reacted as did Miles. For example, Thomas Wentworth Higginson, who had commanded the first black regiment in the Union Army, actively opposed the Anti-Catholicism of many of his peers. People like Miles, when mentioning the draft riots, often overlooked the fact that 140,000 Irish-Americans served in the Union Army, many of them barely off the boat.[15] Finally, the extraordinary liberalization of American Catholicism during the latter half of the twentieth century would never have occurred if anti-Catholic sentiment had been as great as it was in the 1920s. The efforts of organizations such as the Guardians of Liberty could only have served to make American Catholics defensive and insular.

Nelson Miles was not a bigot with regard to other unpopular ethnic groups. He had much contact with the vitriolic anti-Semite Henry Adams by virtue of the very close relationship between Adams and his sister-in-law, Elizabeth Cameron. However, he never publicly showed an inclination to anti-Semitism and, to the contrary, maintained a close personal friendship with the New York Jewish philanthropist, Nathan Strauss. At Strauss' behest Miles spoke at the dedication of a monument to the Jewish Civil War dead on Long Island in May, 1905.[16] Similarly, when Strauss turned his milk purification facilities over to the city of New York in 1920, General Miles publicly and effusively praised him, comparing Strauss to a heroic soldier.[17]

---

[15] Prominent among these troops was the Irish Brigade of the First Division of the Second Corps, which was under Miles' command during the Petersburg Campaign and is generally considered one of the best units in the Army of the Potomac.

[16] New York Times, May 8, 1905, 14:5.

[17] Ibid, Sept. 2, 1920, 8:8.

Miles also retained strong sympathies with American blacks. For example, in August, 1914, the general addressed a large gathering in Harlem. The New York Times' account of his appearance is as follows:

> The visit of General Miles to Harlem formed a very interesting part of the propaganda which has been conducted to secure recognition of colored men in the Fire Department, on the police force, and in the National Guard. To further these objects the Equity Congress of New York was formed in 1910, and it was before the members that General Miles spoke in their rooms at 84 West 134th Street.

The Times quoted the general as saying that:

> You might be better off if there were a recognized nation of colored people which they could call their own. We never can tell what the future may bring forth, but perhaps the intelligence acquired in the past few years by your race may be utilized as a great civilizing force for the great black belt of Africa with its 160 million inhabitants which need the intelligence of such teachers and missionaries as your race has already raised up in this country.[18]

General Miles' anti-Catholicism was related to another of his great passions--temperance. During his military career, he was constantly concerned with alcoholism, a problem which plagues our Army to this very day.[19] Almost naively he searched for ways to wean the troops from liquor and keep them involved in "wholesome" pursuits, particularly physical fitness. Indeed, one of his great achievements as a military

---

[18]N.Y. Times, Aug. 3, 1914, 11:2 "Gen. Miles to Negroes."

[19]The Miles papers in Carlisle contain a February 8, 1876 letter from Miles to the Chairman of the House Military Committee recommending that drinking saloons be abolished on Army posts and that the selling of liquor be prohibited.

commander on the Plains is that he always had his troops prepared from whatever physical challenge presented itself. The forced march made by Miles to intercept the Nez Perce could not have been made by most other regiments.[20]

In 1915, General Miles was chosen to be the presiding officer for the convention of the Anti-Saloon League of America in Atlantic City. There was a brief controversy stemming from the general's refusal to appear on the same platform as the ex-prize fighter John L. Sullivan, publicly predicated on his aversion to prize-fighting but possibly also based on his aversion to Irish-Catholics. In any event, the general did preside over the convention and told his audience that the devastation then being caused by the First World War in Europe was less serious than the devastation caused by alcohol.[21]

In addition to his commitment to temperance and his dabbling in anti-Catholicism, General Miles maintained an active interest in military affairs, politics, and international relations, in his later life. Once Theodore Roosevelt bolted to the Progressive Party, the General felt comfortable being a Republican again. In 1913, he made his only effort

---

[20] Another admirer of General Miles' training methods was Lt. John J. Pershing, who arrived in the Southwest shortly after the surrender of Geronimo. His biographer, Frank Vandiver, notes:

> Good commanders hate laziness. Now that the Indians menaced less and badmen were reforming, Miles worried that his departmental garrisons had almost nothing to do. Routine post duties brought boredom; there seemed no challenge to efficiency. Miles provided the challenge. He ordered widespread field maneuvers by troops and companies, maneuvers under simulated campaign conditions. As they worked out, these maneuvers had refreshing originality and difficulty. Designed to test ingenuity, acumen, guile, and leadership, they stimulated the able and taught the dull. Black Jack: The Life and Times of John J. Pershing, Vol. 1, p. 67. [In September 1887, the future five-star general received personal congratulations from Miles upon his capture of another cavalry troop in field maneuvers. Ibid, p. 69.]

[21] New York Times, July 3, 1915, 16:6; July 8, 1915, 22:5

for elected office when he announced his candidacy for the Republican nomination for Congress from Massachusetts' Third Congressional District; his candidacy was unsuccessful.[22]

During the same year, Miles traveled to the Balkans and became a partisan observer of the events in that region of the world. After uniting with Greece, Serbia, and Romania to fight the Turks, Bulgaria had a territorial dispute with its former allies and went to war with them. In July, 1913, the Greek Army had cut the Bulgarian capital, Sophia, off from the rest of the world except for sporadic telegraph communication. A few westerners, including General Miles, were stranded in the city. On July 25, 1913, Miles telegraphed his assessment of the situation to the New York Times and was rewarded with the recognition of a byline and placement of his dispatch on page one. Miles took the side of the Bulgars, asserting that they had been invaded and that they were not guilty of atrocities as alleged by the Greeks and Serbs. The general asserted that the War was completely unnecessary and that the territorial dispute between Bulgaria and her neighbors should have been resolved by the International Court of Arbitration at the Hague. He warned that unless the war ended it could lead to a much wider war, noting that Austria was beginning to mobilize its troops. Miles concluded with an appeal for generous aid to the Bulgarians, noting that he had already cabled an appeal for help to the American Red Cross.[23]

After Bulgaria agreed to terms forced upon it by Greece, Serbia, and Romania, Miles traveled to London, where he appealed to Great Britain to force the Turks to live up to their treaty obligations and evacuate recently captured Adrianople. Not even Miles could have foreseen just how dangerous the situation in the Balkans had become. Less than a year later, the heir to the Austrian throne would be

[22]New York Times, Sep. 21, 1913, II, 1:7.

[23]New York Times, July 23, 1913, 1:3; July 24, 1913, 3:1; July 25, 1913, 1:1 ("Gen. Nelson Miles Defends Bulgars"); July 28, 1913, 6:7; Aug. 7, 1913, 1:6; Aug. 10, 1913, II. 10:5.

assassinated by Serbian nationalists and all of Europe would march off to war.

As the European War dragged on with its frightful casualties, many in the United States began to urge that the country get ready for the possibility that it might be drawn into the conflict. There emerged the "Preparedness" Movement, which advocated universal military training through conscription of a large national reserve army. If his association with the Massachusetts National Guard, which was threatened with eclipse by the movement, wasn't enough to make General Miles an outspoken opponent of "preparedness," the identity of three of its most prominent advocates--Theodore Roosevelt, Leonard Wood, and Elihu Root--would have been.[24] President Wilson, under pressure from the preparedness advocates to increase the size of the national army and intervene in Europe on the side of the Allies, adopted a half-way measure that included federalizing the State-controlled National Guard.

In February, 1916, the Senate and House Military Committees held hearings on the Wilson administration's plans. A major witness opposing the plan on behalf of the National Guard was retired Lt. General Nelson Miles. The General told the Senate Committee that the United States should have a standing army of 150,000 men in peacetime so organized that it could be rapidly expanded to 394,000 in the event of war. His plan called for 97 Infantry Regiments of 1,000 men each, which would be enlarged to 3,000 men in wartime. Similarly each artillery battery would be enlarged from four guns to eight. No new officers would be needed because, under his plan, each officer would simply command more men.

Miles told the Senators, "There is nothing to indicate that a larger military force will be required in the near future, if ever." He took a dim view of conscription, saying that "you can't Germanize the American people." He said if the need did arise for a larger army, the country

---

[24]One can make too much of Nelson Miles' spitefulness, because another prominent advocate of a large national army raised through conscription, Major-General Hugh Scott, was a protege from whom Miles was not alienated.

could increase it to 1.2 million simply by transforming regiments into brigades, battalions into regiments, and so forth. Insofar as the required manpower was concerned, Miles said he had absolutely no fear that a sufficient number of men would not volunteer in a serious emergency. Finally, he dismissed concerns that a European enemy might be able to land 300,000 troops in the United States, saying that even if this could be accomplished that the foreign troops would be in a very precarious position while waiting for reinforcements.[25]

A week later before the House Committee on Military and Naval Affairs, Miles again ridiculed the concern over an invasion of the United States and denounced Wilson's "Continental Army Plan" which would establish a national ready reserve. The General stated that this plan "would put tremendous power into the hands of some future President. It is un-American. Why try to Germanize the American people? You cannot Germanize American citizens." Possibly recalling the response of his own generation to Lincoln's call to arms, the old soldier proclaimed:

> If 500,000 men were landed on either of our coasts and we were not able to raise enough men to drive them out, I would want to move to a different country.

Again drawing on the experiences of his youth, Miles asserted that conscription just wouldn't work in the United States, recalling that troops had to be rushed directly from the battlefield at Gettysburg to suppress the draft riots in Philadelphia. He also reiterated his opinion that the State-controlled National Guard, not a reserve force controlled by Washington, should constitute the contingency military force of the nation.[26]

---

[25]New York Times, February 1, 1916, 7:1.

[26]Ibid, Feb. 9, 1916, 1:3.

As American involvement in the European War drew nearer, the 77-year-old soldier wrote to the War Department to offer his services if war came. His disappointment in not having this offer accepted was most likely minimized by the fact that President Wilson also spurned repeated offers from Miles' arch-foe Theodore Roosevelt to lead American troops into battle and totally ignored Leonard Wood in passing out opportunities for greater glory as well. At a three-day meeting of the National Guard Association a few weeks before our entry into the war, Miles again opposed the centralization of all military power in Washington on the grounds that it opened the door for future usurpation or autocracy. He urged perfection of the present system of reliance on the State forces instead.[27]

Apparently undaunted by the frightful losses and lack of success of the Allied offensives on the Western front, Miles told the National Guardsman that if America entered the war it should wage offensive, not defensive, warfare and confidently predicted that we could bring an end to the war in six to twelve months. Indeed, the prediction turned out to be fairly accurate. Seven months after the infusion of American troops into the Western front, the German government collapsed and the enemy sued for peace.

The old soldiers of the Civil War generation and Cuba were eclipsed by new heroes: General Pershing, Sergeant York, and the flamboyant Brigadier-General, Douglas MacArthur. During World War I General Miles suggested on several occasions that he be sent to Siberia at the head of an American Army to hold the Trans-Siberian railroad for the Allies. In a March 8, 1918 letter to Senator James H. Lewis, he proposed that the force be composed of Americans of Russian descent, particularly those who had once served in the Russian Army. He viewed the role of this army as protecting United States interests on the Trans-Siberian and giving support to the Russian people and

---

[27]Personnel Records of Nelson Miles, Letter of March 17, 1917, National Archives; New York Times, March 28, 1917, 3:1.

government. As to the latter, which was now controlled by Lenin and the Bolsheviks, Miles stated:

> It matters not so much what the character of the Russian Government may be, so long as it is actively opposing the common enemy...I believe there is yet time to hold that great power on the side of the Allies.[28]

Sherman Miles, Nelson's son, was attached to the U.S. First Army during the offensives of 1918, but gained none of the martial glory achieved by his father.

In 1919, Theodore Roosevelt died after speculation had begun that he might be the Republican Presidential candidate in 1920. After flirting with another Miles arch-enemy, Leonard Wood, the Republicans nominated Ohio Senator Warren G. Harding. Miles, obviously relieved by the frustration of the ambitions of his life-long foes, commented favorably on the Harding candidacy in The Guardian of Liberty and received a warm acknowledgement from the candidate.[29] Just before the election the general publicly announced his support for the Republican ticket. He said Harding and Coolidge believed in the adjudication of international disputes by arbitration, but that they were, as he was, opposed to the surrender of our national sovereignty to a super-government.[30]

The publicity attending the general's announcement gave the pro-Democratic New York Times one final opportunity to chastise the 81-year-old soldier. The day after Miles' announcement a Times editorial observed that "One of the humors of the campaign is the hailing of General Nelson A. Miles, who has 'come out' for Harding and Coolidge

---

[28]Miles papers, Carlisle. See also letters of April 24, 1917, November 13, 1917, and June 15, 1918.

[29]Harding to Miles, August 9, 1920, Miles-Cameron Papers, Library of Congress.

[30]New York Times, Oct. 27, 1920, 3:4.

as a Democrat." The paper recalled the general's unsuccessful bid for the Republican nomination for Congress from his district in 1913 and what it termed his "savage and extravagant" attacks on Theodore Roosevelt in 1912, made at the behest of the Republican National Committee. The Times went back further to 1896 and said that Miles had alienated President Cleveland by sending a congratulatory note to Republican candidate McKinley. The editorial concluded that while the general was a gallant soldier, "in politics he has never been of value to any party and his skirmishes with public questions have not shown any strategic merit...As a bolting Democrat; the General is a good deal of a joke."[31]

In his last years, the General remained close to his family and stayed in remarkably good health. At the West Point graduation ceremonies in 1923, he was given a seat of honor next to General Pershing and watched his grandson, Miles Reber, receive his commission. At 85 he spoke to the Press Club of Chicago on Lincoln's birthday and reminded them of the great concern that the emancipator had expressed about alcoholism. Several weeks later he appeared before the House Special Committee on Aviation and National Defense, which was investigating the conduct of Brigadier-General William Mitchell, accused of insubordination in his advocacy of air power. Miles, described as a "convert to the importance of aviation in preparedness," criticized the conservatism of the Army leadership in exploring the military uses of aircraft.[32]

Two and a half months later, the general would make his final appearance on the front pages of America's newspapers. The first page of the New York Times on May 16, 1925 carried his picture with a headline underneath proclaiming "GEN. NELSON A. MILES DIES AT THE CIRCUS" and described him as a Civil War "Boy General." Next to the story of his death was a harbinger of the next war which would

---

[31]N.Y. Times, Oct. 28, 1920, 14:4.

[32]New York Times, June 13, 1923, 13:1; Feb. 13, 1925, 5:3; March 3, 1925, 3:1.

pose the only challenge to the United States that is even remotely comparable to that met by Nelson Miles and his generation. The adjacent column told of the activities of the young Italian premier, Benito Mussolini, who in the next decade with his sidekick, the former World War I Lance Corporal, Adolph Hitler, would set the world on fire once more.

POSTSCRIPT

Nelson Miles' son, Sherman, was the Acting Chief of U.S. Army Intelligence at the time of Pearl Harbor, and as a result was involved in the post-war controversy concerning responsibility for the disaster that befell the country on December 7, 1941. At the close of his testimony before Congress in January 1946, Major-General Walter C. Short, the senior Army commander at Pearl Harbor, charged that Sherman Miles, George C. Marshall, Army Chief of Staff, and General Leonard Gerow, Chief of War Plans, had unfairly censured him at the time of the Japanese attack.

Sherman Miles graduated from West Point in 1905, served as U.S. military attache to Russia from 1914-16, and occupied a staff position in France after our entry into World War I. He was commanding officer at Ft. Sill, Oklahoma, in 1938 and then went to London as a military attache in 1939. Following his stint at the War Department in 1941, he was appointed commander of the First Corps Area in Boston in 1942 and retired with the rank of Major-General in November 1945. Sherman Miles died at the age of 83 on October 7, 1966. [New York Times, October 8, 1966, 31:1 (obituary).] The Miles-Cameron Papers indicate a fairly close relationship between Sherman Miles and George Patton. This collection also includes a congratulatory note to Sherman Miles from Lt. General Simon B. Buckner, son of the Confederate general, remarking on the fact that the sons of Civil War adversaries were fighting together in the common cause of the 1940s. General

Buckner, during the battle of Okinawa, became the highest ranking American soldier to be killed in World War II.

General Miles' daughter, Cecilia, his oldest child, was often escorted to the Executive Mansion in 1896 by one of her father's aides, Lt. John J. Pershing.[33] In 1901 she married Samuel Reber, the chief signal officer on her father's staff. Colonel Reber served in France during World War I (close enough to the front to be gassed) and ultimately became a vice-president of RCA.[34]

Cecilia's two sons both achieved some notoriety. Her oldest son, Major-General Miles Reber, was a member of the Army general staff in Washington from 1943 to 1950. In 1950 he became the Army's chief legislative liaison and later was appointed Commanding General of the Western Area Command in Europe. In 1954 he received substantial publicity when he testified before Congress that Wisconsin Senator Joseph McCarthy had sought favors from the Army on behalf of Private G. David Schine, a former investigator on McCarthy's Communist-hunting committee. General Reber was the first witness called by the Army in the Army-McCarthy hearings, and told the Senators that Senator McCarthy had called him to seek a commission for Private Schine. He also testified that the Senator and his chief aide, Roy Cohn, had attempted to pressure him when he declined to grant the favor. McCarthy's first question to the General on cross-examination was whether Sam Reber was the general's brother (see below). Then McCarthy asked if the General was aware that his brother had been allowed to resign from the diplomatic corps when charges had been made against him that he was a bad security risk as a result of an investigation of McCarthy's committee. The motivation for this nationally-televised smear was apparently to establish bias towards McCarthy on the part of the general and to retaliate against his brother for his failure to assist McCarthy's aides, Schine and Roy Cohn, in their

---

[33]Vandiver, Frank E., Black Jack: The Life and Times of John J. Pershing, 159.

[34]New York Times, April 18, 1933, 15:1 (obituary of Samuel Reber); New York Times, September 11, 1952, 32:4 (notice of death of Cecilia Miles Reber).

probe of one of his subordinates in Europe. After a bitter exchange between other senators and McCarthy over the question, Miles Reber said that as far as he knew his brother retired upon reaching the age of 50. General Reber died in 1976 at the age of 74.[35]

Possibly the most distinguished of General Miles' descendants was Cecilia's son, Samuel. A graduate of Groton and Harvard College, General Miles' grandson was a career foreign service officer. He was the deputy to Robert Murphy, President Franklin Roosevelt's special representative in North Africa in 1943, and was later political adviser to General Eisenhower at Allied Headquarters. After the war, Reber was Deputy U.S. High Commissioner for Germany and played an instrumental role in the establishment of the West German government and in the negotiations with the Russians concerning the future of Austria. At the time of his retirement from government service in 1953, Samuel Reber was acting U.S. High Commissioner for Germany. He died in 1971 at the age of 68.[36]

---

[35] New York Times, Nov. 28, 1976, 44:2. Adams, John G., Without Precedent, 1983, pp. 58, 164-167, 186 [an account of General Reber's appearance in the Army-McCarthy hearings].

[36] Current Biography, 1949, pp. 505-06; New York Times, Dec. 26, 1971, 49:2.

CHAPTER XII: AN APOLOGY FOR AN APOLOGIA

One cannot help but be struck by the incredible contrast between the Nelson Miles that emerges from his autobiographical accounts and the two prior favorable biographies written by Virginia Johnson and Newton Tolman, on the one hand, and the conventional portrayal of the general as a totally unscrupulous self-promoter, on the other. What is also difficult to understand is how a man who was held in such high regard by many of the most enlightened people of his time, i.e., the survivors of the great crusade to save the Union, the anti-imperialists, and reformers, could have acquired such an unsavory reputation. One reason may be that his arch-rival, General Crook, had several dedicated subordinates who wrote the books that serve as the basis for almost all the current histories of the Indian Wars. John Gregory Bourke and Britton Davis, in particular, portrayed General Miles as a villain. Miles had his dedicated supporters, but they didn't write. Miles' memoirs do not have the pretense of objectivity that have won the works of Bourke and Davis the deference of historians.

Looking at General Miles through the prism of the Vietnam experience of my own generation, there is a powerful temptation to portray the General as all-knowing and wise and a victim of the unenlightened forces of his time, specifically imperialism. How often does one with a jaundiced view of the military find a war hero like Nelson Miles, who as head of the United States Army invited trouble to assure the proper treatment of enemy prisoners? What other chief of his nation's armed forces would admit, as did Miles about the Spanish-American War, that his victorious country had no justification for going to war? Like Newton Tolman, in his The Search for General Miles, I almost fell into the trap of attributing Miles' demise as a public figure simply to the jealousy of those less talented and the venality of the imperialists.

Unfortunately, Nelson Miles had some very real and some very large shortcomings as a human being. I think the dark side of his personality was best described by his wife's uncle, William Tecumseh

Sherman, Commanding General of the Army, in a 1879 letter to General Philip Sheridan, then commanding the Military Division of the Missouri:

> General Miles is too open to mistake the dictates of his personal ambition for wisdom and I am sorry to say he is not just and fair to his comrades and superiors. He will absorb all power to himself and ignore his immediate commanders if not supervised and checked--
>
> ****
>
> I have done him hundreds of favors but because I withhold one he forgets all else and considers the sending of General Ruger to Montana as taking from him his personal right. He wants me to send away any officer who ranks him so that he may have full sway(?) from St. Paul to Missoula.[1]

I will readily admit that Nelson Miles' conduct can support a portrayal of a man so concerned with his personal ambition that he was devoid of any integrity or principles. His enlightened pronouncements about the Indians and the Filipinos and against imperialism could be legitimately regarded as mere lip service to ideals held dear by those whose political assistance he needed for his own advancement. Yet, I am inclined to believe that for all his faults, Nelson Miles did have principles and in many ways was a man worthy of the adulation he received during his lifetime.

As for his shortcomings, nothing can justify General Miles' anti-Catholic activities, and not much more can justify his destruction of the reputation of Commissary General Eagan in the embalmed beef scandal of 1899. Eagan may have made a tremendous mistake in relying so much on "experimental" canned beef to feed the U.S. Army during the

---

[1]Sherman to Sheridan, July 19, 1879, P.H. Sheridan Papers, Vol II, Container 39, Reel # 17, Library of Congress, Manuscript Division (the question mark in the quotation indicates that I could not read Gen. Sherman's handwriting).

Spanish War. However, he did not poison the troops with chemicals, as Miles alleged with incredibly little evidence. Even if all he sought was to rectify an erroneous policy by the Commissary Department, Miles could have done so without necessarily ruining Eagan personally.

Although I'm very sympathetic with General Miles in his relations with Theodore Roosevelt and Elihu Root, his opposition to the Army Reorganization Bill in 1902 and 1903 has little to recommend it. It makes no sense to argue that vesting power in an autonomous commanding general, who owes his position primarily to longevity, is more democratic and more in keeping with American principles than making the entire military establishment directly answerable to the Secretary of War. Miles was frequently motivated by personal spite, and I think this was clearly the case with regard to Root's plan to institute a general staff system.

The general's contribution to the debate over military manpower just prior to the First World War also does him little credit. His position that the volunteer system proved successful in the Civil War and therefore needed no modification was at best an oversimplification. The Union Army came perilously close to running out of men to fight the war in 1864. By fortunate circumstance the enlistments of most of the troops did not run out until after Grant's offensive got underway. In the prior months the Army was able to secure many re-enlistments through bonuses and 30-day furloughs because the soldiers knew there was a good chance that if they didn't re-enlist that they would be dead before their enlistments expired anyway.

Having covered his negatives, there is much that can be said on Nelson Miles' behalf. First, he was brave, incredibly brave. Second, he seems to have had an ability to move and motivate men. The judgment of Francis Barlow as to his military abilities is borne out by all the campaigns he waged. He also seems to have made a point of accomplishing his objectives with as little bloodshed as possible. His miscalculation when he charged the Nez Perce is understandable by virtue of the fact that most of the Indian leaders paid no attention to defensive tactics. One can hardly fault Miles for the fact that Chief

Joseph was unusual in this respect. Most of all, Miles was one of the few Army commanders on the frontier who showed initiative and perseverance; many others were perfectly content to rest on the laurels they had won in the Civil War.

Most important, in assessing the career of Nelson Miles, it is difficult to dismiss all the enlightened things he said and did as having been done with an ulterior motive. He persisted in seeking justice for the Nez Perce, and it is difficult to see how his career would have been damaged if he had not done so.

He kept his promises to Geronimo, and his career would not have been hurt if Geronimo had been hanged in Arizona. Although one can fault him for his initial handling of the Ghost Dance Crisis, he clearly tried to avoid violence and successfully defused an explosive situation after Wounded Knee.

At the outbreak of the Spanish War the best thing for Miles' career might have been to tell McKinley and Alger what they wanted to hear. Instead, Miles told the President, based on historical research, that a summer invasion of Cuba was too risky due to the threat of disease. Although things worked out for the American expedition, the Santiago campaign was almost an unmitigated disaster for precisely the reasons advanced by General Miles.

As someone whose reputation is that of an unprincipled glory-seeker, Miles' conduct at the outbreak of the Spanish War deserves closer scrutiny. Rather than trying to get the lion's share of the action as would many in his position, General Miles advocated reliance on naval power to defeat the Spanish and openly expressed the opinion that a large invasion of Cuba might prove to be unnecessary. The impetus for a massive invasion of the island came from other quarters. To my mind, Miles' behavior in early 1898 conclusively establishes that as vain and ambitious as he was, he put the interests of his country first. Moreover, one cannot attribute Miles' opposition to a Cuban invasion to an aversion to taking risks. More than any of the Civil War veterans who stayed in the Army, Nelson Miles was the epitome of the "can-do" soldier.

In the invasion of Puerto Rico, Miles again demonstrated that he did not place his personal glory above regard for human life. Wouldn't a bloody battle for San Juan better have served his interests than the almost bloodless flanking movements he employed? With regard to the Philippines, his detractors claimed presidential ambition motivated his public statements about the torture tactics employed by some American troops. Aside from the fact that the General affirmatively spurned the presidency, there is little logic to these accusations. Bryan's overwhelming defeat by President McKinley in 1900 had already established that anti-imperialism and concern for the Filipinos were hardly world-beating issues in American politics. Moreover, Theodore Roosevelt was immensely popular from the outset of his presidency, and even Nelson Miles would have realized that, absent an economic depression, the chances of defeating him in 1904 were not very good.

The proposition that General Miles thought he would ride revulsion to the torture of the Filipinos to the White House in 1904 is not supported by his actions or the context in which they occurred. His Philippine report did not condemn the Army wholesale but pointed out that many of the commanders in the islands had in fact made it clear that torture tactics were strictly prohibited. Moreover, Miles' political alliance in this matter was with the Democrats, and he had to have known that he could never be the Democratic presidential candidate with Varina Davis lurking in the background. Moreover, the prospects for a Democratic victory in 1904 were nonexistent. Roosevelt, in succeeding the martyred McKinley, enjoyed the same advantages that Lyndon Johnson derived from succeeding John F. Kennedy. Even William Jennings Bryan realized this and let Judge Alton B. Parker be the Democrats' sacrificial lamb in 1904.[2]

---

[2]Another indication of how seriously the Democrats regarded their chances of success against Roosevelt in 1904 is their nomination of a Vice-Presidential candidate, Henry Davis, who was almost 81 years old.

Finally, Miles at the outbreak of World War I stood in refreshing contrast to Theodore Roosevelt and others who were foaming at the mouth for an opportunity to get America involved in the conflict. He also, I think, deserves credit for his unwillingness to join the chorus of those advocating the largest standing army the country could support.

How does one explain the harsh treatment Miles has received? Some of it is due simply to a matter of perspective. If one is writing a favorable biography of George Crook, Varina Davis, Theodore Roosevelt or Elihu Root, Miles almost has to come out the heavy. While I think one can excuse some of what has been written on this basis, I think many writers have found the General an easy mark due to his pompous personality and have gone overboard in their criticisms. Margaret Leech, for example, ridicules Miles' obsession with the threat of disease when he arrived in Cuba and some of the measures he ordered to combat it. At the same time she concedes that his orders to burn down all the buildings in Daiquiri, the Army's staging area, were valuable in stopping the spread of malaria and yellow fever.

However, the more serious accusations against the general, I think, are the product of gross unobjectivity. Varina Davis' accusations against Miles were clearly fueled by an ulterior motive. I simply do not accept the portrait she paints of the General as a sadist, whose conduct had no relationship to legitimate security concerns. The treatment of Miles by revisionists such as Angie Debo is even less legitimate; their accusations are not even supported by the facts on which they based their conclusions. While one can excuse the harsh treatment of Miles by Mrs. Davis, on the grounds that one can hardly expect her to have appreciated her husband's imprisonment from Miles' perspective, it is difficult to excuse Debo's ravaging of Miles' historical reputation on behalf of a cold-blooded murderer.

The real Nelson Miles was, in my view, an essentially well-intentioned man who was to some extent blinded by the incredible achievements of his youth. One can hardly blame a man, looking back at his survival and meteoric rise through the battles of Antietam, Fredericksburg, Chancellorsville, Spotsylvania, Cold Harbor, and the

Appomattox campaign, from concluding that he was something out of the ordinary. Add to that his achievements in Montana against the Plains Indians, and you can understand his growing belief in his infallibility. In this respect, there is an obvious parallel to Douglas MacArthur, whose early rise to general was followed by other great achievements, and who like Miles came to believe that his wisdom entitled him to disregard the duly elected President of the United States.

The historical lesson to be drawn from Miles' career, I believe, is the necessity of maintaining the control of the military by civilian authority and the danger inherent in America's infatuation with military heroes. The American people have selected or at least flirted with a war hero as President after virtually every major conflict.[3] We have

---

[3] The following men became President, or were nominated, or were seriously considered as a candidate by a major party, in part on the basis of their military service:

Revolutionary War:	George Washington
War of 1812/ Indian Wars:	Andrew Jackson William Henry Harrison
Mexican War:	Zachary Taylor Franklin Pierce Winfield Scott (lost to Pierce) Lewis Cass (an 1812 general who lost to Taylor)
Civil War:	U.S. Grant Rutherford B. Hayes James A. Garfield Winfield Scott Hancock (lost to Garfield) Benjamin Harrison William McKinley
Spanish War	Theodore Roosevelt Admiral George Dewey (not nominated)
World War I	John J. Pershing (not nominated) Leonard Wood (not nominated)

been fortunate in that the generals we have elevated to the Presidency have been men like Washington, Grant and Eisenhower, who had some humility. But for the accident of his tenure at Fort Monroe, we may have had Nelson Miles, who was for all his talents, like Douglas MacArthur, particularly unsuited to the leadership of a democracy.

World War II	Dwight D. Eisenhower
Korean War	Douglas MacArthur (not nominated)

* I have excluded such junior officers as James Monroe (Revolution), Cpt. Harry Truman (World War I), John F. Kennedy, Gerald Ford, and George Bush (World War II), whose combat experience helped but was incidental to their political careers.

CHAPTER XIII: FORGOTTEN HISTORY

The genesis of this book was a visit I made to the Harvard University campus in 1982. In the alcove of Memorial Hall, a building constructed just after the Civil War to honor the University's Union war dead, are plaques commemorating each student who died in the war, giving his name, and the place and date of his death. The contrast between the patriotic fervor of the college students of 1860-61 and my attitude and that of most of my generation toward military service during the Vietnam War was striking. I thought that maybe I could write a book about those who idealistically volunteered to save the Union and died for it.

After writing a few chapters, based largely on the Harvard Memorial Biographies (1866), I realized I needed more material. I started looking for Civil War survivors whose stories might be interesting to people living in the Twentieth Century. The most obvious subject was Oliver Wendell Holmes, Jr., whose Civil War experience is probably the most popular among twentieth century writers of any Union soldier who was not a general officer. I then went to the Union veterans who became president after the War; Grant, Hayes, Garfield, Harrison, and McKinley. I still needed more material and discovered much to my amazement that most of the commanders of the United States Army at the time of the Spanish-American War were not only Civil War veterans but that several of them had been general officers at the close of the war, which ended thirty-three years earlier.

Major-General Joseph Wheeler interested me because he had been a Confederate general, and so did Arthur MacArthur, Jr., because of his son. The other commanders were people I had never heard of before so I tried to see what had been written about them. I could find no biographies of Generals Shafter, MacArthur, or Merritt, but four of General Miles (including the two he wrote himself); I read them all.

My initial reaction was that the books contained surprisingly little detail about his Civil War experiences, and I was curious about what accounted for his incredible rise to Major-General.[1] My next step was to go through the index of the Official Record of the War of Rebellion (the O.R. to Civil War buffs) to check out every reference to Miles; this was very helpful in tracking his career until he made Brigadier-General; then, since every movement of his brigade and later division appeared in the index, it became too cumbersome. It was also through the O.R. that I became aware that there was another part of the Miles' story that had been left out in the four previous books: his tenure at Ft. Monroe [if it is mentioned at all it is just in passing].

That the General was far more controversial than I had imagined was revealed to me by Margaret Leech's In the Days of McKinley and David Trask's The War With Spain in 1898; both treat him rather harshly. I looked at every magazine article I could find written at the time of his Philippine report and his retirement several months later and was surprised to discover how poorly his report, which to me appeared commendable, was received. I was even more puzzled after I went to the Library of Congress and read the report; I couldn't ascertain what in the report any right-thinking person could find objectionable.

My next step was to look at Miles through the eyes of his adversaries. I read Varina Davis' book about her husband and Miles' defense of his conduct in the February 1905 Independent. I read Crook's autobiography (as expanded by Martin Schmitt), and I was thrilled to find that Theodore Roosevelt's letters were published and that the President had had all those incredibly nasty things to say about Nelson Miles.

---

[1]Virginia Johnson's Unregimented General is a good book, but it is uncritical and focuses mostly [and in much greater detail than mine] on the Indian Wars; Newton Tolman's The Search for General Miles is easier to read and more provocative but is also extremely uncritical. Moreover, Tolman purposely omitted any footnotes or bibliography, which I view as unfortunate. Miles' autobiographies are fairly readable, although Personal Recollections is a bit long; I did find it useful in looking at what claims Miles actually made with regard to the Geronimo campaign. Serving the Republic is surprisingly readable for a book authored by one as pompous as General Miles. None of these books discusses Miles' tenure at Ft. Monroe, his reconstruction service, the substance of his rivalry with Crook, or anything about his career after the Spanish War in any detail.

The New York Times, on which I relied on heavily, is the only American newspaper that I know of that is indexed back into the nineteenth century. Not only are references to Nelson Miles listed under his name all the way back to his Reconstruction duty in North Carolina, there is a book that indexes the various chronological indexes by the names of individuals. I checked virtually every reference to Nelson Miles in the Times between 1867 and 1925. I also cross-checked other newspapers if I had a specific citation (e.g., from Schmitt's book on Crook I was able to find the Washington Evening Star's account of the 1890 hearings in Congress on the Apaches), and looked at probably a dozen papers' assessments of the general at the time of his retirement.

I am indebted to Brian Pohanka for apprising me of the depth of the New York World's support for Miles in his feud with Secretary Alger and the embalmed beef scandal. Brian also alerted me to the World's political cartooning on the General's behalf, reviewed my manuscript, and offered many helpful suggestions. I am also grateful to him for loaning me the photographs for this book.

I found General Miles' personnel records at the National Archives to be of surprisingly little value--with one exception. In them I found a postcard from an Irish-American complaining about Miles' activities with the Guardians of Liberty. It is my recollection that until that point (which came fairly late in my research) I had no inkling as to Miles' anti-Catholicism.

The discovery of Angie Debo's biography of Geronimo, which provided me much to write about, I owe to a co-worker, Steve Jones, who saw a 1970s television interview of Debo on Public Broadcasting. After reading the book I immediately went back to Personal Recollections to see what the general had in fact said about the surrender of the Apache warrior, as well as concentrating on the contemporary accounts in the New York Times.

I also tried to find books written by and about officers who were closely associated with General Miles. I looked at the biographies of Major-General Hugh Scott, Chief of Staff 1914-17, and General James

Wilson, and found them of surprisingly little value. However, General Schofield's account of the Pullman strike was very useful and made me explore other books about the incident, including Almont Lindsey's pro-labor, anti-Miles account. Frank Vandiver's biography of General Pershing was surprisingly informative as to what it was like to be under Miles' command in Arizona and during the Ghost Dance crisis.

The Miles-Cameron Papers in the Library of Congress were helpful in humanizing the general, as were the Miles papers at the U.S. Army Military History Institute Archives in Carlisle, Pennsylvania. The Carlisle collection contains Civil War letters in Miles' own hand and the incredible exchange between Miles and General Meade during Reconstruction about how far Miles could go in assisting the loyalist government. A doctoral thesis by Peter de Montraval on Miles' career through the Indian Wars was helpful in confirming my understanding of other things I had read, leading me to new sources--particularly the marvelous assessment of Miles' character by General Sherman. Finally, I am indebted to the authors of the general works covering the various historical episodes in which Nelson Miles took part. Bruce Catton and James McPherson's Battle Cry of Freedom are my principal sources of knowledge about the Civil War. The works of S.L.A. Marshall and Robert Utley served the same purpose for the Indian Wars.

I obtained a good overview of the Spanish-American War from David Trask's The War with Spain and G.J.A. O'Toole's The Spanish War. For the Philippine insurrection, I relied upon John Morgan Gates' Schoolbooks and Krags: The U.S. Army in the Philippines and Stuart Creighton Miller's Benevolent Assimilation. I would recommend either of the last two books to anyone who is under the impression that anything that happened in Vietnam during the 1960s was unprecedented.

BIBLIOGRAPHY

UNPUBLISHED WORKS

Henry T. Allen Papers, Library of Congress

DeMontravel, Peter K., "The Career of Lt. General Nelson A. Miles from the Civil War through the Indian Wars" Ph.D. diss, St. Johns Univ., 1977.

Miles, Nelson, Letters to the Loyal Legion, 1924, Library of Congress

Nelson A. Miles Papers, U.S. Army Military History Institute Archive, Carlisle Barracks, Pa.

Miles-Cameron Papers, Library of Congress

Personnel Records of Nelson Miles, National Archives

Personnel Records of Francis C. Barlow, National Archives

Rouse, Henry C., Around the World With General Miles, Privately Printed, 1904, Library of Congress, Rare Book Collection

Senate Executive Document No. 117, 49th Congress, 2d Session

Carl Schurz Papers, Library of Congress

Philip H. Sheridan Letters, Library of Congress

Moorfield Storey Papers, Library of Congress

Henry Watterson Letters, Library of Congress

NEWSPAPERS AND MAGAZINES

Baltimore Sun

Boston Herald

City and State (Philadelphia)

Cosmopolitan (circa 1910--not to be confused with the current periodical of the same name)

Current Biography

Dial

Guardian of Liberty

Harper's Weekly

The Independent

Literary Digest

Louisville Courier-Journal

The Nation

The New York Times

The New York World

The North American Review

The Outlook

The Springfield Republican

Washington Evening Star

Washington Post

BOOKS

General Background Works

Adams, Charles Francis, Autobiography, 1916

Adams, Henry, Letters, 1892-1918

Chambers, John Whiteclay, To Raise An Army: The Draft Comes to Modern America, 1987

Dictionary of American Biography

Dyer, John P., From Shiloh to San Juan: The Life of "Fighting Joe" Wheeler, 1961

Faulkner, Harold U., Politics, Reform & Expansion, 1890-1900, 1959

Fuess, Claude M., Carl Schurz, Reformer, 1931

Jessup, Phillip C., Elihu Root, (2 vol.), 1938

Johnson, Virginia Weisel, The Unregimented General: A Biography of Nelson A. Miles, 1962

Letters of H.L. Mencken, 1961

Miles, Nelson, Personal Recollections, 1896

Miles, Nelson, Serving the Republic, 1911

Morison, Etling ed., The Letters of Theodore Roosevelt, 1951

Morris, Edmund, The Rise of Theodore Roosevelt, 1976

Porter, Robert P., Lives of McKinley and Hobart, 1896

Pringle, Henry F., Theodore Roosevelt, 1931

Schmitt, Martin F. ed., General George Crook, His Autobiography, 1946

Schofield, John M., Forty-Six Years in the Army, 1897

Schurz, Carl, Autobiography (an abridgement in one volume by Wayne Andrews), 1906-08, 1961

Scott, Hugh L., Some Memories of A Soldier, 1928

Sullivan, Mark, Our Times, 1930

Tehan, Arline Boucher, Henry Adams In Love: The Pursuit of Elizabeth Sherman Cameron, 1983

Tolman, Newton, The Search for General Miles, 1968

Trefousse, Hans L., Carl Schurz, Univ. of Tennessee Press, 1982

Tuchman, Barbara, The Proud Tower, 1966

Welch, Richard E., George Frisbie Hoar and the Half-Breed Republicans, 1971

Wilson, James H., Under the Old Flag, 1912

Watterson, Henry, Marse Henry (Autobiography), 1919

Vandiver, Frank E., Black Jack: The Life and Times of John J. Pershing, 1977

CIVIL WAR ERA

American Heritage Picture History of the Civil War (2 vols.), 1960

Catton, Bruce & William, Two Roads to Sumter, 1963

Catton, Bruce, This Hallowed Ground, 1955

-------------, Reflections on the Civil War, 1982

-------------, The Coming Fury, 1961

Fuller, Charles A., Personal Recollections of the War of 1861, 1906

Grant, U.S., Personal Memoirs, DeCapo Press, 1985

Higginson, Thomas Wentworth ed., The Harvard Memorial Biographies, 2 vol., 1866

Lindeman, Gerald, Embattled Courage: The Experience of Combat in the American Civil War, 1987

McPherson, James M., Battle Cry of Freedom: The Civil War Era, 1988

Merrill, James M., William Tecumseh Sherman, 1971

Nevins, Allan, The War for the Union (vol. 1), 1959

Oates, Stephen B., With Malice Towards None: The Life of Abraham Lincoln, 1977

O'Connor, Richard, Sheridan, the Inevitable, 1953

Palmer, Bruce, Chancellorsville, MacMillan, 1967

Putnam, Elizabeth Cabot, Memoirs of the War of '61, George H. Ellis, Boston, 1920

Sears, Stephen W., Landscape Turned Red: The Battle of Antietam, 1983

Stackpole, Edward J., They Met at Gettysburg, 1956

Tucker, Glenn, Hancock the Superb, 1960

War of Rebellion, A Compilation of the Official Records of the Union and Confederate Armies (O.R.), War Department, 1902

Warner, Ezra J., Generals in Blue, 1964

Williams, Kenneth, Lincoln Finds a General (vol. 1), 1949

Wilson, Edmund, Patriotic Gore, 1962

Vandiver, Frank, Their Tattered Flags: The Epic of the Confederacy, 1970

JEFFERSON DAVIS AND RECONSTRUCTION

Carter, Hodding, The Angry Scar, Doubleday, 1959

Davis, Burke, The Long Surrender, Random House, 1985

Davis, Varina Howell, Jefferson Davis (2 vols), 1890

Hirshson, Stanley, Farewell to the Bloody Shirt, 1962

Wellman, Manley Wade, Giant in Gray: A Biography of Wade Hampton of South Carolina, 1949

THE INDIAN WARS

Beal, Merrill D., I Will Fight No More Forever: Chief Joseph and the Nez Perce War, 1963

Bourke, John Gregory, On the Border With Crook, 1891

Davis, Britton, The Truth About Geronimo, Yale Univ. Press, 1929

Debo, Angie, Geronimo, 1976

Erlanson, Charles B., General Miles, The Red Mans' Conqueror and Champion, 1969

Faulk, Odie B., The Geronimo Campaign, 1969

Haley, James L., The Buffalo War, 1976

Marshall, S.L.A., Crimsoned Prarie: The Indian Wars on the Plains, 1972

Porter, Joseph C., Paper Medicine Man: John Gregory Bourke and his American West, 1986

Thrapp, Dan L., The Conquest of Apacheria, Univ. of Oklahoma Press, 1967

Utley, Robert, Frontier Regulars, 1973

Utley, Robert, The Last Days of the Sioux Nation, 1963

THE PULLMAN STRIKE

Lindsey, Almont, The Pullman Strike, 1942

Meltzer, Milton, Bread and Roses: The Struggle of American Labor, 1865-1915, 1977

Warne, Colston, ed., The Pullman Boycott of 1894: The Problem of Federal Intervention, 1955

THE SPANISH AMERICAN WAR

Heald, Edward Thorton, The William McKinley Story, Stark County Historical Society, 1964

Leech, Margaret, In the Days of McKinley, 1959

Morgan, H. Wayne, William McKinley and His America, 1963

O'Toole, G.J.A., The Spanish War, W.W. Norton, 1984

Trask, David, The War With Spain in 1898, MacMillan, 1981

Watterson, Henry, History of the Spanish-American War, 1898

THE PHILIPPINE INSURRECTION

Bain, David Haward, Sitting In Darkness: Americans in the Philippines, 1984

Gates, John Morgan, Schoolbooks and Krags: The U.S. Army in the Philippines, 1898-1902, 1973

Hahn, Emily, The Islands: America's Imperial Adventure in the Philippines, 1981

Karnow, Stanley, In Our Image: America's Empire in the Philippines, 1989

Miles, Nelson, The Philippine Report, Anti-Imperialist League, 1909

Miller, Stuart Creighton, Benevolent Assimilation, 1982

Schott, Joseph L., The Ordeal of Samar, 1964

INDEX

Adams, Charles F., Jr. 157, 171
Adams, Henry 108, 186
Aguinaldo, Emilio 155-159
Aircraft (military) 194
Alger, Russell 112, 118-143
Altgeld, John 100
Amelia Court House (battle) 28
American Railway Union 97-106
Anderson, Finley 180
Andrew, John 6, 10
Antietam (battle) 13-14
Anti-Imperialist League 157
Anti-Saloon League 188
Apaches 63-89
-deportation of Chiricahua band from Arizona 72, 82-85
-proposed relocation to Ft. Sill 85-87
Appomattox 28
Army Reorganization bill (1902) 162
Arnold, Lt. Frederick 167

Balangiga massacre 159
Baldwin, Frank (Lt., later Gen'l) 53, 93
Balkan War (1913) 189-90
Bannock tribe 60-61
Barlow, Francis C. 4, 7, 8, 9, 10, 11, 13, 14, 20-22, 23, 26, 51, 68 and passim
Bear Paw Mountain (battle) 57-60
Beauregard, P.T. 30
"Beef Court" 134-43
Bell, Gen. 169
Big Foot (Sioux Chief) 92-94
Black, John (Maj.) 130-31
Blacks 5n, 48-49, 122, 187
Bolsheviks 193
Bourke, John G. 75, 87, 198
Bradford, Gamaliel 179
Bragg, Braxton 30
Bristoe Station (battle) 19
Brooke, Col. John R. 23, 24
Bryan, William Jennings 145, 157-8
Bulgaria 189-90
Bull Run (2nd battle) 11
Burnside, Ambrose 13, 14, 26

Caldwell, John 9, 14, 17, 18
Calhoun, John C. 39

Cameron, Elizabeth (Miles' sister-in-law)	108, 137, 186
Cameron, James Donald (Senator)	108
Carnegie, Andrew	157
Catholic Church	182-86
Catton, Bruce	11
Centreville, Va.	11
Cervera, Pascual (Admiral)	116-22
Chaffee, Adna (Gen.)	159-78
Chancellorsville (battle)	16-19
Chatto (Apache warrior)	63-4, 83
Clay, Clement	31, 33
Cleveland, Grover	66, 81-2, 97, 100
Cody, William F., "Buffalo Bill"	91
Cogswell, William	5-6n.
Cohn, Roy	196-7
Cold Harbor (battle)	23-25
Conscription	190-92
Cook, Levi F.	144
Cooper, Dr.	42-44
Corbin, Henry (Gen.)	109, 129, 131, 145-6, 162
The Crater (battle)	25-26
Craven, Dr. John J.	36-9, 40-43
Crawford, Cpt. Emmett	64
Crazy Horse	54-55
Crook, Gen. George	53-4, 63-89, 111
Culberson, Sen.	167
Custer, Gen. George A.	4, 48, 53-4
Dana, Charles A.	32-3
Davis, Britton Lt.	75, 198
Davis, Cushman Sen.	137
Davis, Gen. George	169
Davis, Jefferson	30-46
Davis, Richard Harding	125
Davis, Varina Howell (Mrs. Jefferson)	31-46, 90, 197, 223-5
Debo, Angie (Geronimo's biographer)	63-89, 202-03 and passim
Debs, Eugene V.	97-106
Dewey, Adm. George	146-55
"Dodge Commission"	128-134
Dodge, Grenville	110, 128, 133-134
Mr. Dooley (Finley Peter Dunne)	3
Dorman, C.A.	44-5
Eagan, Charles (Gen.)	128-143, 199-200
Eliot, Charles (Pres., Harvard)	138
"Embalmed Beef" scandal	128-143
Fair Oaks (battle)	8, 9
Fish, Sgt. Hamilton	120
Foraker, Sen. Joseph	137, 148

Forsyth, James (Col.)	92-94
Fort Sumter	5
Fredericksburg (battle)	15
Freedman's Bureau	48
Fuller, Charles A.	15
Funston, Gen. Frederick	159, 169
"Gary Plan" (NYC schools)	183-4
Gatewood, Lt. Charles	71, 73, 76-7, 87-88
Geronimo	63-89
Ghost Dance Crisis	91-96
Gibbon, Gen. John	22, 24, 26
Glenn, Maj. Edwin F.	172-75
Gordon, Gen. John B.	20n, 23
Grant, U.S.	22, 23, 25, 27
Guardians of Liberty	182-86
Halleck, Gen. Henry	38, 47
Hancock, Gen. Winfield Scott	14,18-9, 25, 46, 51
Harding, Warren G.	193-4
Harrison, Benjamin	85, 91-2, 96, 157
Harvard University	138
Hay, John	108
Hayes, Rutherford B.	58, 63n., 69, 111
Higginson, Henry	110
Higginson, Thomas W.	47, 186
Hill, Gen. A.P.	13
Hoar, Sen. George F.	157, 170-71
Holden, W.W.	49
Holmes, Oliver Wendell, Jr.	13
Hood, Gen. John Bell	30
Hooker, Gen. Joseph	15, 16, 18, 19
Howard, Gen. O.O.	7, 9, 48, 57-60, 68, 80-1
Hughes, Gen. Robert	169, 172
Humphreys, Gen. A.A.	29
Jackson, "Stonewall"	11,12,19
Jews	186
Johnson, Andrew	31
Johnson, Virginia W.	198
Johnston, Joseph E.	8, 9, 10, 27, 30
Jones, Pvt. Edwin A.	40-41
Joseph, Chief of the Nez Perce	57-60
"The Jungle"	141
Kearney, Gen. Philip	10
Kent, Gen. J. Ford	93, 120
Lame Deer (Sioux Chief)	56
Lamont, Daniel	109-10
Lawton, Gen. Henry W.	70-71, 77-79, 86, 120, 157

Lee, Fitzhugh 113
Lee, Maj. Jesse 140-41
Lee, Robert E. 9-12, 15, 18, 22-3
Leech, Margaret 3
Lenin, V.I. 193
Lincoln, Abraham 8,15-16
Lindsey, Almont 103-5
Livermore, T.L. 88
Lodge, Henry Cabot 112
Long, John D. 150-51
Longstreet, Gen. James 11-12
"Lost Order" (Antietam campaign) 12
Louisville Courier-Journal 178

Mabini, Apolinario 168-171
MacArthur, Gen. Arthur, Jr. 157-59
Mackensen, Gen. August von 2
Mackenzie, Gen. Ranald 53, 62
Maine (battleship) 113
Malvern Hill 10
Maus, Gen. Marion 65, 87, 96, 142
McCarthy, Sen. Joseph 196-7
McClellan, Gen. George 8-15, 27
McCullough, Hugh 42
McKeen, Col. H. Boyd 25
McKinley, William 69, 110-14, 131, 145, 156-58
Meade, Gen. George Gordon 19-22, 49-50
Mencken, H.L. 2
Merritt, Gen. Wesley 125, 128, 131-2, 142, 144, 155
Miles, Cecilia (Reber)(daughter) 196
Miles, Daniel (brother) 6, 17
Miles, Mary (wife) 51, 180-81
Miles, Sherman (son) 193, 195-6
Mitchell, Gen. Billy 194
Morgan, Gov. Edwin 7, 10
Mosby, John Singleton 114
Mussolini, Benito 195

Natchez (Apache chief) 65
"The Nation" 177
New Hope Church, Va. 20
The New York Times 74, 143, 146, 151-2, 163-5, 174, 193-194 and passim
The New York World 143, 173, 178
Nez Perce Indians 57-60

Olney, Richard 100
Osgood, Col. Henry B. 129-130, 136
Otis, Gen. Elwell 155-57
"The Outlook" 174

Parker, Alton B. 179-181
Pershing, Gen. John J. 3, 95, 188n.
Petersburg campaign 25-29
Philippine Insurrection 155-181
Miles' inspection tour 168-71
Miles' report 171-75
Pope, Gen. John 10-12, 53, 68
Porter, Gen. Fitz-John 11
Powell meat preservative process 139-40
"Preparedness" movement 190
Puerto Rico (invasion) 123-26
Pullman Strike 97-106

Reams Station (battle) 26
Reber, Gen. Miles (grandson of N. Miles) 194, 196-7
Reber, Samuel (son-in-law) 196
Reber, Samuel (grandson) 196-7
Red River War 52-3
Richardson, Gen. Israel 13
Roosevelt, Theodore 6, 45, 112-13, 118-19, 120, 126-27, 128, 132-33, 138-39, 145-54, 160-78, 179-82, 190-93
Root, Elihu 144-54, 160-78,
Ropes, John C. 89
Ross, Edmund G. 68-70, 75-76
Rouse, Henry C. 168
Ruger, Gen. T.H. 62, 107, 109

Sampson, Adm. William 116-22, 146-54
Sanderson, J.W. 44
San Juan Hill 120
Santiago de Cuba (naval battle) 121-22, 146-54
Schley, Adm. Winfield Scott 117-22, 146-54
Schine, G. David 196-7
Schofield, Gen. John M. 93-95, 100-103
Schurz, Carl 157, 171
Scott, Gen. Hugh 190n.
Sedgwick, Gen. John 16,19
Sewell, Sen. William 58
Shafter, Gen. William 76, 116, 121-23, 128, 140
Sharp, Col. Henry 130
Sheridan, Gen. Philip 62, 66, 111
Sherman, Sen. John 58, 108
Sherman, Mary Hoyt [See Mary Miles]
Sherman, Gen. William T. 27, 51, 56, 62, 199
Short Bull 91
Sickles, Gen. Daniel 182&n
Sinclair, Upton 141
Sioux War (1876-77) 54-57
Sitting Bull 54-5, 62, 91-2
Smith, Gen. Jacob 159, 166-69

Spanish-American War 112-127
Spotsylvania (battle) 23
Strauss, Nathan 186
Sullivan, Mark 2,3
Sumner, Gen. E.V. 9, 10
Sutherland Station (battle) 28

Taft, William Howard 159, 160-78
Temperance 187-88
Terry, Gen. Alfred 54, 62, 68
Titlow, Cpt. Jerome 35-37
Tolman, Newton 198

Utley, Robert 75, 83-84

Wade, Gen. James F. 73, 82, 134-143
Walker, Edwin 100
Waller, Maj. Littleton 166
Warren, Gen. Gouverneur 27-28n
Washington Evening Star 85, 180
"Water Torture" 167
Watterson, Henry 153, 163
Weir, Pvt. Andrew K. 167
Welsh, Herbert 83, 163, 171, 173-74
Weston, Gen. J.F. 136
Weyler, Gen. Valeriano 112
Wheaton, Gen. Lloyd 157
Wheeler, Gen. Joseph 31, 32, 120-123
Wilderness (battle) 22
Wilson, Henry 5
Wilson, Gen. James H. 28-29, 124
Wilson, Woodrow 191-92
Wolf Mountain (battle) 55
Wood, Gen. Leonard 70-71, 133, 192-93
World War I 190-93
    Russians 192-93
Wounded Knee Massacre 92-95

ABOUT THE AUTHOR-ARTHUR J. AMCHAN

I won't be pretentious and talk about myself in the third person. I was born in Washington, D.C. in 1946, and was introduced to the study of history and current events by my father at the age of five while listening to Elmer Davis report the nightly news on CBS radio. In response to my question, "What is the 38th parallel?", my father pulled out a map and explained the Korean War to me.

I graduated from Miami University, Oxford, Ohio, in 1967, magna cum laude with a B.A. in political science. I attended Harvard Law School from 1967-69, at which time I was drafted into the United States Army. I was assigned to the United States Army Procurement Agency in Saigon, April 1970-March 1971, and returned to finish my legal education in 1972. Suffice it to say that nobody in the Army ever confused me with Nelson Miles.

I worked from 1972 to February 1989 with the United States Department of Labor and now work for the United States Environmental Protection Agency. I have previously published two articles in the CCH Labor Law Journal on occupational safety and health law and the inequities of the exclusive remedy provisions of workers compensation. In 1985 I self-published the Slower Runner's Guide.

I live in Arlington, Virginia, with my wife, Susan, and my children Steven, Adele, and Nathan, all of whom have heard far more about Nelson Miles that anyone could reasonably wish. My father died in 1987, but I regard this book as fulfilling in a very small way the enormous debt I owe him.

ORDER FORM

AMCHAN PUBLICATIONS
P.O. BOX 3648
ALEXANDRIA, VA. 22302

THE MOST FAMOUS SOLDIER IN AMERICA:
NELSON A. MILES 1839-1925

Send $14.95 per copy plus $1.00 for shipping to the address above.

Please send me THE MOST FAMOUS SOLDIER IN AMERICA. I enclose $__________ for __________copies. Va. residents add 4 1/2 % sales tax ($0.67).

NAME ______________________________
ADDRESS ______________________________
____
STATE ______________ ZIP CODE ______________

ORDER FORM

HEROES, MARTYRS, AND SURVIVORS OF THE CIVIL WAR

by Arthur J. Amchan

Estimated Publication date: January 1991

Includes the stories of:

THE FIVE UNION VETERANS WHO BECAME PRESIDENT
Grant, Hayes, Garfield, Harrison and McKinley

THE FLOWER OF NEW ENGLAND
Oliver Wendell Holmes, Jr., Paul Joseph Revere, Robert Gould Shaw, Charles Russell Lowell, Jr., Josephine Shaw Lowell, Henry L. Abbott, Thomas Wentworth Higginson

THE MAN BEHIND AN INNOCUOUS HISTORICAL MARKER
Julius Peter Garesche

THE GERMAN REVOLUTIONARY AND AMERICAN REFORMER
Carl Schurz

THE OTHER SIDE
Robert E. Lee, Nathan Bedford Forrest, Wade Hampton

THE CIVIL WAR VETERANS WHO COMMANDED THE ARMY IN THE SPANISH-AMERICAN WAR AND THE PHILIPPINES
Joseph Wheeler, CSA, USV; Nelson Miles, Arthur MacArthur, Jr.

THE NEW GENERATION
Theodore Roosevelt

SPECIAL PREPUBLICATION OFFER $12.95 per copy, plus $1.00 shipping.

I enclose $__________ for ________copies. Va. residents add $0.58 sales tax.

NAME ____
ADDRESS ____
____
____
STATE ____________________ZIP CODE____________________

ORDER FORM

SOMETHING LIGHTER FROM AMCHAN PUBLICATIONS:

THE SLOWER RUNNER'S GUIDE
by Arthur J. Amchan

Send $5.95 per copy, plus $0.50 for shipping to:

AMCHAN PUBLICATIONS
P.O. BOX 3648
ALEXANDRIA, VA. 22302

Va. residents add $0.27 for sales tax.

I enclose $__________ for __________copies.

NAME ____

ADDRESS ____

____

____

STATE ____________________ZIP CODE____________________

"If I was buying a book for a midlife (or) beginning runner...it would be this one." Len Wallach, THE SAN MATEO (CA) TIMES

"the most practical runner's manual I've ever read." (Mayor) Jim Moran, THE ALEXANDRIA (VA) GAZETTE PACKET

"...hilarious but very useful..." THE WASHINGTON POST

"for those of us who dream of aging gracefully" THE ALEXANDRIA (VA) GAZETTE

"full of worthwhile information...in an interesting breezy style." Phil Jackman, THE BALTIMORE SUN

"...the perfect book for people...who...have little hope of becoming a consistent front runner." Bob Forest, ON THE RUN, Newsletter of the Lake Area (La.) Runners.